COMPETITION LAWS, GLOBALIZATION AND LEGAL PLURALISM

Building upon a theoretical framework and empirical research, this book provides a thought-provoking analysis of the interests, strategies and challenges that China has faced in developing its Anti-Monopoly Law (AML) in the context of economic globalization.

The book comprises three main parts: Part I reviews the directions of convergence of global competition law; Part II provides a contextual analysis of China's market governance and its strategic interests; and Part III examines the latest enforcement of the Anti-Monopoly Law by focusing on the interactions between global actors and China, the relationships between Chinese competition and sectoral regulators, and the enforcement of global competition law norms in the Chinese context.

This book is one of the first to provide a critical understanding of China's experience as a new competition regulator, set against the background of the plural sources of global competition laws.

Volume 5 in the series Hart Studies in Competition Law

Hart Studies in Competition Law

Volume 1: *Intellectual Property, Antitrust and Cumulative Innovation in the EU and the US*
Thorsten Käseberg

Volume 2: *State Aid and the European Economic Constitution*
Francesco de Cecco

Volume 3: *The Private Enforcement of Competition Law in Ireland*
David McFadden

Volume 4: *Cross-Border EU Competition Law Actions*
Edited by Mihail Danov Florian Becker and Paul Beaumont

Competition Laws, Globalization and Legal Pluralism

China's Experience

Qianlan Wu

·HART·
PUBLISHING
OXFORD AND PORTLAND, OREGON
2013

Published in the United Kingdom by Hart Publishing Ltd
16C Worcester Place, Oxford, OX1 2JW
Telephone: +44 (0)1865 517530
Fax: +44 (0)1865 510710
E-mail: mail@hartpub.co.uk
Website: http://www.hartpub.co.uk

Published in North America (US and Canada) by
Hart Publishing
c/o International Specialized Book Services
920 NE 58th Avenue, Suite 300
Portland, OR 97213-3786
USA
Tel: +1 503 287 3093 or toll-free: (1) 800 944 6190
Fax: +1 503 280 8832
E-mail: orders@isbs.com
Website: http://www.isbs.com

Hart Publishing is an imprint of Bloomsburg Publishing Plc

British Library Cataloguing in Publication Data
Data Available

ISBN: 978-1-84946-432-1

Typeset by Compuscript Ltd, Shannon
Printed and bound in Great Britain by
TJ International, Padstow

FSC www.fsc.org
MIX
Paper from responsible sources
FSC® C013056

To my parents

FOREWORD: CHINA AS A LABORATORY OF LEGAL CHANGE

FRANCIS SNYDER*

Since the beginning of reform and opening under Deng Xiaoping in December 1978, China has been gradually yet continually engaged in building a market economy. China's accession to the World Trade Organization (WTO) in December 2011 provided further impetus for a wide range of reforms which mostly were already underway. Market-oriented reforms have been part of a long-term process, complex, complicated, and creating and embracing numerous conflicting interests. They have stimulated legal and other institutional developments, and they also, to some extent, demand and are conditioned by these developments.

There is no single model of a market economy, regardless of what some pundits, politicians or scholars may have claimed in the past or even may claim today. Today we are aware of the plurality and diversity of human economic, political, social, legal and institutional arrangements. Contemporary China takes its place among this array. But here, however, faced with the dynamism, energy and complexity of modern China, our understanding is often deficient. This is true of insiders, outsiders or those who straddle both (overlapping) worlds, as generations of anthropologists frequently remind us. Lack of cultural knowledge or sympathy, poor empirical research, hence lack of basic understanding, insufficient theoretical tools, an analytical lens clouded by stereotypes or unfounded assumptions—a host of factors—frequently prevent us from seeing China and its process of marketization as they really are: incredibly complex, often contradictory, characterised by many layers and types of social relations, and deeply embedded in a longstanding and specific society and culture, which regardless of changes during the past century remains vastly different from that of other countries, especially the USA and the EU.

For years, if not centuries, in China there has been a lively debate about who makes rules, what kinds of rules and how rules are most effectively applied. The labels 'rule by man', 'rule by law' and 'rule of law' capture some aspects of this debate. They do not however really express directly the extent to which, in recent

* CV Starr Professor of Law, EU Jean Monnet Chair *ad personam* and Co-Director of the Centre for Research on Transnational Law, Peking University School of Transnational Law, Shenzhen Graduate School, China; Visiting Professor, formerly Centennial Professor, London School of Economics; Emeritus Professor, CERIC, Aix-Marseille Université, France; Visiting Professor, College of Europe, Bruges.

decades, China has again become part of international society and the world economy. This process of participation, sometimes hidden but never absent during many centuries of history, has been especially in evidence when China was an original Contracting Party to GATT 1947, resumed its seat in the United Nations in 1971, signed the Shanghai Communiqué with the United States in 1972, established full diplomatic relations with the European Union, then the European Economic Community, in 1975, and acceded to membership in the World Trade Organization in 2001. Today China is a laboratory for legal change, informed not only by domestic social and economic forces, domestic institutions and domestic norms, but also by international law, global legal pluralism and transnational law. These sources of change, whether domestic, international or transnational, have continued to stimulate and shape the development of China's market economy, in a context in which China has become one of the leading countries in the world market.

Legal scholarship, including law and society scholarship, is beginning to come to terms with this transformation. In recent years an increasing number of publications, in many forms and from numerous sources, have seen the light of day to analyse and to inform us about legal and institutional changes in China, their domestic and international sources and their impact, or lack of impact, on everyday economic, legal and social life. Very few, however, have tackled the crucial subject of Chinese competition law; fewer still result from research by Chinese legal scholars, whether in China, Europe, the United States or elsewhere; hardly any of these have done so from a law and society perspective; and one wonders if there are any at all who have dared to combine their empirical research with a broad theoretical perspective.

This book by Qianlan Wu is a pioneering study. It aims to innovate in the field of Chinese legal studies, bringing a new theoretical perspective to a relatively new field of legal research about China, and notably to a field of law that is absolutely crucial to the construction and management of a market economy as China resumes its place in the world. The Chinese Anti-Monopoly Law (AML) is the result of a very thorough process of governmental and academic study of relevant laws throughout the world, as well as being based on domestic experience following the well-known but little studied Chinese approach of trial, experimentation and gradual change.[1] It draws upon many sources, international, transnational and national. Dr Wu's book provides an indispensable guide to these developments. Setting the creation of the AML in its international, transnational and domestic contexts, it examines the past, present and (so far as possible) the future of competition law in China.

China's framework for policy-making has very special characteristics. Two features in particular stand out. First, since 1949, China has been and is still a party-state. The Chinese Communist Party (CCP) is an integral part of government at every level, including the judiciary. Dean Zhu Suli argues that the CCP has played

[1] Sebastian Heilmann and Elizabeth J Perry (eds), *Mao's Invisible Hand: The Political Foundations of Adaptive Governance in China* (Harvard University Press, Cambridge MA, 2011).

a key role in constituting the nation-state, it is internal rather than external to government and 'there is no such thing as government policy independent from the CCP'.[2] Second, far from being highly centralised, China's policy-making framework has been described as 'fragmented authoritarianism', as several generations of scholars from Doak Barnett[3] through Ken Lieberthal, Michel Oksenberg and David Lampton[4] to Andrew Mertha[5], not to mention Lucien Pye[6], have pointed out. As a result, it differs profoundly from the legal, institutional and other parameters of policy-making in other countries, especially the United States or the EU. Unfortunately, the latter frequently are simply presumed to be appropriate comparators for understanding and benchmarks for evaluating law-making and the implementation of law in China.

Dr Wu's book should be useful in helping us to revise some of these misguided presumptions. It stands out by virtue of its analysis of the historical sources of the AML, its basic provisions and assumptions, and its application and administration so far. There is no doubt that Dr Wu's book will be incredibly useful to scholars and others who seek to gain a greater understanding of Chinese competition law and its current and likely future role in the construction and management of a market economy in China.

2 Zhu Suli, 'Political Parties in China's Judiciary', Duke Law, Center for International and Comparative Law Occasional Papers (CiCLOPs), 2009, available at www.law.duke.edu/cicl/ciclops.

3 A Doak Barnett, *Cadres, Bureaucracy, and Political Power in Communist China* (Columbia University Press, New York and London, 1967).

4 Kenneth Lieberthal and Michel Oksenberg, *Policy-Making in China: Leaders, Structures, and Processes* (Princeton University Press, Princeton, 1988); Kenneth G Lieberthal and David M Lampton (eds), *Bureaucracy, Politics, and Decision-Making in Post-Mao China* (University of California Press, Los Angeles, 1992).

5 Andrew C Mertha, *The Politics of Piracy: Intellectual Property in Contemporary China* (Cornell University Press, Ithaca, NY, 2007).

6 Lucien Pye, *The Spirit of Chinese Politics* (JMIT Press, Cambridge MA, 1968, new edition Harvard University Press, Cambridge MA, 1992); Lucien Pye, *The Dynamics of Chinese Politics* (Oelgeschlager, Gun & Hain, Cambridge MA, 1981).

ACKNOWLEDGEMENTS

When I started my PhD in London, I was brave and stupid enough to try to find solutions to the many challenges raised by the complex relationships between competition law, globalization and China. The LSE's motto, *rerum cognoscere causas (to know the causes of things)*, has fundamentally changed the perspective of my research and has given me an intellectual experience that has been stimulating and eye-opening. I am eternally grateful for the guidance I received throughout this process from Professor Francis Snyder and Dr Andrew Lang of the LSE's Law Department. I am indebted to Professor Snyder for his support and faith in me throughout years.

The research for the book started with my PhD Programme at the LSE, in respect of which I am grateful for the support of Professor Dr Hong Zhou, Director of the Institute of European Studies, and Professor Dr Xiaoye Wang, Institute of Law of the Chinese Academy of Social Sciences. The book, in its development into a monograph, benefited from the financial support provided by the British Academy research grant I received in 2011 on the subject 'When International Legal Norms Speak Chinese'. The grant has enabled me to conduct up to date empirical research in Europe and China and I am thankful to the British Academy for this kind support.

The book is a also a product of the inspiration, help and encouragement I received from Dr Sunari Senaratne, Dr Guoming Li, Dr Carmen Haddadin and many friends I met at the Goodenough College, London. I thank my husband Dr Bowen Tian for his unconditional tolerance and support in the writing process. I thank Hart Publishing, especially Ms Rachel Turner, Ms Charlotte Austin and Ms Melanie Hamill, for their professional, efficient and patient work. I thank the School of Contemporary Chinese Studies at the University of Nottingham for its administrative support.

Writing the book has been a valuable learning experience and I therefore thank everyone who has facilitated, helped and supported me in this journey.

TABLE OF CONTENTS

LIST OF ABBREVIATIONS

ABC	Agriculture Bank of China
AIC	Administration of Industry and Commerce
AML	Anti-Monopoly Law
AQSIQ	General Administration of Quality Supervision, Inspection and Quarantine of the PRC
BOC	Bank of China
CBRC	China Banking Regulatory Commission
CCB	China Construction Bank
CCP	Chinese Communist Party
CFIUS	Committee on Foreign Investment in the US
CNOOC	China Offshore Oil Corporation
CSRC	China Securities Regulatory Commission
DOJ	Department of Justice
DRD	Development and Reform Department
DSM	Dispute Settlement Mechanism
ECJ	European Court of Justice
ECMR	European Commission Merger Regulation
ECSC	European Coal and Steel Community
EEC	European Economic Community
FIE	Foreign Invested Enterprises
FTC	Federal Trade Commission
GATS	General Agreement on Trade and Services
GATT	General Agreement on Tariffs and Trade
GPA	Government Procurement Agreement
HHI	Herfindahl Hirschman Index
ICBC	Industrial and Commercial Bank of China
ICN	International Competition Network
ICPAC	US International Competition Policy Advisory Committee
IMF	International Monetary Fund
ITO	International Trade Organization
LAO	Legislative Affairs Office
MFN	Most Favoured Nation
MOFCOM	Ministry of Commerce
MOFTEC	Ministry of Foreign Trade and Economic Cooperation
MOU	Memorandum of Understanding
NDRC	National Development and Reform Commission
NORSMEO	National Office of Rectification and Standardization of Market Economic Order

NPC	National People's Congress
OECD	Organisation for Economic Cooperation and Development
PBOC	People's Bank of China
PDEs	Private Domestic Enterprises
PMC	People Mediation Centre
SAIC	State Administration of Industry and Commerce
SASAC	State-owned Assets Supervision and Administration Commission
SETC	State Economic and Trade Commission
SIEC	Significant Impediment of Effective Competition test
SOCB	State-Owned Commercial Bank
SOEs	State-Owned Enterprises
SPC	Supreme People's Court
SSNIP	Small but Significant Non-transitory Increase in Price
TEC	Treaty Establishing the European Community
TRIPs	Trade-Related Intellectual Property Rights
TVE	Township and Village Enterprises
UNCTAD	United Nations Conference on Trade and Development
WGTCP	Working Group on Trade and Competition Policy
WTO	World Trade Organization

TABLE OF CASES

European Union

United States of America

World Trade Organization

TABLE OF LEGISLATION

European Union

United States of America

People's Republic of China

Japan

Turkey

TABLE OF TREATIES

European Coal and Steel Community (ECSC)

European Economic Community (EEC)

European Union

WTO Agreements

Regional Agreements

Bilateral Agreements

Other Treaties

Declarations

Introduction

I. COMPETITION LAW AND ECONOMIC GLOBALIZATION

In the context of economic globalization, various economies have adopted competition law as the main legal instrument for market governance. Interestingly, these competition laws have exhibited the following common features: first, the structure of competition law in almost all competition regulation regimes includes, the regulation of anti-competitive agreements, dominance and mergers; second, competition law has been enforced by one independent regulator or, increasingly, by private litigation; and, third, the goals pursued by these competition laws shift between social and economic goals based on fairness or pure efficiency concerns. In recent years, many competition authorities have chosen to emphasize the efficiency concern and have adopted a more economics-based approach in enforcing competition laws.

China adopted its first comprehensive competition law, the Anti-Monopoly Law (AML), in 2007 and has quickly risen to be the one notable competition regulator in the global markets. The AML emerged out of the convergence of international competition law norms, generated by leading competition law regimes and international organizations. However, further examination reveals that China has attempted to build a competition regime of its own in order to achieve its strategic goals.

Given the fact that legally binding harmonization rules on competition law have not been in place, the following questions can therefore be asked: why have the competition laws of various economic systems converged, seemingly independently? Why do the economies of varying backgrounds adopt competition laws showing a certain level of convergence with international norms? And why do competition regimes choose to converge more with certain international norms on competition law than with others in a legally pluralistic world?

II. COMPETITION LAW AND GLOBAL LEGAL PLURALISM

Global competition law convergence has been advocated on plural grounds. It is advocated on the grounds of efficiency, where the convergence can reduce transaction costs for the international business circle, which otherwise may be subject to the duplication or contradiction of extra-territorial application of competition law.[1] It has also been advocated where the convergence can complement trade liberalization worldwide, leading to the maximization of efficiency.[2] It is advocated on the ground of development, where competition law has been increasingly linked with market economy construction and the development of the economies of former communist countries. However, it is argued that competition law in these economies has goals that are different from those of mature market economies and that the functioning of the law requires a level of economic development and the institutional set-up of the economies.[3]

Plural actors participate in global competition law development, which transcends the sovereign state. Leading competition regimes become the generators of norms in order to influence the convergence of competition law, through networks as well as international organizations.[4] Competition law regimes of influential developing economies such as those of the members of BRICS have become more assertive, which has a far-reaching impact on global competition law convergence.[5] Furthermore, plural mechanisms have been used to promote global competition law convergence. These include the transformation from hard law harmonization towards non-legally binding dialogue, on a voluntary basis, at both the bilateral and multilateral levels. This is accompanied by the increasing emphasis on responding to the embeddedness of the recipient competition regime by the generators of the competition law norms.

Hence, the development of global competition law in the context of economic globalization can best be understood through the theories of global legal pluralism. Global legal pluralism argues that sources for law include the formal norms articulated by sovereign powers and the informal norms generated by any social field inhabited by individuals.[6] It emphasizes the existence of hybrid legal spaces, where more than one legal regime exists concurrently; for example, the application of sovereign and international laws, and the interaction of various legal regimes has an impact on the development of the legal space as a whole.[7]

[1] J Basedow, 'Jurgen International Antitrust: From Extraterritorial Application to Harmonization' (1999) 60 *Layola Law Review* 1037.

[2] Ignacio Garcia Bercero and Stefan D Amarasinha, 'Moving the Trade and Competition Debate Forward' (2001) 4(3) *Journal of International Economic Law* 481–506.

[3] William E Kovacic, 'Institutional Foundations for Economic Legal Reform in Transition Economies: The Case of Competition Policy and Antitrust Enforcement' (2001) 77 *Chicago-Kent Law Review* 265; Eleanor Fox, 'Economic Development, Poverty and Antitrust: The Other Path' (2007) 13 *Southwestern Journal of Law & Trade in Americas* 211; Mark Palim, 'Worldwide Growth of Competition Law: An Empirical Analysis' (1998) 43 *Antitrust Bulletin* 105.

[4] Imelda Maher, 'Competition Law in the International Domain: Networks as a New Form of Governance' (2002) 29(1) *Journal of Law and Society* 112–36.

[5] Adrian Erich, Vassily Rudomino and Jose Regazzini, *Competition Law in the BRICS Countries* (Kluwer Law International, 2012).

[6] Sally Falk Moore, *Law as Process: An Anthropological Approach* (Routledge & Kegan Paul, 1978) 55.

[7] Sally Engle Merry, 'Legal Pluralism' (1988) 22(5) *Law & Society Review* 869–896.

Given this background, two main theories have emerged with respect to the understanding of market governance, legal changes and globalization: the theory on autopoietic law and law without state and the theory on sites of governance and legal pluralism.

The theory of autopoiesis of the law argues that law is a self-referential and self-reproductive system with normative closure and environmental openness.[8] In the face of the convergence of legal norms, it argues that the relationship between law, as an autopoietic system, and fragments of society is selective, ranging from being coupling to interwoven. In other words, where the legal system is loosely coupled with certain fragments of the social system, the legal transplant can be easier, although it is subject to the social embeddedness of the society. The legal change would exert a fundamental impact on both the rules transplanted and the social systems that the rules are transplanted into, as the meaning of the external rules would be reconstructed and the internal context would undergo fundamental changes.[9]

Regarding legal pluralism and globalization, the theory argues that the fragmentation of world society creates a form of global law that is apolitical and autopoietic yet cannot be measured by positive law standards. It suffers from the underdevelopment of political and institutional support at the global level, and is dependent on other social processes, such as economic and social transactions in globalization. However, it is these economic and social transactions which would eventually serve as the premise for the politicization of these laws decentred from the state.[10]

The theory of the autopoiesis of law is largely based on the premise of private law and contract, and it applies the private law principle to examine the development of both private and public law in globalization. Furthermore, the theory has emphasized the autopoietic reproduction of the legal system based on its own elements and has argued that the autopoietic closure can create effective restraints on the political instrumentality of the law.[11] However, in the context of economic globalization, not all legal systems enjoy the same level of normative closure and environmental openness in society, and their relationship with fragments of social processes varies from society to society.

The theory of the sites of governance and legal pluralism argues that globalization is governed by the totality of strategically determined, situationally specific and often episodic conjunctions of a multiplicity of sites throughout the world.[12]

[8] Gunther Teubner, 'Breaking Frames: Economic Globalization and the Emergence of *Lex Mercatoria*' (2002) 5(2) *European Journal of Social Theory* 199–217.

[9] Gunther Teubner, 'Legal Irritants: Good Faith in British Law or How Unifying Law Ends Up in New Differences' (1998) 61 *Modern Law Review* 11–32.

[10] Gunther Teubner, '"Global Bukowina": Legal Pluralism in the World Society' in Gunther Teuber (ed), *Global Law Without a State* (Dartmouth, 1997) 3–31.

[11] Gunther Teubner, *Autopoietic Law: A New Approach to Law and Society* (Walter De Gruyter, 1988) 4–5.

[12] Francis Snyder, 'Governing Economic Globalization: Global Legal Pluralism and European Union Law' (1999) *European Law Journal* 334–74.

Sites may be public, private or mixed. Some are market-based, while others are polity-based. Actors in these sites include private parties, for example, companies, governments, non-governmental organizations and others. These actors influence the development, characteristics and the competitiveness of sites.[13]

Each site has structural aspects and relational aspects. The structural aspects examine the institutions, norms and dispute resolution processes of the site.[14] With respect to the relational aspect among sites of governance, each site, actively or passively, interacts with other sites under legal pluralism. The sites of governance theory argues that the structural and relational aspects of the sites of governance have a dialectical relationship, in that the development of the structural aspect of a site impacts the sites' relationships with other sites, and the sites' external relations, in turn, shape the structural development of the site.[15] The totality of sites represents a new form of global legal pluralism.[16] However, it should be noted that the strategic interests of actors may not be consistent in the long term and that many strategic actors may not be driven only by strategic calculations, but may also be influenced by factors such as loyalty, familiarity and tradition.[17]

The development of competition law worldwide shows that competition laws have a high divisibility of goals, and continue to communicate and converge with each other within various legal spaces. Competition regimes cross-reference each other with the aim of achieving their own strategic goals in tackling challenges brought by globalization.

Hence, this book builds upon global legal pluralism and in particular the sites of governance and legal pluralism. It focuses on the experience of China, one of the world's rising powers, in terms of its AML development, with the aim of answering the questions raised. The book argues that in the face of challenges brought by globalization, competition regimes are incentivized to export their own competition regulation norms with the aim of reducing the communication barrier with each other and becoming the leader in generating norms influencing the development of competition law. Soft law norms generated by dominant sites, such as the US, the European Union (EU) and the World Trade Organization (WTO), on competition regulation have exerted a far-reaching impact on the development of global competition law. In developing its AML, China has learned to strategically handle international competition law norms to effect its own

[13] LK Mytelka and M Delapierre, 'Strategic Partnership, Knowledge Based Network Oligopolies and the State' in A Claire Culter et al (eds), *Private Authority and International Affairs* (State University of New York Press, 1999) 129–53.

[14] Snyder (n 12).

[15] This is built upon the original model proposed by Bratton and McCahery in the cross-reference in corporate governance around the world. See William Bratton and Joseph McCahery, 'Comparative Corporate Governance and the Theory of the Firm: The Case against Global Cross Reference' (1999) 38(2) *Columbia Journal of Transnational Law* 213–298.

[16] Francis Snyder, 'Economic Globalization and the Law in the Twenty First Century' in Austin Sarat (ed), *Companion to Law and Society* (Blackwell Publishing, 2004) 629.

[17] Brian Tamanaha, 'Understanding Legal Pluralism: Past to Present, Local to Global' (2007) 29 *Sydney Law Review* 375–411.

development and to build up its own conceptual framework, compatible with its development goals and legal doctrines, when international competition law norms fail to do so. As such, competition regimes driven by respective strategic interests choose to converge with and compete against each other in competition regulation. It is this process that largely complicates, influences and, to a certain extent, shapes the outcome of global competition law development.

III. OUTLINE OF THE CHAPTERS

The book is composed of three parts. Part I aims to answer the following question: given that the harmonization effort of competition law has failed, why do competition laws worldwide converge to a certain extent on a voluntary basis?

Part I answers this question in two chapters. Chapter 1 reviews the development of US antitrust law and EU competition law, and argues that the convergence of US antitrust law and EU competition law has generated an important soft law norm which influences the development of competition law worldwide. This is the pursuit of allocative efficiency based on economic analysis. Chapter 2 reviews the roles played by international organizations in competition law development, including the Organisation for Economic Co-operation and Development (OECD), the United Nations Conference on Trade and Development (UNCTAD), the WTO and the International Competition Network (ICN). It argues that the WTO has the structural capacity to exert an impact on competition law development; however, its impact is constrained by its own normative framework. Consequently, the WTO has generated the norm of the non-discrimination principle aiming at market access in order to influence the development of competition law. Part I concludes that the soft law norms generated by leading competition law regimes and international organizations play a pivotal role in promoting global competition law convergence. Hence, these two interlinked norms—the pursuit of allocative efficiency and the non-discrimination principle—continue to serve as normative framework to impact the convergence of competition laws worldwide. However, Part I argues that the two norms contain fundamental clashes in the context of competition regulation.

Part II, on China's market governance and the making of the AML, aims to answer the following question: why do economies with various backgrounds adopt competition laws showing a certain level of convergence with international norms? It answers this question by examining China's market governance, the restraints on competition in the Chinese market and the making of the AML in China. Chapter 3 examines the institutional transformation, normative framework and dispute settlement of China's market governance. It argues that market governance in China is unitary and administrative where the party-state remains a dominant, strategic and resilient actor. Chapter 4 analyses the progress and fragmentation in China's economic transformation. It indicates that the marketization levels in China vary as a result of state control over market entry, financial markets and labour markets, and of the segmentation of regional markets. Restrictions on competition in China can result from intrinsic market failure as well as from the state-controlled discriminatory market environment. Chapter 5 examines the process of creating the AML. It shows that China's law-making process, its communication with international actors and its market regulation embeddedness shaped the outcome of the enactment of the AML. Hence, the AML pursues a diversity of goals that are beneficial to China's developmental needs in its substance, and adjusts to the incumbent market regulatory framework in its enforcement.

Part III aims to answer the following question: why do competition regimes choose to converge more with certain international norms on competition law than with others? It attempts to answer this question by examining the institutionalization of the AML enforcement frameworks in China and to what extent the AML refers to the principle of allocative efficiency and the principle of non-discrimination in its enforcement from 2008 to 2012. Chapter 6 examines the public enforcement, private enforcement and judicial review of the AML. It argues that the anti-monopoly authorities, namely the National Development and Reform Commission (NDRC), the State Administration of Industry and Commerce (SAIC) and the Ministry of Commerce (MOFCOM) have engaged in capacity building and the rationalization of enforcement procedures by adopting secondary legislations. However, the coordinated segmentation among the anti-monopoly authorities, between the anti-monopoly authorities and sectoral regulators within the State Council Anti-Monopoly Commission, as well as between the private and public enforcement, have contributed to influencing the decision-making in the enforcement of the AML. Chapter 7 examines how China refers to international competition law norms by analysing the decisions issued by the anti-monopoly authorities. The analysis shows that China refers to the pursuit of allocative efficiency by revealing efforts to build up the economic analysis of markets, particularly in the field of concentration regulation by MOFCOM and that it refers to the non-discrimination principle by applying the AML to all business operators in the market and to administrative monopoly. However, the practice reveals that the reference to the two principles faces limits, resulting from the embeddedness of China's market governance and China's own legal doctrines. More importantly, the theoretical and empirical gap existing between the two principles is unable to provide China with an effective and realistic tool to pursue the diversified developmental goals concurrently within the framework of the AML. Consequently, China is searching for its own conceptual framework for its competition regulation on the one hand, while, on the other hand, it applies a dual-track enforcement of the AML to pursue both efficiency goals and non-efficiency goals.

Part I

Where Do the Norms Come From?

1

US, EU and Global Competition Law Development

I. INTRODUCTION

Part I of this volume reviews the impact of leading competition regimes, such as US antitrust law and EU competition law, and of international organizations, including the WTO, the OECD, UNCTAD and the ICN on global competition law development. This chapter reviews the development of US antitrust law and EU competition law from a historical perspective. It argues that both laws have experienced a transformation of goals but show, to a certain extent, convergence between the two in terms of goals and enforcement. It then argues that EU competition law has, strategically, cross-referenced US antitrust law with the aim of improving its own interest—for example, market integration or modernization—and of strengthening the EU's position as a major actor in globalization. Nevertheless, this convergence between US antitrust law and EU competition law has generated norms, inter alia, setting the goal for competition law to pursue allocative efficiency and consumer surplus, based on economic analysis. This has profoundly influenced, shaped or led competition law development in the rest of the world.

II. US ANTITRUST LAW

US federal antitrust law has as its core part the Sherman Act, adopted in 1890, the Federal Trade Commission Act and the Clayton Act of 1914.[1] It regulates mainly multilateral and bilateral actions that harm competition in the form of agreement, or in *conspiracy*, as provided by section 1 of the Sherman Act; the unilateral harm of competition in monopolization or the attempt to monopolize, as provided by section 2 of the Sherman Act; and merger and acquisition, the effect

[1] For a brief overview of US antitrust laws, see www.ftc.gov/bc/antitrust/antitrust_laws.shtm.

of which may substantially lessen competition or tend to create a monopoly, as provided by section 7 of the Clayton Act.

With respect to section 1 of the Sherman Act, the US courts have held that it outlaws unreasonable restraints and divides the unreasonable restraints into illegal per se and those found illegal after having been evaluated under the rule of reason doctrine.[2] To challenge a multilateral anti-competitive action in the market, the claimant, either a private party or government authority, must prove that there was an agreement; that the agreement was between two or more parties; that it unreasonably restrained trade or competition in the relevant market; that the restraint affected interstate commerce; and, in the case of private action, that the agreement injured the plaintiff and, in a criminal action, that the defendant acted with criminal intent.[3]

With respect to section 2 of the Sherman Act, the claimant must prove the possession of market power in the relevant market and the wilful acquisition and maintenance of this power through improper means. Monopoly power, according to the US court, is the power to control market prices or exclude competition.[4] The establishment of market power in the relevant market is based on the delineation of product and geographic markets, mainly through a demand substantiality cross-elasticity test. The examination of wilfulness is more complicated, but, nevertheless, includes predatory pricing; refusal to deal with competitors or to allow competitors to use essential facilities for effective competition; use of market power in one area as leverage to obtain or maintain market power in another; misuse of product information to gain a competitive advantage; misuse of litigation to harm competitors; and customer restrictions designed to exclude competition.[5]

With respect to section 7 of the Clayton Act, based on US court case law, the US Department of Justice and the Federal Trade Commission (FTC) issued horizontal merger guidelines in 1967, 1982, 1984, 1992, 1997 and 2010 to provide detailed rules by which the legality of proposed mergers, acquisitions and joint ventures could be examined.[6] According to the 1997 merger guidelines, the US competition authority needs, first, to delineate the antitrust market based on the test of elasticity of demand substitutability of the product, namely the SSNIP (Small but Significant and Non-transitory Increase in Price) test, and measure market concentration based on the Herfindahl-Hirschman Index (HHI), before and

[2] *Standard Oil Co of New Jersey v United States*, 221 US 1 (1911); and *United States v American Tobacco Co*, 221 US 106 (1911).

[3] Section 4 of the Sherman Act.

[4] *United States v EI du Pont de Nemours & Co*, 351 US 277 (1956).

[5] Douglas Broder, *A Guide to US Antitrust Law* (Sweet & Maxwell, 2005) 100.

[6] US Merger Guidelines 1997, available at: www.justice.gov/atr/public/guidelines/horiz_book/hmg1.html.

after the proposed transaction.[7] It then assesses the merger in the light of market concentration and other market factors, including potential adverse competitive effects. In particular, the authority assesses whether entry would be timely, likely and sufficient either to deter or to counteract the competitive effects of concern. The authority also assesses any efficiency gains that can be generated from the merger, which cannot reasonably be achieved by the parties through other means. Finally, the authority assesses whether, without the merger, either party would be likely to fail, causing it to exit the market.[8]

On 19 August 2010, the US issued one new Horizontal Merger Guideline. Among other changes, the new guideline emphasizes that merger analysis does not use one single methodology, but is a case-specific process. The Guideline downplays the market shares as the indicator for potential adverse competitive effects. Instead, it requires to be considered, where available, natural experiments (eg, empirical data assessing the impact of mergers, entry or expansion in the relevant or similar markets) or substantial competition between the merging parties and other factors. The 2010 Guideline also de-emphasizes the role played by relevant market definition in merger regulation, which is no longer the first step to be taken by regulators.[9]

The application of antitrust law to the restraint on competition has produced rich case law in the past 100 years. In reviewing antitrust case law, leading US antitrust scholars, such as William Kovacic, have summarized some emerging, basic principles which have come into being with respect to the analysis of competition restraints. These principles include, first, the application of cognizable theory of anti-competitive effects, most typically collusive or exclusionary effects;[10] and, second, the examination of evidence of actual or predicted anti-competitive effects, whether presumed, direct or circumstantial. Direct evidence of anti-competitive effects may include reduced output, diminished quality, diminished innovation, diminished buyer choice and actual exclusion of rivals, while circumstantial evidence can be derived from the establishment of market power based on market shares. The third principle is the evaluation of the conditions of entry and the fourth is the evaluation of business justification for the restraint of competition, in particular, justification on the grounds of efficiency.[11]

With respect to the institutional setting for the application of antitrust law, the FTC and the Department of Justice are complimentarily responsible for its administrative enforcement. However, the antitrust statutes have remained vague

[7] US Merger Guidelines 1997, s 1.5, available at: www.justice.gov/atr/public/guidelines/horiz_book/15.html.

[8] US Merger Control Guideline 1997.

[9] Horizontal Guidelines, issued by the US Department of Justice and Federal Trade Commission on 19 August 2010, available at: http://ftc.gov/os/2010/08/100819hmg.pdf.

[10] *Brunswick Corp v Pueblo Bowl-O-Mat, Inc*, 429 US 477 (1977).

[11] Andrew I Gavil, William E Kovacic and Jonathan B Baker, *Antitrust Law in Perspective: Cases, Concepts and Problems in Contemporary Policy* (West Publishing, 2002) 776–922.

and open-ended.[12] Under the American common law tradition, US antitrust law gave federal judges extraordinary power to interpret and develop it through case law. Consequently, the federal judges looked into the common law tradition, in particular, the restraint of trade doctrine, and later into modern economic theories to support their interpretation of antitrust law.[13] The US courts have especially emphasized the need to recognize and adapt to the changing circumstances and lessons of accumulated experiences in antitrust cases.[14] As economic studies have evolved, the theories chosen by the court to interpret antitrust laws have transformed accordingly. This has, in turn, shaped the development of antitrust law.

It can be seen that US antitrust law is characterized by its juridical approach and the strong influence of evolving economic thought focused on effect analysis. The FTC has claimed that the aim of antitrust law is to enforce rigorous competition and to improve consumer welfare.[15] However, a historical review of antitrust law development reveals that, subjected to the influence of opposing ideologies underpinning the US market economy and because of the social embeddedness of business development and US legal culture, it has not had one consistent and uniform goal, but a diversity of goals through its transformation.

A. The Early Stage

The nineteenth century saw the entrenchment of American laissez-faire political liberalism, which, on the one hand, embraced classical economic theory with a faith in free and universal competition as upheld by Adam Smith and, on the other hand, emphasized the protection of individual rights against power, including economic power.[16] Under the influence of this political liberalism, American classical economic theory evolved to be based more on individual rights.[17] Along with the protection of individual liberty, the right to property and the right to exchange, competition became an integral part of the values upheld by the laissez-faire constitutionalism of this progressive era.

The emergence of trusts as powerful business organizations attracted much controversy in nineteenth-century US society. The social controversy over the

[12] Robert H Bork, 'Legislative Intent and the Policy of the Sherman Act' (1966) 9 *Journal of Law and Economics* 7–48.

[13] Marc Allen Eisner and Robin Stryker, *Antitrust and the Triumph of Economics: Institutions, Expertise and Policy Change* (University of North Carolina Press, 1991) 228.

[14] William Kovacic and Carl Shapiro, 'Antitrust Policy: A Century of Economic and Legal Thinking' (2000) 14(1) *Journal of Economic Perspectives* 43–56.

[15] www.ftc.gov/bc/antitrust/index.shtm.

[16] Walter Adams and James W Brock, 'The Sherman Act and the Economic Power' in Theodore P Kovaleff (ed), *The Antitrust Impulse, An Economic, Historical and Legal Analysis* (ME Sharpe, 1994) 505.

[17] Rudolph JR Peritz, *Competition Policy in America, 1888–1992: History, Rhetoric, Law* (Oxford University Press, 1996) 11.

accumulation of wealth in the hands of big corporations in the US market revealed two opposing ideologies: namely, the evolutionist and interventionist visions with respect to the relationship between the state and the market.[18] On the one hand, the evolutionist vision, based on property and contract protection, viewed the market as a mechanism to facilitate exchanges among individuals in their pursuit of best interests. Monopolies would emerge, but would not last long, given the entry of new players and the lack of state privileges. Thus, the market has a self-correcting function and state intervention should be kept at a minimum. On the other hand, the interventionist vision, although upholding the market mechanism, viewed the trusts as a result of the market's susceptibility to manipulation by powerful business, and hence demanded direct government control.[19]

The adoption of the Sherman Act was, according to scholars such as Walter Adams and James Brock, a compromise between the two ideologies.[20] The birth of the Sherman Act showed that the US Congress wished to endorse competition as a general principle for its market economy and that antitrust law would contribute to the long-established ideals of economic opportunity, security of property, freedom of exchange and political liberty.[21] It also showed that Congress refused to rely completely on the self-regulating function of the market mechanism and preferred a certain degree of government regulation.[22]

However, in the early stages of antitrust law development, the evolutionist vision played a very influential role in the application of antitrust law by both the judiciary and the administration. When Congressman Sherman was lobbying for the adoption of the Sherman Act, he assured his colleagues that the statute did not announce a new principle of law, but applied old and well-recognized principles of common law.[23] The US judiciary rarely invoked any formal economic theories, but construed antitrust cases largely through common law doctrines, in particular, restraint of trade doctrines, which functioned to prevent any party from gaining undue power in the market.[24]

In *Standard Oil*, which famously set out the rule of reason as the main method used in the application of antitrust law, Chief Justice White's opinion was largely individual rights-oriented, built upon common law doctrines, and contained little economic analysis.[25]

[18] William Hage, 'The Ideological Origins and Evolution of Antitrust Law' in *Issues in Competition Law and Policy* (ABA Section of Antitrust Law, 2008).

[19] Ibid.

[20] Walter Adams and James Brock, 'Antitrust, Ideology, and the Arabesque of Economic Theory' (1994) 66 *University of Colorado Law Review* 257.

[21] James May, 'Antitrust in the Formative Era: Political and Economic Theory in Constitutional and Antitrust Analysis, 1890–1918' (1989) 50 *Ohio State Law Journal* 258–395.

[22] Ibid.

[23] 21 Congress Report 2456 (1890).

[24] AD Neale, *The Antitrust Laws of the United States of America: A Study of Competition Enforced by Law* (Cambridge University Press, 1970) 11.

[25] *Standard Oil Co of New Jersey v United States* (n 2).

In interpreting the meaning of sections 1 and 2 of the Sherman Act, Chief Justice White stated that the antitrust law was adopted because of the vast accumulation of power by corporations and the widespread impression that their power had been, and would be, exerted to oppress individuals and injure the public generally.[26] He then interpreted antitrust law by referring mainly to the restraint of trade doctrine. He pointed out that in common law, monopoly was unlawful because of its restriction on individual freedom of contract and its injury to the public. By relying on contract law principles, he argued that to protect individual freedom of contract was not only in his own interest, but, principally, was in the interest of the common weal. According to him, voluntary restraints imposed upon the individual's right to pursue his calling came to be recognized as generally in accordance with the restraint of trade doctrine and hence as monopolistic, especially those which were thought to unduly diminish competition and enhance prices. He re-emphasized that to protect freedom of contract, when not unduly or improperly exercised, was the most efficient means of preventing a monopoly. He also endorsed the common law assumption that markets are self-correcting and that government has a limited role in preserving this capability by preventing only private actions that inhibit free exchange. The jurisprudence of US antitrust law at this stage reflects the evolutionist vision's view that market transactions, even between actors with vastly unequal endowments of wealth, are not coerced and are therefore legitimate.[27]

This jurisprudence corresponds to the classical economic theory upheld by American liberalism. Classical Smithian economic theory relies little on empirical economic analysis, but views competition as leading to a perfect and static market condition where the demand and supply curve reaches equilibrium in a transparent market environment and each actor behaves rationally.[28] In other words, in the eyes of classical economists, competition exists as the norm in a market economy.[29] Similarly, the court's approach seems to endorse a principle of competition enshrined in the natural value of individual liberty as a cornerstone of American classical economic theory and invokes little empirical economic analysis.[30]

Hence, antitrust law at this stage was interpreted to protect individual freedom from the coercive power held by large business players in the market. The Sherman Act was interpreted further to achieve non-economic goals, as Senator Kefauver claimed that without any proper regulation of the trusts, there would be a loss of public faith in the legitimacy of the market system that would lead to the collapse of democratic government.[31]

[26] Ibid.

[27] Hage (n 18).

[28] Adam Smith, *The Wealth of Nations* (Modern Library, 1954) 56.

[29] Paul McNulty, 'Economic Theory and the Meaning of Competition' (1968) 82(4) *Quarterly Journal of Economics* 639–56.

[30] William Kovacic and Carl Chapiro, 'Antitrust Policy: A Century of Economic and Legal Thinking', University of California, Berkeley, Working Paper No CPC99-09.

[31] Robert Pitofsky, 'The Political Content of Antitrust' (1978–79) 127 *University of Pennsylvania Law Review* 1051.

However, the court's approach at this time has been criticized as formalistic, as it invoked the freedom of contract principles with no further explanation and left key concepts in antitrust law such as agreement, markets and anti-competitive restraints undefined. The common law doctrines had limits in the interpretation of antitrust law and the court began to look to other disciplines, for example, economics, for support.

B. The Golden Age, 1955–80

Following the Great Depression, American society became disillusioned with the market. The Roosevelt administration re-emphasized competition as a core value of American society, but showed a preference for the interventionist view of markets, embracing necessary government regulation. In the 1940s, the US Supreme Court was mainly composed of Roosevelt appointees who favoured the interventionist view of markets. This, synchronizing with the appointment of Thurman Arnold as Head of the Antitrust Division, marked the start of the active application of antitrust law in US history.[32]

In dealing with antitrust cases, the US courts began to seek support from the now-influential economic theories. Economic theories on the market and competition evolved rapidly in the US. In contrast to the static view of competition in classical economic theory, marginalism revolutionized industrial economics in the US in the early-twentieth century, leading to the development of mathematical models which divided markets into degrees of competitiveness. Therefore, economists began to view markets as imperfect[33] and to focus more on market structures. They now viewed the market as impaired either by ruinous competition, with prices being forced so low that they could not cover fixed-cost investments, or by too little competition given the oligopoly problem. Thus, economists started to view competition as an exception rather than the norm for the economy. The task of competition regulation, at least from an economic point of view, seemed to be formidable. However, in 1940, John Clark proposed the idea of workable competition, which argued that while imperfect competition did exist, its impact was limited. According to Clark, it was workable competition, not the perfect competition of classical economics theory, that the government should aim to identify and enforce.[34] It was the proposal of the workable competition idea that provided the foundation for antitrust law to become the main competition regulation tool in the US.[35]

[32] Arthur M. Johnson, 'Theodore Roosevelt and the Bureau of Corporations' (1959) 45(4) *Mississippi Valley Historical Review* 571–90.

[33] Joan Robinson, *Economics of Imperfect Competition* (Macmillan, 1933).

[34] John Maurice Clark, 'Towards a Concept of Workable Competition' (1940) 30 *American Economic Review* 243.

[35] Herbert Hovenkamp, 'Neoclassical Crisis in Competition Policy 1890–1955', *University of Iowa Legal Studies Research Paper*, 8 July 2008, No 08-32.

From 1940 to the 1980s, the Structure-Conduct-Performance Harvard School of economic thinking was one of the dominant economic rationales influencing US antitrust law. This built upon Joe Bain's work on industrial organization theories, which, among other things, emphasized that the high entry barrier is associated with higher degrees of monopolistic output restriction and that the main deficiency of the antitrust policy was that it failed to tackle the important product differentiation entry barrier.[36] Building upon Bain's industrial organization theory, the Harvard approach emphasized that the structure of the market influenced the conduct of players, which, in turn, determined the performance of the market.[37] The number of competitors in the market, barriers to entry and the economy of scale are important factors when examining market structures.[38]

The influence of structuralism can best be illustrated by the jurisprudence in the Warren Court and its treatment of mergers. The *Brown Shoe*[39] case was the first case to come before the US Supreme Court under section 7 of the Clayton Act. The case involved a merger between Brown Shoe, the second largest shoe manufacturer in the US, and Kinnery, a retailer and manufacturer of shoes. Justice Warren examined the restraints on competition by the horizontal aspect of this merger. As section 7 of the Clayton Act requires the prohibition of any merger that substantially reduces competition in the market, Justice Warren argued that in this case, the substantial reduction of competition should be measured by the market share foreclosed by the merger in question, according to various economic and historical factors. The most important of these factors included the parties' intention to merge and the trend of the industry towards concentration.[40] In examining the future trend of the industry, Justice Warren argued that as the industry had a tendency towards oligopoly, the merger would in the future prove to be anti-competitive, although Brown argued that the shoe industry at that moment was competitive. Justice Warren went on to argue that the merger would be anti-competitive because Congress wanted to prevent the formation of further oligopolies, with their attendant adverse effects on the local control of industry and on small businesses.

Similar logic was applied by Justice Warren in his examination of the vertical aspect of the merger in this case. He held that the merger imposed vertical restraints on competition in that in 31 cities the combined market share, after the merger, was high, which intensified the existing market power held by the parties to the merger. According to him, the high concentration level based on the market share would be conducive to an oligopoly, which was something that Congress

[36] Joe Bain, 'The Rise of Structure Conduct Performance' in Jack High and Wayne Gable (eds), *A Century of the Sherman Act: American Economic Opinion* (George Mason University Press, 1992) 54.

[37] Hovenkamp (n 35).

[38] Edward Mason, *Economic Concentration and the Monopoly Problem* (Harvard University Press, 1957).

[39] *Brown Shoe Co, Inc v United States*, 370 US 294 (1962).

[40] Ibid.

aimed to avoid.[41] Furthermore, even if the merger would result in relatively small market control, the fact that it was held by one of the largest national chains in the US could adversely affect competition. The fact that the national chain was combined with a manufacturing operation aggregated the restraints on competition.[42] The merger between the supplier and retailer, according to Warren, would incur predatory pricing that would squeeze out small business players in the industry. As emphasized by Warren, one should not fail to recognize the desire of Congress to promote competition through the protection of small, viable, locally owned businesses.[43]

The Warren Court decision in *Brown Shoe* clearly reflects the influence of Harvard structuralism. In examining the restraints on competition by the merger, the court focused on the impact of the merger on the market structure, namely the impact on market foreclosure, which would prevent newcomers entering into the market, and the impact of the combined market power on small business players in the market. The logic of the court illustrates that competition was viewed as rivalry to promote better market performance and, to this end, the task of antitrust law was to safeguard a market structure in which the number of business players would not be affected and which was thus conducive to competition.

However, the Warren Court antitrust jurisprudence received wide criticism, mainly from the later Chicago School of economic thinking. As held by the Chicago School, the Harvard Structuralist School regulated business practice, which did not harm competition and eventually led to the loss of efficiency and consumer welfare in total.[44]

C. The Chicago and Post-Chicago Stages

In the Reagan and Bush administrations, evolutionist ideology prevailed. Deregulation was enforced thoroughly, in almost all sectors of the US economy, and the role of the state was minimal. The Reagan administration defined its role as helping enterprises, but not standing in their way.[45]

The emphasis from the Chicago School of antitrust economic theory on efficiency came into influence in the 1970s. Judges who were well informed about economics, such as Robert Bork and Richard Posner, readily translated the Chicago School's economic thinking into language which could be understood by legal practitioners. By the 1970s, the US Supreme Court judgments had shown

[41] Ibid.
[42] Ibid.
[43] Ibid.
[44] Richard Posner, *Antitrust Law: An Economic Perspective* (University of Chicago Press, 1976).
[45] Marc Allen Eisner, *Antitrust and the Triumph of Economics: Institutions, Expertise and Policy* (University of Chicago Press, 1991) 184.

an ascendancy of economic analysis in antitrust cases, such as in *GTE Sylvania*.[46] Furthermore, US companies were faced with intense competition in the global market and were concerned with increasing their efficiency, which encouraged the acceptance of the efficiency argument by American society.[47] As a result, the Chicago School of thought became the leading economic theory influencing US antitrust law.

Embracing the classical price theory, members of the Chicago School argue that as long as market entry is kept open, the demand and supply curve will encourage any profit-seeking business player to enter the market and keep competition rigorous.[48] Instead, efficiency should be the main yardstick in the application of antitrust law.

According to antitrust economics, efficiency in the market includes mainly allocative efficiency and productive efficiency. In the situation of perfect competition, market players, as rational and self-interested driven actors, are keen to maximize their profits. Marginal revenue refers to the extra revenue generated by one additional unit of product or service. Marginal cost refers to the cost of producing one additional unit of product or service. Allocative efficiency refers to the situation where in seeking the maximization of profits, the players have reached a point where the cost for the production of one extra unit (marginal cost) exceeds the price he or she would obtain for it. In this scenario, the market player would stop expanding the production and consumers can obtain the products at the price they are willing to pay for them.[49] Productive efficiency is achieved when a producer produces the product or service at the lowest possible cost. In perfect competition, the production exceeding the marginal cost would cause customers to switch to other products supplied by competitors on the market. As long as the cost for production does not exceed marginal cost, the producer has the incentive to produce more efficiently with an aim to maximize marginal revenue.[50]

In contrast to the perfect competition where producers act as price-takers, a monopoly exists when the producer can set the price and ignore its effect on other sellers.[51] Restraint imposed by the monopoly of the market can impair both productive and allocative efficiency. With respect to allocative efficiency, monopolistic producers tend to set price above the marginal cost, which entails higher producer surplus, but not high enough to compensate for the reduction in consumer surplus caused by higher prices. With respect to production efficiency, monopolistic producers have less incentive to make effort in increasing product

[46] *Continental TV, Inc v GTE Sylanvia Inc*, 433 US 36 (1977). See also Maxwell Blecher, 'The Impact of GTE Sylvania on Antitrust Jurisprudence' (1991) *60 Antitrust Law Journal* 17–26.

[47] McNulty (n 29).

[48] Posner (n 44).

[49] Richard Whish, *Competition Law* (Oxford University Press, 2008) 3.

[50] Maher Dabbah, *EC and UK Competition Law: Commentary, Cases and Materials* (Cambridge University Press, 2004) 7.

[51] Hugh Gravelle and Ray Rees, *Microeconomics* (Longman Group, 1992) 269.

efficiency and inefficient monopolistic producers can continue to exist in the market due to no competition.[52]

The Chicago School of economic thought stresses that it should be the consumer welfare enhancing allocative efficiency, not productive efficiency, which the antitrust law aims to achieve. According to Bork, antitrust law aims to pursue the exclusive goal of allocative efficiency for consumer welfare, without impairing productive efficiency so much as to produce no gain or loss in consumer welfare.[53]

Bork's idea is clearly illustrated by the following graph.

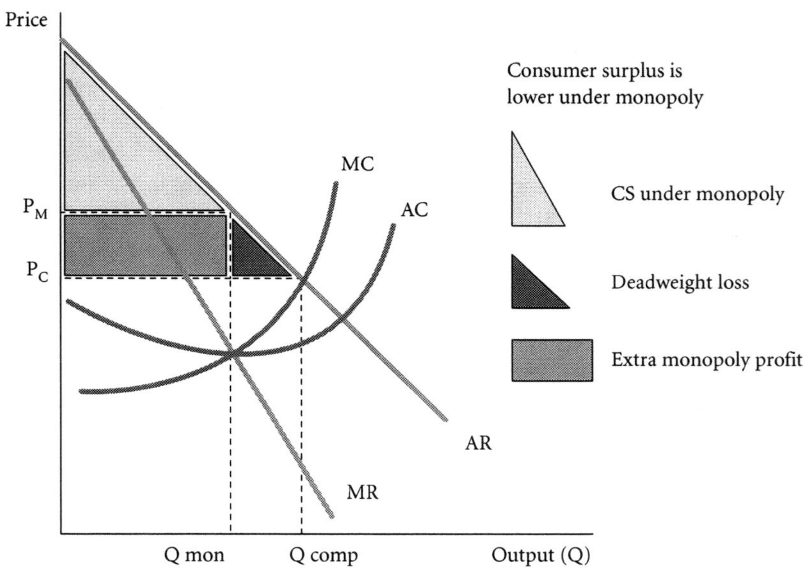

The graph compares the case of perfect competition, where P_C (price in perfect competition) = MC (marginal cost) and the quantity sold to consumers = Qcomp (quantity in perfect competition) with the case of maximum market power, where the monopoly charges a price of P_M (price in monopoly) and produces a quantity of product at Qmon (quantity in monopoly). It can be seen that the social welfare generated when P_M = Qmon is less than that generated when P_C = Qcomp, and the lost welfare is shown in the triangle, which cannot be recovered and is deadweight welfare loss. Therefore, the pursuit of allocative efficiency with consumer surplus, namely when P_C = Qcomp, is regarded as the most efficient way to avoid the deadweight loss and maximize social welfare.

Bork attacked the Warren Court approach in the *Brown Shoe* case. He argued that it was impossible to see any harm to competition in the case, that the Supreme

[52] Massimo Motta, *Competition Policy: Theory and Practice* (Cambridge University Press, 2004) 43 and 47.

[53] Robert Bork, *The Antitrust Paradox* (Free Press, 1993) 9.

Court failed to notice that more than 800 shoe manufacturers were operating in a national market and that the industry was as close to pure competition as is possible outside a classroom model.[54] The mistake the Court made was to treat the vertical merger as exclusionary and thus as inherently anti-competitive. Furthermore, the Warren Court ruled that the horizontal aspect of the merger provided a five per cent market control in the shoe industry and that this would be a negative reassurance for the acquisition of a market share by similar future mergers. However, Bork argued that as long as market entry was easy and rapid, the Court's apprehension of oligopoly was groundless.[55] Bork also criticized Justice Warren's argument that to protect small business players vis-a-vis large national chains as a result of a merger served more social purpose and protected market egalitarianism, pointing out that he had failed to note the fact that large national chains operate on an efficiency basis and bring consumer benefits.[56]

The Chicago School has had a far-reaching impact on the transformation of antitrust law in substantive rules, which can be observed clearly in the fields of merger regulation, vertical restraints and predatory pricing.

With respect to merger regulation, the FTC adopted a series of merger guidelines from 1968 to 1997 in line with the transformation of economic thought. Compared with the 1968 merger guidelines, which were reluctant to approve mergers on the ground of efficiency and treated vertical merger foreclosure and the increase in entry cost as a primary target, the merger guidelines in 1997 were more efficiency oriented and based on economic analysis. The 1997 guidelines aimed to assess whether the merger would substantially reduce competition in the market. The competition authorities use the assessment of market concentration, potential adverse competitive effects, entry, efficiency and failure in order to answer the ultimate question: is the merger likely to create or enhance market power or to facilitate its exercise?

Vertical agreements can be challenged under section 1 of the Sherman Act as unreasonable restraint on trade, and under section 2, of the Sherman Act as exclusionary conduct. Chicagonian thinking holds that vertical agreement has its efficiency enhancing functions. As manufacturers and retailers have different incentives in business, by setting up a vertically exclusive dealing agreement, the manufacturer is able to motivate the retailer to engage more in production promotion services and prevent the free-riding problem caused by other distributors. This leads eventually to the increase of consumer welfare. Hence, the Court held that vertical agreements are not anti-competitive per se and that all non-price vertical agreements should be subject to a rule of reason analysis.[57] In order to challenge vertical agreements, under section 1 of the Sherman Act, the claimant must prove that the agreement is likely to have a genuine adverse effect on competition

[54] Ibid, 211.
[55] Ibid, 214.
[56] Ibid, 216.
[57] *Continental TV, Inc v GTE Sylanvia Inc* (n 46).

based on empirical market analysis and is going to harm interbrand competition. To challenge vertical agreements, under section 2 of the Sherman Act, the claimant must prove that there is a causal link between the monopolist's action and its market power and the adverse effect on competition in the market.[58]

With respect to predatory pricing, Chicagonian economic thinking holds that predatory pricing, as a low pricing strategy aiming to squeeze competitors out of the market or deter them from entering it, is actually rarely used by business players, as such behaviour is irrational, unlikely and only happens in exceptional circumstances.[59] Under the influence of the Chicago School, the US Supreme Court in the case of the *Brooke Group*[60] held that to challenge predatory pricing under section 2 of the Sherman Act, the claimant must prove that the defendant has employed below-cost pricing and that there is a dangerous probability that the defendant will recoup the investment. According to the Chicago School, as long as market entry remains easy, the entry of new competitors will threaten the durability of predatory pricing and will substantially lessen its anti-competitive effect. Hence, the Court requires proof of the probability of recoup. Under the influence of the Chicago School, the Court has obviously adopted a market effect approach, which thus leads to narrow regulation with respect to predatory pricing.

Based on the above, it can be seen that the Chicago School of economic thinking has had a sweeping influence on US antitrust law, substantially reshaping its direction. First of all, it clarified that allocative efficiency leading to consumer welfare was the one and only goal of antitrust law. This argument has been augmented by Bork and Posner[61] and the US Supreme Court through case law. It was a watershed in the development of US antitrust law, because it meant the law stopped experimenting with other goals and restricted its concerns to consumer welfare. It is argued that by restricting the goals of antitrust law to consumer welfare, US antitrust law has been given certainty and has achieved rigorous enforcement of competition.[62]

Second, the Chicago School developed detailed methods for the evaluation of anti-competitive restraints in antitrust law. In *Sylvania*,[63] the Court officially stated the need to carry out an economic analysis to evaluate the anti-competitive restraints in the case. Hence, empirical economic analysis by the claimant, the defendant and the judiciary began to play a significant role in antitrust cases. In the economic analysis, the entry barrier was no longer the a priori target. Instead, US antitrust law adopted an effect analysis by looking at the verification of effect in

[58] James C Cooper, Luke M Froeb, Dan O'Brien and Michael G Vita, 'Vertical Antitrust Policy as a Problem of Inference' (2005) 23(7–8) *International Journal of Industrial Organization* 639–64.

[59] John S McGee, 'Predatory Price Cutting: The Standard Oil Case' (1958) *Journal of Law and Economics* 137.

[60] *Brooke Group Ltd v Brown & Williamson Tobacco Corp* (92-466), 509 US 209 (1993).

[61] Bork (n 53); Posner (n 44).

[62] John J Flynn, 'Antitrust Jurisprudence: A Symposium on the Economic, Political and Social Goals of Antitrust Policy' (1977) 125(6) *University of Pennsylvania Law Review* 1182–90.

[63] *Continental TV, Inc v GTE Sylanvia Inc* (n 46).

allocative efficiency enhancement against the restriction of competition brought about by the restraints.[64] Effect analysis thus departed from the notion of protecting individual liberty upheld by the earlier enforcement of antitrust law.

The political economy for antitrust law development in the post-Chicago era changed slightly from that of the Chicago era. Both the Clinton and George W Bush administrations pledged to have more rigorous antitrust enforcement. However, such vigorous enforcement by the Clinton administration has been viewed as developing no new rules of substance.[65] The resurgence of national and global price-fixing prosecution during the George W Bush administration added more teeth to US antitrust enforcement.[66]

The post-Chicago stage has seen a greater reliance by antitrust law on leading economic theories. These mainly include the mathematical reconstruction of industrial organization theory using game theories.[67] As seen in the *Kodak* case,[68] the central question, when Kodak's dominant position in the manufacturing market could not be established, was whether it was possible to establish that Kodak had abused its market power in the linked service market. The Court pushed aside the Chicago School price theory and ruled that consumers in the case had experienced a locked-in effect and had suffered from imperfect information. The Court then argued that it was possible to establish the abuse of dominance on the part of Kodak in the linked market. However, it should be noted that the Chicago School of economic thought has made a distinctive mark on US antitrust jurisprudence, and the criticism mainly focused on the fact that the Chicago School has been oversold in antitrust law, but has little dispute over the basic approaches that the Chicago School uses.[69]

From over a century of antitrust law application in the US, it can be seen that the goals of the law have not been single or consistent, but, on the contrary, divisible. The goal of antitrust law, to put it simply, has changed from protecting individual liberty based on the principle of competition to protecting the market structure fostering competition, and to protecting consumer benefit based on the maximization of allocative efficiency. These goals are divided, but nevertheless interlinked, as all of them are rooted in classical economic theory and American liberalist ideology, and serve to make the market work better.

[64] Ingo Schmidt and Jan B Rittaler, *A Critical Evaluation of Chicago School of Antitrust Analysis* (Kluwer, 1989) 106.

[65] Robert Pitofsky, 'Antitrust at the Turn of the Twenty-First Century: The Matter of Remedies' (2002) 91 *Geogetown Law Journal* 169–82.

[66] John Connor, 'Effectiveness of Antitrust Sanctions on Modern International Cartels' (2006) 6 *Journal of Industry, Competition and Trade* 195–223.

[67] Jonathan Baker, 'A Preface to Post-Chicago Antitrust' in Antonio Cucinotta, Roberto Pardolesi and Roger Van den Bergh (eds), *Post-Chicago Developments in Antitrust Law* (Edward Elgar, 2002) 69.

[68] *Eastman Kodak Co v Image Tech SVCS*, 504 US 451 (1992).

[69] Richard Shmalensee, 'Thoughts on the Chicago Legacy in US Antitrust' in Robert Pitofsky (ed), *How the Chicago School Overshot the Mark: The Effect of Conservative Economic Analysis on US Antitrust* (Oxford University Press, 2008) 11.

The divisibility of goals also confirms that in the search for an interpretation of antitrust law, the US judiciary and administrative authorities chose to rely, first, on the common law restraint of trade doctrine. When faced with the limits of the doctrine, they chose to invoke evolving economic thought for support. As a result, the enforcer's choice of which strand of economic thought to use as an instrument for construing antitrust law has, on the one hand, been influenced by the developments in political economy, ideology and leading economic theories, and, on the other hand, bound these enforcers to their chosen strand of thought. Hence, today the US antitrust law is characterized by its goal of efficiency and empirical economic analysis.

III. EU COMPETITION LAW

EU Competition Law is one regime that is comparable to US antitrust law in terms of its magnitude and influence. The core provisions of EU competition law include Articles 101, 102 and 106 of the Treaty on the Functioning of The European Union (TFEU). Article 101 of the TFEU provides that agreements that have as their object or effect the prevention, restriction or distortion of competition within the common market are automatically void, unless they can be exempted by satisfying conditions set out in Article 101(3).[70] Here, EU competition law has held that a rule of reason principle is not upheld under the Article 101 analysis because a systematic exemption clause has been provided under Article 101(3).[71]

Article 102 provides that abuse of a dominant position by one or more players in the market that affects trade among Member States shall be prohibited.[72] Although the prohibited abuse of dominance provided under Article 102 is mainly exploitative abuse, the European Court of Justice (ECJ) has held that the list under Article 102 is not exhaustive and that Article 102 aims to regulate both exploitative and exclusionary abuse.[73]

Article 106 provides that in the case of public undertakings in Member States, Member States shall not enact or maintain any measures that restrict competition. However, public undertakings entrusted with the operation of service of general economic interests or having the character of a revenue producing monopoly can be exempted from Article 106 when the competition regulations obstruct the performance of the undertakings in law and, in practice, of the tasks assigned to them.[74]

[70] Art 101 TFEU.
[71] Whish (n 49) 131.
[72] Art 102 TFEU.
[73] Case 6/72, *Europemballange Corporation and Continental Can Company Inc v Commission* [1973] ECR 215.
[74] Art 10 TFEU.

Under the EU legal order, the Council of the European Union has the competence to issue regulations or directives to give effect to the principles set out in Articles 101 and 102.[75] The EU issued Regulation on the control of concentration between undertakings in 1989, which was superseded by the EC Merger Regulation in 2004.[76]

The European Commission had acted as the sole agent responsible for the enforcement of EU competition law before the modernization reform in 2004.[77] As a result of the reform, the national competition authorities and national courts share the enforcement of Articles 101 and 102 together with the European Commission. A European Competition Network (ECN), composed of the European Commission and the national competition authorities, was set up to undertake public enforcement of EU competition law. While the Commission has the ultimate control in competition cases,[78] the ECN shows the decentralized enforcement of EU competition law. Furthermore, national courts of Member States can now apply Article 101 (in particular, Article 101(3)) and 102 in full. While the Commission and the national competition authorities have the referral system for competition regulation with community dimension, the Commission has the exclusive competence to apply the EU merger regulation.[79] The General Court of the EU and the European Court of Justice are responsible for the judicial review of the legality of Commission decisions.[80]

On the surface, EU competition law diverges from US antitrust law in various aspects. First, whereas the US is a federal sovereign state, the EU is one union based on economic and political partnership among 28 Member States.[81] Given the different social and political contexts between the US and the EU, EU competition law claims to have a model of its own, pursuing goals different from antitrust law. Second, EU competition law regulates both private and public restraints on the market, and plays an active role in sector liberalisation in the common market,[82] while US antitrust law mainly targets private restraints and, when in conflict with sector regulation, the latter prevails.[83] Third, US antitrust law is juridical and relies extensively on private enforcement given the treble damage provided under US

[75] Art 103 TFEU.

[76] Council Regulation (EEC) No 4064/89 of 21 December 1989 on the control of concentrations between undertakings, OJ L395, 30 December 1989 1–12; Council Regulation (EC) No 139/2004 of 20 January 2004 on the control of concentrations between undertakings (the EC Merger Regulation), OJ L24, 29 January 2004, 1–22.

[77] For the European Commission as the sole agent responsible for EU competition law enforcement, see Council Regulation No 17 of 6 February 1962, OJ 013, 21 February 1962, 204–11.

[78] For example, the competition authorities of Member States are automatically relieved of the case when the Commission initiates its own proceedings. Council Regulation 1/2003 on the Implementation of the Rules on Competition Laid Down in Articles 81 and 82 of the Treaty, OJ L1, 4 January 2004, 1–25.

[79] OJ L24, 29 January 2004, 1–22.

[80] Articles 256, 260 and 267 TFEU.

[81] http://europa.eu/abc/panorama/index_en.htm.

[82] Council Regulation No 130/2004, OJ C 20, 28 January 2003, 4.

[83] *Verizon Communication Inc v Law Offices of Curtis V Trinko*, LLP, 540 US 682 (2004).

law. EU competition law relies more on public enforcement by the administrative system of the EU.

However, in recent years, and especially after the modernization reform, EU competition law declared its pursuit of the goal of consumer welfare and integrated economic analysis into its application of competition law.[84] The European Commission has encouraged private enforcement in Member States by issuing Green and White Papers on the private enforcement of EU competition law in national courts in 2005 and 2008, respectively.[85] It is therefore interesting to observe why and how EU competition law chose to converge, at least in some aspects, with competition regulation across the Atlantic and analyze to what extent this convergence has been achieved. To this end, it would be helpful to review the development of EU competition law in recent decades, in which the transformation of the goals of the law serves as the central thread.

A. The Historical Legacies of EU Competition Law

Europe at the end of the Second World War was at a crossroads. European states were, on the one hand, faced with the task of recovering from the war and seeking economic development; on the other hand, they were wary of the possible resurgence of totalitarian power in Europe. During Europe's reconstruction period, the US made efforts to ensure economics prevailed over politics and to de-ideologize issues of political economy into questions of output and efficiency.[86] Compared with the US, most European governments, although aiming to build up a market economy, did not have the same strong faith in the self-correcting function of the market and preferred direct government intervention or even nationalization.[87] Antitrust law based on statute regulation by one independent authority was a new and imported concept in Europe. This was partly because of the political influence of the US in the post-war period and partly because of Europe's wish to garner economic growth through similar laws.[88]

Against this background, the European Coal and Steel Community (ECSC) Treaty of 1951 contained anti-cartel provisions similar to the provisions provided

[84] Commission Green Paper on Vertical Restraints in EC Competition Policy in 1997, available at: http://europa.eu/documents/comm/green_papers/pdf/com96_721_en.pdf.

[85] Green Paper on Damages Actions for Breach of the EC Antitrust Rules, COM (2005) 672 final, available at http://eur-lex.europa.eu/LexUriServ/LexUriServ.do?uri=CELEX:52005DC0672:EN:NOT; and White Paper on Damages Actions for Breach of the EC Antitrust Rules. COM (2008) 165 final, available at: http://eur-lex.europa.eu/LexUriServ/LexUriServ.do?uri=CELEX:52008DC0165:EN:NOT.

[86] Charles S Maier, 'The Two Postwar Eras and the Conditions for Stability in Twentieth-Century Western Europe' (1981) 86(2) *American Historical Review* 327–52.

[87] G Majone, 'The Rise of Statutory Regulation in Europe' in G Majone (ed), *Regulating Europe* (Routledge, 1996) 51.

[88] Imelda Maher, 'Re-imaging the Story of European Competition Law' (2000) 20(1) *Oxford Journal of Legal Studies* 155–66.

in the Sherman Act, the Clayton Act and the Federal Trade Commission Act. The ECSC Treaty provides that:

> Article 65(1): There are hereby forbidden all agreements among enterprises, all decisions of associations of enterprises, and all concerted practices, which would tend, directly or indirectly, to prevent, restrict or impede the normal operation of competition within the common market, and in particular:
>
> (a) To fix or influence prices;
> (b) To restrict or control production, technical development or investments;
> (c) To allocate markets, products, customers or sources of supply.[89]
>
> Article 66: Except as provided in paragraph 3 below, any transaction which would have in itself the direct or indirect effect of bringing about a concentration, within the territories mentioned in the first paragraph of Article 79, involving enterprises at least one of which falls under the application of Article 80, shall be submitted to a prior authorization of the High Authority.[90]

It should be noted that the anti-cartel provisions of the ECSC Treaty were not simply a copy of US antitrust law. For instance, the High Authority of the ECSC was provided with interventionist powers in crisis situations.[91] These provisions reflected the US intention to prevent the occurrence of large coal and steel trusts in Germany. However, as the ECSC was a forerunner of the EU, the influence of US antitrust law in competition regulation development in the EU should not be denied.[92]

The formation of the ECSC as an economic community carried a hidden intention to seek long-term peace in Europe. Its progress encouraged political leaders to pursue the ideal of establishing a political union in Europe. The political ideal soon failed, but it nevertheless pushed politicians to focus more on the economic integration of Europe.[93] The Spaak Report, which led to the final establishment of the European Economic Community (EEC), stated that a common market would be beneficial to European business. In order to create a common market, government restrictions on the movement of goods, services, persons and capital had to be removed. Accordingly, private restraints should not act as private barriers to economic integration, and competition rules had to be applied to guarantee that

[89] Art 65.1 ECSC Treaty. The ECSC Treaty expired on 23 July 2002. Decisions of the Representatives of the Member States meeting within the Council on the Consequences of the expiry of the European Coal and Steel Community, [2002] OJ L194/35.

[90] Art 66 ECSC Treaty.

[91] Ibid, Articles 59 and 61.

[92] Sigrid Quark and Marie-Laurie Djelic, 'Adaptation, Recombination and Reinforcement: The Story of Antitrust and Competition Law in Germany and Europe, in Wolfgang Streeck and Kathleen Thelen (eds), *Beyond Continuity: Institutional Change in Advanced Political Economies* (Oxford University Press, 2005) 256.

[93] R Cardozo, 'The Project for Political Community (1952–4)' in R Pryce (ed), *The Dynamics of European Union* (Croom Helm, 1987).

cartels and monopolies would not frustrate the common market goal.[94] The EEC Treaty followed the Spaak Report's interpretation and conferred a market integration imperative on EC competition rules. Compared with the indirect influence of US antitrust law, the Spaark Report had a much more direct and far-reaching influence on EC competition law.

Apart from the political economy of economic integration in Europe, different ideologies on the relationship between the state and market have also played influential roles in shaping EC competition laws. One of the most influential ideologies has been the 'ordoliberalism' upheld by German competition law.

Ordoliberalism reflects on prior traditions of liberalism and argues that liberalism had been narrowed down to laissez-faire capitalism and isolated from social reality. Ordoliberalism returned to the fundamental values of liberalism and added new elements which transformed the direction of the liberalist tradition.[95]

While embracing competition as the main means to generate wealth rapidly, ordoliberalism emphasizes human values instead of pure efficiency. It emphasizes the importance of protecting social goals, including the pursuit of social justice. Hence, although the market and competition are upheld as the driving forces for economic growth, the market should function in a way which is fair and equitable to everyone within it.

Ordoliberalism aims to create a society built on a set of social, political and economic values that protect individual rights and democratic institutions. Competition, as one of its core economic values, should function in an equitable way so as to achieve the right social values. The state is obliged to build the necessary institutions to protect these values.[96] Here, ordoliberalism requires a state strong enough to protect the individual against private abuse, including abuse caused by monopolies.

Therefore, in ordoliberalism's view, competition is conceived not as spontaneous activities on the part of players during transactions in the market; it is conceived as an order in which no firm has the power to coerce conduct by other firms in that market.[97]

Ordoliberalism converges with American liberalism in its emphasis on competition's role in wealth accumulation and on the protection of individual rights. However, ordoliberalists view that, based on the protection of individual freedom, the notion of competition is an order free from coercive power in the market, which in other words means a process, structure and even an institution installed and supported by the state that, in turn, supports the functioning

[94] Brussels Report on the General Common Market (commonly known as the Spaak Report) 1956, Title II, ch 1b, Monopolies, 59–60.

[95] David Gerber, *Law and Competition in Twentieth-Century Europe: Protecting Prometheus* (Oxford University Press 1998) 239.

[96] Ibid, 240–41.

[97] Ibid, 245.

of society.[98] This differs fundamentally from American liberalism's faith in the self-correcting function of the market and from the notion upheld by classical economic theory of competition as spontaneous transactions leading to static equilibrium, or as leading to the maximization of allocative efficiency, as upheld by the Chicago School.

The rapid growth of ordoliberalism and its acceptance outside Germany in Europe influenced the European integration process, as its advocacy of the state's role in a market economy was regarded as well suited to the task faced by the EEC of building up a common market.[99]

Ordoliberalism has had a far-reaching impact on EU competition rules, which can be appreciated even today. First, the TFEU explicitly calls for concerted action to guarantee steady expansion, balanced trade and fair competition.[100] Second, ordoliberalism has influenced the development of substantive rules under EU competition law, in particular Article 102. In *Continental Can*, the Court held that EU law provided for the installation of a system to ensure that competition in the common market was not distorted. Hence, Article 102 meant that competition structure, in other words a competitive process, should be maintained with the ultimate purpose of protecting undistorted competition, to serve consumer benefit and to promote market integration.[101] This showed clear overtones of the ordoliberalism influence. In *Hoffman La Roche*, the Court held that dominant players should act as if they were in a competitive market to prevent the abuse of their dominance,[102] which pointed to ordoliberalism's notion of competition as a competitive process—the elimination of competitors would make competition difficult or impossible and would thus impair the institution of a functioning market economy.

B. The Foundational Period: The Market Integration Imperative

By the mid-1950s, when the fear of a resurgent Germany had lessened, the Treaty of Rome competition rules had become rather muted. This is because, first, European society was lacking enthusiasm towards the new supranational organization[103] and, second, the European Commission lacked experience in dealing

[98] Wernhard Moschel, 'Competition Policy from an Ordo Point of View', in A Peacock and H Willgerodt (eds), *German Neo-Liberals and the Social Market Economy* (Macmillan, 1989) 146.

[99] John Gillingham, *European Integration, 1950–2003: Superstate or New Market Economy?* (Cambridge University Press, 2003) 10.

[100] The Preamble to the TFEU.

[101] *Europemballange Corporation and Continental Can Company Inc v Commission* (n 73).

[102] Case 85/76, *Hoffmann-La Roche & Co AG v Commission of the European Communities* [1979] ECR 461.

[103] Cardozo (n 93).

with competition cases and the first procedural enforcement regulation was not adopted until 1962.[104]

Although the early application of competition law was quiet, it was embedded in the EU's primary task of building up a common market free from trade barriers among the Member States. Both the European Commission and the European courts have relied on or even stretched EU competition law to achieve this end.[105] The fact that the Commission has chosen market integration over other goals for its competition rules can be observed from the following points.

First, in this period, the European Commission focused on vertical agreements, in particular, the territorial market allocation provisions contained in vertical agreements. In *Consten Grundig*,[106] the German electronic goods manufacturer Grundig set up a vertical exclusive dealing arrangement with its distributors in EC Member States, including Consten in France, to prevent parallel import. UNEF, another retail company, bought Grundig goods from Germany and sold them on the French market for a much cheaper price. Consten took legal action against UNEF regarding the parallel import. UNEF, before the European Commission, challenged the validity of an exclusive dealing agreement between Grundig and Costen under Article 101 of TFEU. The Commission held that the arrangement fell under Article 101(1) and could not be exempted under Article 101(3) as Article 101 covers interbrand as well as intrabrand competition. Furthermore, it held that the territorial ban constituted the restraint of competition on the common market.[107] Grundig appealed against the Commission's decision before the ECJ. The ECJ upheld the decision, stating that although vertical distribution agreements did not necessarily fall under Article 101(1), agreements capable of constituting a threat, whether direct or indirect, actual or potential, to freedom of trade between Member States in a manner that might harm the attainment of the objectives of a single market between states should be caught by the EU competition law. For the Court, the territorial ban of trade contained in the provision had as its object the restriction of competition in the market, and there was no need to examine its actual effect on the competition.[108] The Court's broad interpretation of agreements and its teleological method showed its supportive role in guiding the Commission towards achieving economic integration.[109]

As discussed above, in the development of US antitrust law under the influence of the Chicago School of economic thinking, the exclusive dealing agreement can be beneficial to consumers as it prevents free-riding from other competitors and increases interbrand competition. This can, in most cases, outweigh its negative

[104] Council Regulation No 17, Regulation implementing Articles 85 and 86 of the Treaty, OJ 13, 21 February 1962, 204–11.

[105] Giorgio Monti, *EC Competition Law* (Cambridge University Press, 2007) 39.

[106] Cases 56 and 58 /64, *Consten & Grundig v Commission* [1966] ECR 299.

[107] Valentine Korah, *Cases, Materials on EC Competition Law* (Hart Publishing, 2006) 13.

[108] *Consten & Grundig v Commission* (n 106).

[109] Grant Kelleher, 'The Common Market Antitrust Laws; The First Ten Years' (1967) *Antitrust Bulletin* 1219.

effect on intrabrand competition.[110] In other words, the Commission and the courts, preoccupied with the target of creating a common market, were aggressive in attacking vertical agreements, in particular, vertical agreements with a territorial ban.[111]

Second, the Commission examined horizontal agreements through the lens of market integration. Compared with its attitude to vertical agreements, the Commission was much more cautious in the application of competition rules against horizontal agreements. In examining the agreement's effect on competition, it tended to exempt those that contributed to the formation of a common market and to economic integration.[112]

Third, in the beginning, the Commission made little use of Article 102 on the regulation of the abuse of dominance. During this period, tackling dominant players on the emerging common market remained a sensitive issue, as most of these players continued to be national champions of Member States. Member States were keen to develop their industrial competitiveness and were reluctant to let their national champions be subjected to EU competition law.[113] However, in the 1970s, Europe was hit by an oil crisis and the resulting high inflation. The Commission started to use Article 102 to discourage dominant players from adding to the pressure on the economy.[114]

The application of Article 102 has been seen as one of the most controversial areas of EU competition law. For the Commission to apply Article 102 to unilateral anti-competitive behaviour, it must establish dominance and then the abuse of dominance. However, both the Commission and the Court have failed to set out a consistent interpretation of the concepts of dominance and abuse, to which the following serve as evidence. First, with respect to the establishment of dominance, the Court in *United Brands* held that:

> The Dominant Position referred to in article 102(86) relates to a position of economic strength enjoyed by an undertaking which enables it to prevent effective competition being maintained on the relevant market by giving it the power to behave to an appreciable extent independently of its competitors, customers and ultimately of its consumers. In general, a dominant position derives from a combination of several factors which taken separately are not necessarily determinative.[115]

The Court's definition contains two aspects, namely the ability to prevent competition and the ability to behave independently.[116] While the Court has

[110] *Continental TV, Inc v GTE Sylanvia Inc* (n 46).

[111] B Hawk, 'System Failure: Vertical Restraints and EC Competition Law' (1995) 32 *Common Market Law Review* 973.

[112] Monti (n 105) 364.

[113] Rein Wesseling, *The Modernisation of EC Antitrust Law* (Hart Publishing, 2008) 48.

[114] David Gerber, 'The Transformation of European Community Competition Law' (1994) 35(1) *Harvard International Law Journal* 97–148.

[115] Case 27/76, *United Brands Company and United Brands Continental BV v Commission of the European Communities* [1978] ECR 207.

[116] Whish (n 49) 174.

not explained the relationship between these two aspects, the Commission emphasizes market share[117] in the establishment of dominance and takes into consideration other factors, such as the market entry barrier, the conduct and performance of the alleged dominant player, and buyer power in the market.[118] However, the Commission's and the Court's definition of dominance have not relied consistently on objective economic analysis, but on a mix of subjective controversial criteria, and are criticised for a lack of reasoning.[119] For example, in *Hoffman-la Roche v Commission*, the ECJ held that 'evidence of the view may legitimately be taken that very large shares are in themselves and save in exceptional circumstances evidence of the existence of a dominance position'.[120] In *Michelin v Commission*, the Commission established Michelin's dominance in the marketplace on the ground of its price discrimination conduct. Based on the establishment of dominance, the Commission argued that the conduct of price discrimination was an abuse of dominance. Although Michelin argued before the Court that the Commission's approach was circular, the Court affirmed the Commission's decision.[121]

Third, the establishment of abuse is even more complicated. Article 102 aims to regulate both exploitative and exclusionary abuses on the market, but the Commission has, throughout the years, acted with benign neglect towards the regulation of exploitative abuse and has focused on exclusionary abuse, which impacts on the competitive process and market integration.[122]

The definition of abuse has been controversial. In *Hoffman-La Roche*,[123] abuse is defined as influencing the structure of a market, having the effect of hindering the degree of existing competition on the market and, the growth of that competition. The definition of abuse of dominance is further elaborated by the Court in *Continental Can*.[124] The Continental Can Company sought to annul the Commission's decision that the company infringed Article 102 by acquiring about 80 per cent of the shares of another competitor. The Court stretched Article 102 on the abuse of dominance to cover mergers and acquisitions. It held that abuse may occur when an undertaking with a dominant position strengthened its position to a degree that would substantially fetter competition, in this case causing the only remaining undertaking in the market to be dependent on the dominant one. It has therefore been argued that the Court deemed restraint on market

[117] *Hoffmann-La Roche & Co AG v Commission of the European Communities* (n 102).

[118] 111 *United Brands Company and United Brands Continental BV v Commission of the European Communities* (n 105).

[119] Maher Dabbah, 'Conduct, Dominance and Abuse in "Market Relationship": Analysis of Some Conceptual Issues under Article 82 EC' (2000) 21 *European Competition Law Review* 45.

[120] *Hoffmann-La Roche & Co AG v Commission of the European Communities* (n 102).

[121] Case 322/81, *NV Nederlandsche Banden Industrie Michelin v Commission of the European Communities* [1983] ECR 3461.

[122] Eleanor M Fox, 'We Protect Competition, You Protect Competitors' (2003) 26 *World Competition* 149–65.

[123] *Hoffmann-La Roche & Co AG v Commission of the European Communities* (n 102).

[124] *Europemballange Corporation and Continental Can Company Inc v Commission* (n 73).

access and the individual liberty of competitors on the market as important factors in considering abuse.[125]

Hence, at this stage, both Articles 101 and 102 were broadly applied with the objective of establishing a common market for the EU. Article 101 aggressively attacked vertical agreements with a territorial ban, while Article 102 was particularly concerned with the behaviour of a dominant player that might impact on the competition process and thus impair economic integration. However, the application of Articles 101 and 102 received increasing criticism due to its tendency to be formalistic and its lack of solid economic analysis.

C. EU Competition Law and Public Policy

By the early 1990s, the picture of the political economy of EU competition law had changed. The internal market was declared to be established by 31 December 1992, when the main national trade barriers blocking the formation of a common market had been removed.[126] As a result, the European economy experienced a radical industrial reorganization. A wave of mergers and acquisitions occurred in both national and European markets.[127] Encouraged by the achievement, the EU enlarged and European leaders sought further integration proposals in subsequent EU summits.[128] Against this backdrop, EU competition law was expanded to adopt one merger regulation in 1989.[129]

In this period, the relationship between the Commission and the Court experienced subtle changes. Given the progress achieved in the formation of a common market, the Court decided to become less active in economic integration.[130] As the formalistic and subjective approach adopted by the Commission in competition cases received increased criticism, the Court began to require the Commission to base its decisions more on economic analysis. The Court indicated in *Reima* that: 'As a general rule, the Court undertakes a comprehensive review of the question whether or not the conditions for the application of Article 101(1) are met. It is clear that in determining the permissible duration of a non-competition clause

[125] Heike Schweitzer, 'Parallels and Differences in the Attitudes Towards Single Firm Conduct: What are the Reasons? The History, Interpretation and Underlying Principles of Sec. 2 Sherman Act and Article 82 EC', EUI Working Paper.

[126] The goal of the internal market was set out by the Single European Act in 1986, OJ L169 of 29 June 1987.

[127] Gerber (n 114) 97.

[128] During the 1993 European Council meeting at Copenhagen, detailed criteria were set out for membership negotiations, which marked the beginning of the systematic enlargement of the EU. See http://ec.europa.eu/enlargement/policy/glossary/terms/accession-criteria_en.htm.

[129] Council Regulation No 4064/89 on the control of concentrations between undertakings, OJ L395, 30 December 1989.

[130] Thijmen Koopmans, 'The Role of Law in the Next Stage of European Integration' (1985) 35 *International & Comparative Law Quarterly* 925.

incorporated in an agreement for the transfer of an undertaking, the Commission has to appraise complex economic matters.'[131]

However, EU competition law at this stage was often used by the Commission and the Court to pursue goals beyond competition, most of which were in the vein of public policy. In *Metro I*,[132] the Court held that it was at the Commission's discretion to apply competition laws and look for goals beyond antitrust, and that free competition was not a superior value in EU competition law. Furthermore, the Court ruled that it was workable, not perfect, competition that EU competition law aimed to achieve. Competition law should aim to achieve various degrees of competition, given the market conditions. In other words, EU competition law could be interpreted to pursue a combination of policy objectives beyond antitrust.[133]

In this period, EU competition law was actively used as an integral part of EU industrial policy. When the Commission looked for new integration proposals, Member States wished to increase the competitiveness of national industries to survive international competition, but a European industry policy was not in place. The Commission used competition law to guide and promote industrial development with a sectoral approach, for example, in the synthetic fabric and steel production sectors.[134] Article 101(3) was also actively involved in the protection of public policy goals, including environmental[135] and employment protection.[136]

EU competition law, at this stage, was also used to regulate Member States' behaviour, with the aim of creating a level playing field. To this end, the Commission focused on Member States' interference in the competition process in the common market. As a result, the Commission started to apply Article 106 to public undertakings in Member States,[137] issuing directives requiring greater transparency.[138] It strengthened its regulation against state aids, which the Commission gradually regarded as an integral part of competition law.[139]

In 1989, Regulation 4064/89 was adopted with the aim of controlling mergers between undertakings on the Community market.[140] The regulation had two distinct features: namely the one-stop shop that handled mergers at a European level, through the simplified procedure of DG IV (now DG Competition); and the two-step substantive test, namely the establishment of dominance and the

[131] Case 42/84, *Remia v Commission* [1985] ECR 2545.

[132] Case 26/76, *Metro v Commission* [1977] ECR 1875.

[133] Heike Schweitzer, 'Competition Law and Public Policy: Reconsidering an Uneasy Relationship: The Example of Article 81', in Josef Drexl, Laurence Idot and Monéger Joël (eds), *Economic Theory and Competition Law* (Edward Elgar, 2009) 134–50.

[134] Wolf Sauter, *Competition Law and Industrial Policy in the EU* (Oxford University Press, 1997).

[135] *Philips-Osram*, 1994 OJ L378/37.

[136] *Metro v Commission* (n 132).

[137] Case C-202/88, *France v Commission* [1991] ECR 1223; this was described by the DGIV as one of the most important decisions the Court has ever given in the area of competition law.

[138] Commission Directive 80/723/EEC of 25 June 1980 on the transparency of financial relations between Member States and public undertakings, OJ L195, 29 July 1980, 35–37.

[139] Frans GA Van Kraay, 'Public Enterprises and the EEC Competition Rules: The British Telecommunication Decision' (1984) 33(3) *International & Comparative Law Quarterly* 1022.

[140] OJ L040, 13 February 1998, 17.

establishment of a significant impediment to competition in the common market or a substantial part of it. However, in practice, the Commission focused almost entirely on the construing of dominance of the merger.[141] Building on the jurisprudence of Article 102, the Commission's interpretation was that the establishment of dominance under merger control meant the merger would acquire market power, which would allow the merged entity to act independently of its competitors, suppliers and consumers.[142] However, the merger regulation dominance test has been criticized, mainly on the ground that the restraint of competition can result from uncoordinated behaviour among parties to the merger, which does not necessarily create or strengthen dominance in the market.[143]

It can be seen that EU merger control regulation has been built upon the jurisprudence of regulation of abuse of dominance in EU competition law and viewed competition as a process in which the elimination of rivalry would lead to the impossibility of competition on the common market. This contrasts with the efficiency-oriented merger regulation under US antitrust law. This also partly explains the sharp contrasts between EU and US attitudes towards cross-Atlantic mergers.[144]

Nevertheless, faced with increased scrutiny by the Court and criticism from the international community (mainly the US), the Commission began to reflect on its application of competition law and to look to other competition regulation for reference. More importantly, given the increasing interconnectedness of markets, the EU common market has become more closely connected with other markets, in particular, with those of the US, and therefore the EU competition regulation regime is faced with increasing pressure from that of its close business partners to reform.[145]

In the backdrop of the cross-border anti-competitive behaviour on the part of private business players and the conflicts arising from the extra-territorial application of US antitrust law and EU competition law,[146] the US and the EU built up a close cooperation on competition regulation, aiming to resolve the conflicts.

In 1991, the US and the EU concluded an agreement on promoting cooperation between the competition authorities across the Atlantic.[147] The 1991 agreement provides the notification of relevant cases, the exchange of information and coordination between competition authorities. It also upholds the traditional comity principle, which requires either party to take into consideration the interest of the other party where necessary.[148]

[141] Whish (n 49) 853.

[142] Mark Furse, *Competition Law of the EC and UK* (Oxford University Press, 2006) 348.

[143] Massimo Motta, *Competition Policy: Theory and Practice* (Cambridge University Press, 2004) 271.

[144] Daniel J Gifford and E Thomas Sullivan, 'Can International Antitrust Be Saved for the Post-Boeing Merger World: A Proposal to Minimize International Conflict and to Rescue Antitrust from Misuse' (2000) 45 *Antitrust Bulletin* 55.

[145] Monti (n 105) 81–82.

[146] Joseph Griffin, 'Extraterritoriality in US and EU Antitrust Enforcement' (1999) 67 *Antitrust Law Journal* 159.

[147] 1991 EU/US Competition Cooperation Agreement, OJ 95, 27 April 1995, 47–52.

[148] Articles II, III and IV EU/US Competition Cooperation Agreement 1991.

In 1998, the comity principle was further institutionalized by the signing of the US and the EU agreement on the application of positive comity in the enforcement of competition law.[149] Pursuant to the agreement, the positive comity principle provides that one party may request the other party to remedy anti-competitive behaviour that originates in its jurisdiction, but affects the requesting party as well.[150] In 2002, the EU and the US set up the best practice on cooperation in reviewing mergers, which, although not legally binding, provides a structured basis for bilateral communication and cooperation on merger review.[151] EU-US cooperation and communication on competition issues have also facilitated the importation of the latest economic theories and concepts of antitrust law into EU competition law.

By the turn of the millennium, the Commission and the Court had gained experience from decades of application of EU competition law; the awareness of competition law within the Community had increased, and sufficient principles, doctrines and case law had been established to serve as a reference for future enforcement.[152] Thus, the time was ripe for the EU to reflect on its competition regulation and carry out modernization reform.

D. The Modernization Era and the Pursuit of Efficiency

By the late 1990s and early 2000s, the EU had become an increasingly active player in the international economic community.[153] Increased economic globalization promoted more dialogue between the EU and the competition regulation regimes of other countries. The appointment of Mario Monti and Neelie Kroes, both economists, as Competition Commissioner, heading the enforcement of EU competition rules, demonstrated the Commission's increasing emphasis on economic analysis in competition law.

One distinctive feature of EU competition law in this period is its modernization reform in 2003 aiming to decentralize competition regulation in the EU.[154]

[149] Agreement between the European Communities and the Government of the United States of America on the application of positive comity principles in the enforcement of their competition laws, OJ L173 of 18 June 1998, 28–31.

[150] Ibid, Art III.

[151] US-EU Merger Working Group on Best Practice on Cooperation in Merger Investigations, available at: http://ec.europa.eu/competition/international/bilateral/eu_us.pdf.

[152] Commission White Paper on modernisation of the rules implementing Articles 81 and 82 of the EC Treaty (formerly Articles 85 and 86 of the EC Treaty), OJ C132 of 12 May 1999.

[153] Michael Smith, 'The European Union's Commercial Policy: Between Coherence and Fragmentation' (2001) 8(5) *Journal of European Public Policy* 781–802.

[154] The reform means that the enforcement of EU competition law has been decentralized, as the application of Articles 81 (now Art 101 TFEU) and 82 (now Art 102 TFEU) would be coordinated by a competition network composed by the European Commission, national competition authorities and the national courts. Council Regulation 1/2003 on the Implementation of the Rules on Competition Laid Down in Article 81 and 82 of the Treaty, [2003] OJ L1/1.

However, what differentiates EU competition law enforcement, during this stage, from the previous two stages is the law's increasing emphasis on effects-based economic analysis for enforcement, and its declaration to pursue consumer benefit as one of its goals. The transformation was slow and incremental, but nevertheless took place as early as the 1990s and in the areas of vertical agreement, merger regulation and abuse of dominance.

i. Vertical Restraint

In 1996, the European Commission published a Green Paper on vertical restraints, which marked the beginning of legal and cultural changes in EU competition regulation.[155] The Green Paper emphasized that, except for two types of vertical agreement deemed to distort competition outright, namely retail price maintenance and territorial protection, vertical agreement cannot be judged as anti-competitive per se, but requires further analysis in terms of the pros and cons of the effect on competition in the market. Where interbrand competition is fierce, the restraint's positive effect on competition is deemed higher. However, in the Commission Green Paper, it was stated that economic theory is one, but cannot be the only, factor in the design of the policy.[156]

In 1997, the Commission issued a notice on the Definition of Relevant Market for the Purpose of Community Competition Law.[157] This sets out the methodology for the delineation of production and geographical markets, based on the elasticity of demand substitutability faced with a hypothetical, small but permanent relative price increase.[158] It is in this notice that the Commission explicitly introduced the US antitrust law small but significant non-transitory increase in price (SSNIP) test into the definition of the market.[159] However, the Commission also emphasized that in defining the geographical market, consideration should be given to the market integration imperative.[160] Furthermore, the notice contains old-style subjective analysis on product characteristics and it has been criticized as a mixture of old-style formalist analysis and modern economics.[161]

In 1999, the Commission issued Block Exemption Regulation 2790/1999 on the application of Article 101(3) Treaty on European Union (TEU) to categories of vertical agreements and concerted practices,[162] along with a Commission notice

[155] Green Paper on Vertical Restraints, available at: http://europa.eu/documents/comm/green_papers/pdf/com96_721_en.pdf.
[156] Ibid, Art 13.
[157] Notice on the Definition of Relevant Market for the Purpose of Community Competition Law, OJ C 372, 9 December 1997, 5–13.
[158] Art 17 Ibid.
[159] Ibid, Art 40.
[160] Ibid, Art 32.
[161] Roger J van den Bergh and Peter D Camescasca, *European Competition Law and Economics: A Comparative Perspective* (Sweet & Maxwell, 2006) 126.
[162] OJ L336, 29 December 1999.

on Guidelines on Vertical Restraints in 2000.[163] Regulation 2790/1999 expired on 31 May 2010 and the Commission has since issued the new Block Exemption Regulation 330/2010 on the application of Article 101(3) to categories of vertical agreements and concerted practices.[164] Pursuant to the regulation, vertical agreements satisfying the block exemption regulation requirements can be exempted under Article 101(3). Regulation 330/2010 recognizes the efficiency enhancing functions of vertical agreements. The regulation sets out hardcore distribution agreements illegal per se, which include indirect minimum resale price maintenance, territorial and customer restrictions, and restrictions in a selective distribution system. It further provides that other vertical agreements fall outside of Article 101(1) based on economic analysis according to the market share.

It can be seen that compared with the aggressive attack on vertical agreement in the early stages, EU competition law's treatment of vertical agreement has largely converged with the Chicagonian antitrust rules. The EU has recognized the efficiency enhancement function of vertical agreement and has employed a case-by-case empirical approach to evaluate the agreement's effect on competition.

However, EU competition law provides a much more stringent treatment of vertical agreements. First, the US Supreme Court has in the *Leegin* case utilized the rule of reason doctrine to look at the retail price maintenance agreement in question.[165] However, EU competition law continues to treat certain vertical agreements, such as minimum and fixed resale prices, as hardcore anti-competitive agreements and excludes these from block exemption regulation.[166] Second, dominant firms entering into vertical agreements have received stricter treatment in EU competition law than in US antitrust law.[167] As provided by the ECJ, a dominant firm has a special responsibility not to allow its conduct to impair genuine undistorted competition in the common market.[168] Based on this, dominant firms entering into vertical restraints, which have the possibility of causing foreclosure in either up or down markets, are held to be likely to impair undistorted competition in the common market and are thus subject to regulation.[169]

The stringent regulation of vertical agreement provided by the EU competition rules is closely linked with the social embeddedness of EU competition regulation. First, the outright prohibition on territorial ban as hardcore anti-competitiveness is directly relevant to the EU's task of safeguarding economic integration. Second, the dominant player's special obligation in vertical agreements reconfirms ordoliberalism's influence, which views competition as a process and imposes obligation on dominant players. Hence, despite the convergence on economic thinking

[163] OJ C291, 13 October 2000.

[164] OJ L102/1, 23 April 2010.

[165] *Leegin Creative Leather Products, Inc v PSKS, Inc*, 551 US 877 (2007).

[166] Regulation 330/2010, OJ L102/1, 23 April 2010.

[167] James Cooper, Luke Froeb, Dainel Obrien and Michael Vita, 'A Comparative Study of United States and European Union Approaches to Vertical Policy', Vanderbilt University Law School, Law and Economics Working Paper No 05-11.

[168] *NV Nederlandsche Banden Industrie Michelin v Commission of the European Communities* (n 121).

[169] Case T-219/99, *British Airways v Commission* [2003] ECR II-5917.

underpinning vertical agreement regulation, divergence exists due to the social embeddedness of the EU and the US competition regulation regimes.

ii. Merger Regulation

With respect to merger regulation, the Commission issued the EC Merger Regulation (ECMR) 139/2004 in 2004.[170] The ECMR upholds the one-stop shop method, but has more flexibility in the allocation of jurisdiction between the Commission and Member States.[171] In July 2003, the Commission announced the appointment of a Chief Competition Economist and a committee to review the suitability of the economic analysis applied.[172] However, it is the change of substantive test in merger control that shows the Commission's determination to bring more economic analysis into the regulation. This has attracted controversial comments.

As stated above, the dominance test provided by Regulation 4064/89 was deficient on economic grounds. Through the application of merger regulation, the Commission had a series of decisions revoked by the Court of First Instance[173] and started to reflect on how to amend the gap in regulation. To solve this, it amended the dominance test so as to provide that a merger would be blocked if it would significantly impede effective competition in the common market, or a substantial part of it, particularly as a result of the creation or strengthening of a dominant position.[174] The new Significant Impediment of Effective Competition (SIEC) test provides a dual-track system for examining the compatibility of merger by looking at the impediment of competition resulting either from the creation or strengthening of dominance or from restraint where dominance is non-existent.

The ECMR has further integrated economic analysis by setting out principles for the evaluation of anti-competitive effects in horizontal mergers. Pursuant to the Commission *Guidelines on the Assessment of Horizontal Mergers* in 2004,[175] the Commission, in examining the compatibility of horizontal mergers, should examine market share and concentration levels by relying on the HHI levels; should evaluate possible anti-competitive effects, including non-coordinated effects and coordinated effects; should evaluate buyer power in the market; should evaluate market entry; and should consider the efficiency and failing firm justifications.[176]

[170] Council Regulation (EC) No 139/2004 of 20 January 2004 on the control of concentrations between undertakings (the EC Merger Regulation (ECMR)), OJL 24, 29 January 2004, 1–22.

[171] Ibid, Articles 4(4), (5), 9 and 22.

[172] European Commission Press Release, http://europa.eu/rapid/pressReleasesAction.do?reference=IP/06/1050&format=HTML&aged=0&language=EN&guiLanguage=en.

[173] Such as Case T-342/99, *Airtours plc v Commission of the European Communities* [2002] ECR II-2585.

[174] Art 2(3) ECMR.

[175] Guidelines on the assessment of horizontal mergers under the Council Regulation on the control of concentrations between undertakings, OJ C 31, 5 February 2004 5–18.

[176] Articles 14, 15, 16 of the Guideline: OJ C 31, 5 February 2004 5–18.

These principles closely resemble those contained in the evaluation method provided by the 1992 merger guidelines under US antitrust law.

However, the transformation is argued to have brought little fundamental change so far.[177] The SIEC test is seen as a powerful tool for the Commission to provide more effective regulation on mergers. However, one recent empirical study on the implementation of the test since 2004 reveals that in evaluating the compatibility of merger, the market share increase and market entry barrier, and its impact on the contestability of the market have remained the main criteria in the Commission's evaluation. Hence, it can be argued that the switch from the market dominance test to the SIEC test has not brought about fundamental change, and market concentration continues to influence the Commission's final decision.[178] Furthermore, although the guidelines on horizontal merger have set out factors for evaluating mergers, they have not managed to provide detailed instructions on how to carry out the evaluation. As such, it has been argued that the Commission's proposal of the SIEC test was mainly aimed at disentangling the relationship between Article 102 and the merger regulation so that the two regulations could develop independently.[179]

iii. Abuse of Dominance

The application of Article 102 has remained the most controversial part of EU competition law and its reform has been the most difficult. The Commission's formalistic establishment of market dominance and its inconsistent interpretation of 'abuse' have sparked continuous discussion on the ultimate purpose of Article 102. When the rest of EU competition law was experiencing reform to integrate a more economics-based approach, it was suggested that the time had come for the reform of Article 102.

In general, the reform of Article 102 aims to transform its application into a more economics-oriented application, which is in line with modern antitrust economic theories. First, in 2005, the Commission issued a discussion paper on the reform of Article 102 in which it clearly held that the objective of Article 102 is the protection of competition in the market as a means of enhancing consumer welfare and of ensuring an efficient allocation of resources.[180]

Second, the establishment of market power under Article 102 has become more empirical and less formalistic. In 2008, the Commission issued a communication

[177] Giorgio Monti, 'The New Substantive Test in EC Merger Regulation—Bridging the Gap between Economics and Law?' in Catherine Barnard (ed), *The Cambridge Yearbook of European Legal Studies 2007–2008* (Hart Publishing, 2008).

[178] Borja Martinez Fernandez, Iraj Hashi and Marc Jergers, 'The Implementation of the European Commission's Merger Regulation 2004: An Empirical Analysis' (2008) 4(30 *Journal of Competition Law and Economics* 791–809. See also Juan Briones, 'A Balance of the Impact of Economic Analysis on the EU Competition Policy' (2009) 32(1) *World Competition* 27–39.

[179] Monti (n 177) 263–86.

[180] http://ec.europa.eu/competition/antitrust/art82/discpaper2005.pdf, Art 4.

on the guidance of the Commission's enforcement priorities in applying Article 102 of the EC Treaty to abusive exclusionary conduct by dominant undertakings (Guidance).[181] This emphasized that the evaluation of market power should also pay attention to the fact that the alleged dominant player has enjoyed its market power in substance and over a period of time, and that the determination of market power depends on a combination of factors.[182]

Third, the reform introduced an effects-based economic analysis for the evaluation of competition restraints under Article 102. In the 2008 Guidance, the Commission requires that the abuse be evaluated by looking at its effect on market conditions. The Commission further proposes that in the evaluation, it must consider whether an alleged dominant player can prove that its conduct is objectively necessary or demonstrate that its conduct's efficiency gains outweigh the impairment of consumer welfare.[183] Consequently, the substantive application of Article 102 has produced the following change: it has transformed the centre for regulation from exclusionary abuse regulation such as anti-competitive market foreclosure by alleged dominant players to price-based exclusionary abuse, in particular, specific forms of abuse including exclusive dealing, tying and bundling, predation, refusal to supply and margin squeeze.

With respect to anti-competitive market foreclosure, the Commission has adopted an effects-based analysis approach based on a detailed analysis of the market conditions.[184] With respect to price-based exclusionary abuse, the Commission recognizes that vigorous price competition in general improves consumer benefits, requiring only minimum intervention, and that if an equally efficient competitor can compete effectively with the pricing conduct of the alleged dominant player, the Commission in general would not hold the pricing behaviour to be anti-competitive. It can be seen that the Commission has adopted a less interventionist approach in exclusionary abuse regulation, which mirrors the US antitrust enforcement, in line with Chicagonian economic thinking.

However, it is argued that the results of the reform of Article 102 have so far remained limited. First, unlike the discussion paper, the guidance has not provided a clear statement of the goals to be pursued by Article 102. Second, neither the discussion paper nor the guidance has defined or substantiated the terms of consumer welfare, or provided a clear set of tests of harm based on the objective of the protection of consumer benefit.[185]

It can be seen that in the modernization reform of EU competition law, substantive reform has taken place in the regulation of vertical agreement, merger and abuse of dominance. The general tendency of the reform has been to make the EU law more economic analysis-oriented, based on modern antitrust

[181] OJ C (2009) 864.
[182] Ibid, Art 10 OJ C (2009) 864.
[183] Ibid, Articles 28–31. OJ C (2009) 864.
[184] Ibid, Articles 67 and 68. OJ C (2009) 864.
[185] Pinar Akman, 'Consumer Welfare and Article 82 EC: Practice and Rhetoric' (2009) 3(1) *World Competition* 71–90.

economic thinking, and to put consumer welfare, though not clearly defined in the EU context, as one of the main goals to be pursued by the law.

However, the above analysis shows that the reform of vertical agreement regulation bears the market integration imperative, the reform of merger regulation sticks to the old market concentration approach and the reform of abuse of dominance regulation has not provided consistent rules. Hence, the transformation's slowness and minimal impact on the substance of EU competition law leads one to ask why the EU has chosen to reform its competition law into a model that clearly bears US influence.

One explanation is in the economic globalization, the increasing connectedness of the EU and the US markets, has promoted more communication and greater convergence in competition regulation in the two sites. As proven by the US experience, solid economic analysis provides certainty in the enforcement of competition regulation and prioritizing consumer welfare as the main goal dedicates limited resources to enforcing more rigorous competition to achieve higher efficiency. As such, the EU is motivated to do the same.

However, it should also be noted that in the development of EU competition law, the EU has continued to use competition laws to effect its own improvement and consolidate its own values, eg, EU has relied on competition law as a useful instrument for achieving a common market and for promoting public policy. Furthermore, perhaps the speech given by the former Competition Commissioner Mario Monti in 2004 can shed some light on this issue. In the speech, Monti claimed that both EU and US competition regulations embrace the same microeconomic analytical tool, particularly in the field of merger control, and that the EU and the US carry comparable global weight in competition law enforcement, and thus the EU matters and is listened to in global competition regulation. EU competition law, according to Monti, is expected to play a leading role in shaping antitrust policy globally.[186] This shows the EU's wish to strengthen its position in global competition law development and to compete with the US in terms of globalization. Obviously, the EU's convergence with modern antitrust economic thinking, upheld by US antitrust law, serves this purpose well.

IV. US, EU AND GLOBAL COMPETITION LAW DEVELOPMENT

The US has recognized the importance of the internationalization of antitrust rules in order to tackle challenges brought about by globalization and has therefore been keen to export its antitrust law norms. However, its approaches have transformed in recent years. In 1995, it stated that its medium-term and long-term priority in the internationalization of antitrust law was to rely on

[186] Mario Monti, 'Convergence in EU-US Antitrust Policy Regarding Mergers and Acquisitions: An EU Perspective', 2004, available at: http://europa.eu/rapid/pressReleasesAction.do?reference=SPEECH/04/107&format=HTML&aged=0&language=EN&guiLanguage=en.

international-comity-based bilateral enforcement cooperation and the strong enforcement of the US antitrust law globally.[187] In 2000, it started to promote the internationalization of the antitrust norms on the basis of informal multilateral consensus building through the OECD and the global competition initiative.[188] Hence, the ICN was instituted based on the initiative by the US International Competition Policy Advisory Committee (ICPAC) to the US Department of Justice.[189] The ICPAC further set out guiding principles for antitrust internationalization in order to increase the transparency of government actions, to expand and deepen the cooperation between the US and overseas competition enforcement authorities, and to create greater soft harmonization and the convergence of systems.[190] However, in 2011, the US Department of Justice identified the cooperation with newer and more distant jurisdictions on antitrust issues as one of the new challenges it faces in the internationalization of antitrust norms. In responding to the new challenges, the US antitrust authority proposed to adopt new perspectives, which inter alia emphasize respect for the interests and cultures of other jurisdictions, trust building and ongoing dialogue.[191]

The US signed its first bilateral agreement on antitrust cooperation with Germany in 1976[192] and has so far signed bilateral cooperation agreements with Australia (1982), the EU (1991, 1998), Canada (1995), Israel (1999), Brazil (1999), Japan (1999), Mexico (2000) and Russia (2009), with the aim of increasing understanding and cooperation on antitrust enforcement.[193] At the urging of the

[187] Diane Wood, 'The Internationalization of Antitrust Law: Options for the Future', 1995, available at: www.justice.gov/atr/public/speeches/0099.htm.

[188] Douglas Melamed, 'Promoting Sound Antitrust Enforcement in the Global Economy', 2000, available at: www.justice.gov/atr/public/speeches/6785.htm.

[189] ICPAC, *International Competition Policy Advisory Committee: Final REPORT, Washington, D.C, Department of Justice* (Antitrust Division, 2000), available at: www.justice.gov/atr/icpac/finalreport.html.

[190] Ibid.

[191] Rachel Brandenburger, 'International Competition Policy and Practices: New Perspectives?', 2010, available at: www.justice.gov/atr/public/speeches/270980.pdf.

[192] Agreement between the Government of the United States of America and the Government of the Federal Republic of Germany Relating to Mutual Cooperation Regarding Restrictive Business Practices, issued on 23 June 1976, available at: www.justice.gov/atr/public/international/docs/0353.htm.

[193] Australia-United States: Agreement Relating to Cooperation on Antitrust Matters;Agreement between the Government of the United States and the Government of the Federal Republic of Germany Relating to Mutual Cooperation Regarding Restrictive Business Practices, issued on 23 June 1976, available at: www.justice.gov/atr/public/international/docs/0353.htm.

Agreement between the Government of the United States and the Government of Australia Relating to Cooperation on Antitrust Matters.

Agreement between the Government of the United States and the Government of Canada Regarding the Application of Their Competition and Deceptive Marketing Practices Laws.

Agreement of the Government of the United States and the Commission of the European Communities regarding the application of their competition laws.

Agreement between the Government of the United States and the European Communities on the application of positive comity principles in the enforcement of their competition laws.

Agreement between the Government of the United States and the Government of the State of Israel Regarding the Application of their Competition Laws.

Antitrust Division of the US Department of Justice, the US Congress enacted the International Antitrust Enforcement Assistance Act (IAEAA) in 1994,[194] which enables the Antitrust Division and the FTC to sign bilateral mutual assistance agreements with foreign competition authorities.[195] The US has also spread its antitrust norms in regional agreements, eg, the North American Free Trade Agreement (NAFTA). Pursuant to the NAFTA, a working group on trade and competition has been set up where the US, Canada and Mexico as Member States can discuss, draft and publish papers on antitrust and competition policy affecting these countries.[196] The US favours antitrust policy transfers through bilateral agreements over multilateral agreement on competition law.

The EU has been highly active in exporting its market governance norms and values on competition law in both hard and soft law forms. From 2003 to 2010, it has enlarged, with 12 new Member States joining.[197] However, its influence on the development of competition laws in these new Member States can be traced back to long before this enlargement. The 12 new Member States, prior to the enlargement, concluded Association Agreements (Europe Agreements) with the EU, which provided the legal basis for their relations with EU and helped these states to achieve the goal of becoming a member of the EU.[198] These Association Agreements reproduce EU competition law provisions. More importantly, the Association Agreements require the associated states to adopt competition law that

Agreement between the Government of the United States and the Government of the Federative Republic of Brazil Regarding Cooperation Between their Competition Authorities in the Enforcement of their Competition Laws.

Agreement between the Government of the United States and the Government of the United Mexican States Regarding the Application of their Competition Laws.

Agreement between the Government of the United States and the Government of Japan Concerning Cooperation of Anticompetitive Activities.

Memorandum of Understanding on Antitrust Cooperation Between the United States Department of Justice and the United States Federal Trade Commission, on the One Hand, and the Russian Federal Anti-Monopoly Service, on the Other Hand.

Available at: www.justice.gov/atr/public/international/index.html.

194 USC 6201-6212 (1994).

195 Michael Harriss and H Stephen Harris, *Competition Laws Outside the United States* (American Bar Association, 2001) 114.

196 NAFTA, s 1504.

197 In 2004, 10 states joined the EU: Cyprus, the Czech Republic, Estonia, Hungary, Latvia, Lithuania, Malta, Poland, Slovakia and Slovenia. In 2007, Romania and Bulgaria became the latest new Member States. See http://ec.europa.eu/enlargement/5th_enlargement/index_en.htm.

198 Europe Agreement establishing an association between the European Communities and their Member States, of the one part, and the Republic of Bulgaria, Republic of Romania, the Czech Republic, the Slovak Republic, the Republic of Cyprus, the Republic of Estonia, Hungary Republic, the Republic of Latvia, the Republic of Lithuania, the Republic of Malta, Republic of Poland and the Republic Slovenia, OJ L358, 31 December 1994, OJ L357, 31 December 94, OJ L360, 31 December 1994, OJ L359, 31 December 1994, OJ L133 21 May 1977, OJ L68 9 March 1998, OJ L347 of 31 December 1993, OJ L26, 2 February 1998, OJ L51, 20 February 1998, OJ L61, 14 March 1971, OJ L348, 31 December 1993 and OJ L51, 26 February 1999.

converge with EU competition law.[199] As candidate states are required to transpose the *acquis communautaire* as a quid pro quo for being admitted in EU, this guarantees the export of EU competition laws to its new Member States through the application of EU law. Furthermore, Turkey has been a candidate state to the EU since 1999. In 1994, it adopted its Protection of Competition Act (Law No 4054) based on EU competition law. One of the reasons that it adopted its Protection of Competition Act based on EU competition law was to fulfil its obligation under the Custom Union Agreement that it signed with the EU in 1995.[200]

The EU has also exported its EU competition law to its neighbouring countries. In 1995, the EU and 12 neighbouring countries in the North Africa and Middle East issued the Barcelona Declaration for a Euro-Mediterranean partnership.[201] Apart from Turkey, the other 11 neighbouring countries are non-EU candidate countries. So far, the EU has concluded EU-Mediterranean Association Agreements with Egypt, Tunisia, Algeria, Jordan, Israel and Lebanon.[202] In the EU-Egypt Association Agreement, anti-competitive agreements, abuse of a dominant position in the EU or Egypt, and public aid distorting competition that may affect trade between the EU and Egypt are declared to be incompatible with the Association Agreement,[203] which clearly bears the influence of EU competition law.[204]

[199] For example, Art 68 of the Europe Agreement establishing an association between the European Commnities and their Member States, of the one part, and the Republic of Poland of the other part, OJ L348/2, 1996.

[200] The EU and Turkey signed the Ankara Agreement of 12 September 1963, OJ L217, 29 December 1964 and its Additional Protocol of 23 November 1970, OJ L293, 29 December 1972 to define the scope and content of the association relationship. The EU-Turkey customs union is defined in Decision 1/95 of the Association Council of 22 December 1995, OJ L35, 13 February 1996. See also Gulgun Anik, 'Competition Rules of Turkey' (1997) 18(5) *European Competition Law Review* 311–18.

[201] Final Declaration of the Barcelona Euro-Mediterranean Ministerial Conference of 27 and 28 November 1995 and its work programme, available at: http://europa.eu/legislation_summaries/external_relations/relations_with_third_countries/mediterranean_partner_countries/r15001_en.htm. The 12 countries are Algeria, Morocco, Tunisia, Egypt, Israel, Jordan, the PLO, Lebanon, Syria, Cyprus, Malta and Turkey.

[202] Decision 2005/690/EC, OJ L265, 10 October 2005, Decision 2004/635/EC, OJ L304, 30 September 2004, Decision 2002/357/EC, OJL 129, 15 May 2002, Decision 2000/384/EC, OJ L147, 21 June 2000, Decision 2000/204/EC, OJ L138, 9 June 2000, Decision 98/238/EC, OJ L97, 30 March 1998 and Decision 2006/356/EC OJL 143, 30 May 2006 concerning the conclusion of a Euro-Mediterranean Agreement establishing an association between the European Communities and their Member States, of the one part, and, respectively, the People's Democratic Republic of Algeria, the Arab Republic of Egypt, the Hashemite Kingdom of Jordan, the State of Israel, the Kingdom of Morocco, the Republic of Tunisia and the Lebanese Republic.

[203] Art 34 EU-Egypt Association Agreement adopted in 2001 and effective in 2004, available at: www.eeas.europa.eu/egypt/aa/06_aaa_en.pdf.

[204] Damien Geradin and Nicolas Petit, 'Competition Policy and the Euro-Mediterranean Partnership' (2003) 8 *European Foreign Affairs Review* 153–80.

Furthermore, in 2001, the Joint Statement of the EU and China summit laid the foundation for the EU and China to strengthen sectoral dialogues.[205] In 2003, both the EU and China reached an agreement to start a competition policy dialogue.[206] In 2004, they set up an institutionalized and permanent Competition Policy Dialogue with an aim of providing technical assistance to China's development of competition regulation regime and undertaking consultation and exchanges on competition law development.[207] The setting up of the EU-China Competition Dialogue contributed directly to the development of the Anti-Monopoly Law, which was adopted in 2007.[208]

V. CONCLUSION

The development of US antitrust law and EU competition law has shown that competition regulation can be conferred with a diversity of goals, subject to the embeddedness of market governance of the two actors. EU competition law has cross-referenced with US antitrust law in its competition law development, mainly to improve its own interests, for example, promoting the integration of the Common Market or creating space for industrial policy promoting national champions.

However, a certain convergence can be observed from the communication, cooperation and interaction between US antitrust law and EU competition law. First, both competition regulation regimes have explicitly declared the intention to embrace the goal of allocative efficiency and consumer surplus maximization. Second, both competition regulation regimes have, to differing degrees, applied a conceptual framework to undertake economic analysis in the assessment of market power and restraints on competition in enforcement. More importantly, US antitrust law and EU competition law have aligned themselves in such a way as to focus more on effects-based economic analysis in building up the jurisprudence for competition law.

While US antitrust law and EU competition law have converged with each other through communication and positive comity, both the US and the EU have been active in exporting the norms of their competition regulation to the international community.

[205] EU-China Summit Joint Statement in 2001, available at: http://europa.eu/rapid/pressReleasesAction.do?reference=PRES/01/312&format=HTML&aged=1&language=en&guiLanguage=en.

[206] EU-China Joint Declaration on the start of a dialogue on competition between EU and China, available at: http://ec.europa.eu/competition/international/bilateral/cn2a_en.pdf.

[207] Terms of Reference of EU-China Competition Policy Dialogue, available at: http://ec.europa.eu/competition/international/bilateral/cn2b_en.pdf.

[208] Francis Snyder, *The European Union and China: Basic Documents and Commentary, 1949–2008* (Hart Publishing, 2009) 807.

Therefore, US antitrust law and EU competition law have been the main norms generator, providing inspiration to global competition law development. Consequently, the pursuit of efficiency has been transformed from one economic principle into a norm of soft law nature impacting the competition law development worldwide. More importantly, in recent years, the pursuit of efficiency has become the raison d'etre and the symbol for a modern competition regulation, which new competition regimes proclaim to achieve by embracing the implied subsequent economic analysis on competition.

2

International Organizations and Competition Law: Diverging Rationale?

I. INTRODUCTION

This chapter examines the international organizations and convergence of competition laws. It reviews the efforts made by the ill-fated International Trade Organization (ITO), the OECD, UNCTAD, the WTO and the ICN. The experience of these actors shows that soft law convergence is better received than hard law convergence by the international community. Further, the non-discrimination principle derived from the WTO theoretical underpinning is cross-referenced by the OECD and UNCTAD, and emerged as another norm to impact on global competition law. However, this chapter argues that the norm of the pursuit of efficiency and of non-discrimination, both impacting the competition convergence process hold fundamental differences from each other.

II. INTERNATIONAL ORGANIZATIONS AND COMPETITION LAW

A. The ITO and the Havana Charter

In the first 30 years since the end of the Second World War, international players headed by the US were concerned with the rebuilding of the international economic order. The main concern was the generation of wealth and the maintenance of world peace, while at the same time integrating the maximum number of allies into this order, as against the emerging communist camp headed by the USSR.[1]

Post-war US foreign policy was influenced by both the ideologies of American liberalism and realism. On the one hand, with respect to international economic relations, American liberalism, based on individual rights, held that all nations

[1] Charles Kegley, *World Politics: Trend and Transformation* (Wadsworth Publishing, 2007) 108.

were better off with trade liberalization. The idea was that there would be coexistence, based on the harmony of different interests, and that the international economy, based on liberalized trade, should be managed by international regimes set up on an institutional basis so as to ensure that no country would suffer from unfair international competition. Realism, on the other hand, argued that nation states were rational actors and that the stability of an open international economy relied on a single dominant or hegemonic power.[2]

The Bretton Woods system, installed as the result of a US initiative, showed the structure of the US effort in leading the construction of a new international order. It included the International Monetary Fund (IMF) to foster the emerging global financial markets, the General Agreement on Tariffs and Trade (GATT), which was designed to reduce tariff barriers and promote trade liberalization, and the World Bank, an international bank for reconstruction and development.[3]

GATT was treated as a temporary arrangement for trade liberalization and was expected to lead to the eventual establishment of an international trade organization, the ITO. Under the initiative of the US and the UK, the Havana Charter was produced to serve as the basis for negotiations leading up to the establishment of the ITO.

Given this background, in line with the removal of state trade barriers, cross-border private business behaviour, which restricts trade and competition on the market, became another main issue in the preparation of the ITO. The Havana Charter provided detailed provisions on the harmonization of the regulation of private restraints of trade.[4] Chapter V of the Havana Charter states that each member has the obligation to adopt measures to prevent private business practices affecting international trade, restraining competition, limiting access to markets or fostering monopolistic control whenever these practices have harmful effects on the expansion of production or trade and interfere with the economic and development goals set out by the Charter.[5]

This is the first time that restrictive private behaviour was brought onto the agenda of internationally harmonized regulation. By setting out the restrictive behaviour on the part of private or public commercial enterprises,[6] the Charter provides that 'each member shall take all possible measures by legislation or other measures … to ensure … that private or public commercial enterprises do not engage in those practices which have harmful effects on the production of trade, or conflict with development goals'.[7] Obviously, the curtailment of competition, the limit of access to markets and the encouragement of monopolistic control

[2] Stefano Guzzini, *Realism in International Relations and International Political Economy* (Routledge, 1998) 25–29.

[3] Peter Kenen, *Managing the World Economy: Fifty Years after Bretton Woods* (Institute for International Economics, 1994) 3.

[4] www.worldtradelaw.net/misc/havana.pdf.

[5] Article 46.1 Havana Charter.

[6] Ibid, Article 46.3.

[7] Ibid, Article 50.1.

are the three main criteria used to evaluate the restrictiveness of the practices in question. Each of the Member States were required to cooperate with each other, in terms of enforcement,[8] and were subject to a consultation and investigation mechanism instituted by the Havana Charter.[9]

However, while the Havana Charter was under negotiation, the US was faced with increasing public distrust in direct government regulation and an outcry for the market mechanism from society. In assessing its chances in Congress, the US government eventually gave up in its attempt to get the Havana Charter ratified by Congress.[10] The withdrawal of the US from the negotiations led directly to the collapse of the envisaged international trade organization and the Havana Charter never came into force.[11]

The envisaged competition rules contained in the Havana Charter were specifically designed to tackle private anti-competitive business restraints affecting international trade. It advocated a unified application of the same rules to all negotiating parties, and provided a legally binding dispute resolution mechanism to safeguard the application. Thus, it can be seen that the ITO sought to achieve a strong convergence of competition regulation in all Member States, with one indivisible goal, namely to strike down the cross-border private restraint of trade.

B. The OECD and Competition Law

Based on the Organization for European Economic Co-operation (OEEC), which was set up by European countries in 1948 with the aim of promoting European recovery after the Second World War,[12] the OECD was established in 1968 with the mandate of promoting economic growth, individual liberty and general well-being among industrialized economies.[13] The OECD currently has a worldwide membership of 33 industrialized countries/economies. In 2007, the OECD provided enhanced engagement with non-member countries, such as China.[14]

Institutionally, the OECD has a General Council as its decision-making body, composed of representatives of its members. At the second level, it has 250 committees, working groups and expert groups working on the topics of economy, development, governance, sustainability, finance, innovation and society.[15]

[8] Ibid, Article 51.

[9] Ibid, Articles 47 and 48.

[10] William Brown, *The United States and the Restoration or World Trade* (Brookings Institution, 1950) 362–84.

[11] Paul Demaret, 'The Metamorphoses of the GATT: From the Havana Charter to the World Trade Organization' (1996) 34 *Columbia Journal of Transnational Law* 123.

[12] www.oecd.org.

[13] Convention on the Organization of Economic Cooperation and Development, available at: www.oecd.org/document/7/0,3343,en_2649_201185_1915847_1_1_1_1,00 html.

[14] http://www.oecd.org/about/membersandpartners/.

[15] www.oecd.org/0,3348,en_2649_201185_1_1_1_1_1_00,html.

The OECD Competition Committee aims to develop into the world's premier source for policy analysis and advice on issues in relation to competition policy and law. In 2001, it set up a global competition forum to include participation by non-OECD members such as China.[16] By 2012, the Competition Committee has issued 10 recommendations on different aspects of competition law, numerous best practice guidelines and peer review reports of the competition law of its members.[17] Among these, one is the OECD Council Recommendation Concerning Cooperation between Member Countries on Anticompetitive Practices Affecting International Trade issued in 1995.[18] The 1995 Recommendation calls for cooperation between the competition authorities of the OECD members on the notification of cases and consultation on the enforcement of competition laws.[19]

Pursuant to the Convention on the Organisation for Economic Cooperation and Development, it is provided that the Organisation may take decisions, may make recommendations to members and may enter into agreements with members, non-Member States and international organizations.[20] In particular, the Convention provides that the decisions taken by the OECD shall be binding on all members, except as otherwise provided.[21] However, in practice, the OECD decisions do not contain legally binding powers. The decisions are binding on members only when the members consent to its legal effect.[22]

The OECD is playing an increasingly active role in promoting communication on competition laws among members and non-members. Its recommendations and best practice guidelines on competition law are soft laws that in a legally pluralistic world generate an impact on policy making as far as its members or candidate members are concerned.

C. The UN Set of Principles and Model Law

While the developed countries, headed by global powers such as the US, attempted to achieve harmonized rules regulating the private restraint of business with the end of the Second World War, decolonization and the emergence

[16] http://www.oecd.org/competition/globalforum/abouttheglobalforumoncompetition.htm.

[17] OCED decisions, recommendations and other instrument in force, available at: http://www.oecd.org/daf/competition/recommendations.htm.

[18] OECD Council Recommendation Concerning Cooperation between Member Countries on Anticompetitive Practices Affecting International Trade, C(95)130 Final.

[19] Article I OECD Recommendation, C(95)130 Final.

[20] Article 6 Convention on the Organization of Economic Cooperation and Development, available at: www.oecd.org/document/7/0,3343,en_2649_201185_1915847_1_1_1_1,00 html.

[21] Ibid.

[22] Speech by the US Secretary of the Treasury Dillon, at a hearing before the committee of Foreign Relations at the US Senate on the OECD in 1961, 23.

of developmentalism, the world started to pay attention to the developing countries and their integration into the global economy.[23]

UNCTAD was convened in 1962 and was established as an organ of the General Assembly of the United Nations in 1964.[24] With a membership of 193 countries, it aims to develop into a knowledge-based institution that promotes sustainable development in developing countries, and the integration of these developing countries into the global economy.[25]

In terms of the institutional set-up, UNCTAD Quadrennial Conference is the highest decision-making body, at which Member States assess trade and development issues and set out the UNCTAD mandate and priorities every four years.[26] In between the meetings of the Conference, the UNCTAD Trade and Development Board, with representatives from Member States, meets regularly to manage policy and institutional issues.[27] UNCTAD has three commissions, namely: the Commission on Trade and Development; the Commission on Investment, Technology and Related Financial Issues; and the Commission on Enterprises, Business Facilitation and Development. Within the area of work on international trade and commodities, the UNCTAD has one specific programme on competition law and policy.[28] The commissions provide a forum for Member States to express their views and exchange opinions on policies regarding development.

The UNCTAD Competition Policy and Law Programme provides knowledge-based assistance on competition and consumer policies to developing countries through[29] three channels: hosting the *Intergovernmental Group of Experts* (IGE) *on Competition Law and Policy* and ad-hoc meetings on competition policy and law yearly. The meetings provide a forum for members to undertake consultations on competition issues of common concern and undertake informal exchange of experiences and best practices through voluntary peer review; providing technical assistance to developing countries seeking competition law design or development; and acting as a depository of United Nations *Model Law on Competition* and the *United Nations Set of Principles on Competition.*[30]

In 1978, UNCTAD convened the United Conference on Restrictive Business Practices.[31] This adopted a Set of Multilaterally Equitable Principles and Rules for the Control of Restrictive Business Practices (hereinafter the Set) in 1979, which was approved by the UN General Assembly in 1980.[32] The Set has been reviewed in 1985, 1990, 1995 and 2000, respectively. The 2000 review of the Set recommended

[23] Immanuel Wallerstein, 'After Developmentalism and Globalization, What?' (2005) 83(3) *Social Forces* 1263–78.

[24] United Nations Economic and Social Council Resolution 917, 8 March 1962.

[25] www.unctad.org/Templates/Page.asp?intItemID=1530&lang=1.

[26] http://unctad.org/en/Pages/Meetings/UNCTAD-Conferences.aspx.

[27] http://unctad.org/en/Pages/Meetings/TDB.aspx.

[28] http://unctad.org/en/Pages/DITC/CompetitionLaw/Competition-Law-and-Policy.aspx.

[29] Ibid.

[30] www.unctad.org/Templates/StartPage.asp?intItemID=2239&lang=1.

[31] Resolution 33/153, 20 December 1978.

[32] Resolution 35/63, 5 December 1980.

that the UN General Assembly subtitle the Set as the UN Set of Principles and Rules on Competition, and calls upon all Member States to implement the provision of the Set.[33]

By clarifying the basic requirements for competition regulation in developing countries, the Set, in the first place, emphasizes the fair treatment of business operators in the market, as well as market access. It delineates the provisions with respect to enterprises[34] and the state.[35] In terms of the protection of competition on the part of the state, it postulates that the state should adopt, improve and effectively enforce appropriate legislation and implementing judicial and administrative procedures for the control of restrictive business practices.[36] It also elaborates upon the contours of the main goal of appropriate legislation by the state. This includes merger or acquisition, the abuse of the dominant position of market power, and formal or informal, written or unwritten agreements or arrangements. It further provides that four conditions should be considered in evaluating the restrictiveness of business practice. These include: the limit of market access, the undue restraint of competition, the adverse effect on trade, and economic development.[37] Clearly, market access is one of the main concerns in the anti-competitiveness analysis under the Set.

Second, according to the Set, competition law should provide fair and equitable treatment to all players on the market, and its enforcement should conform to the established procedures of law.[38]

Third, the Set highlights the importance of social embeddedness in the development of competition rules in developing countries. It calls for specific concern to be paid to developing countries, in particular their financial and trade concerns.[39] Industrial and sectoral development and participation in regionalization are two particular concerns that developing countries should take into consideration when developing competition protection.[40] The Set also ensures that states pay attention to the extent to which restrictive business practices can be acceptable under domestic law, provided the law is public and accessible.[41]

Fourth, the Set provides a cooperation and consultation procedure for dispute resolution. It makes consultation procedures available and requires that states cooperate with each other in enforcing legislation against international restrictive business practices.[42] It also encourages states to undertake mutually reinforcing collaborations to combat, in particular, transnational restrictive business practices.[43]

[33] UNTAD/RBP/CONF/10/REV.2, available at: www.unctad.org/en/docs/tdrbpconf10r2.en.pdf.
[34] Section D UN Set of Principles and Rules on Competition.
[35] Ibid, Section E.
[36] Ibid, Section E.1.
[37] Ibid, Section E.2.
[38] Ibid, Section E.3.
[39] Ibid, Section C.3.
[40] Ibid, Section C.3.
[41] Ibid, Section C.2.
[42] Ibid, Section F.
[43] Ibid, Section C.1.

The Intergovernmental Group of Experts meetings on Competition Law and Policy requests that the UNCTAD publish non-sessional Model Law on competition law, based on the reviews received from UNCTAD Member States.[44] The latest Model Law was issued on 30 August 2010 upon receiving comments from Australia, Belarus, the EU, Hungary, Sweden and Switzerland. It sets out comprehensive provisions on aspects of competition law, commentaries on the provisions of the Model Law and alternative approaches adopted by UNCTAD Member States with respect to specific aspects of competition law.[45]

The Model Law has set out provisions on the core aspects of competition law, including the Objectives and Purpose of the Law (Chapter I), Definition and Scope of the Law (Chapter II), Restrictive Agreements (Chapter III), Abuse of Dominance (Chapter IV), Notification on Restrictive Agreements (Chapter V), Merger Control (Chapter VI), Organization and Functioning of Competition Administering Authority (Chapters IX and X), Sanction and Relief (Chapter XI) and Review of Administering Bodies (Chapter XII) in relation to the public enforcement of competition law, and Actions for Damages (Chapter XIII) in relation to the private enforcement of competition law. It has further set out provisions with respect to the relationship between Competition Law and Sectoral Regulation (Chapter VII) and between Competition Law and Consumer Protection (Chapter VIII).[46]

The content of the Model Law reflects the latest development of international competition laws and exhibits the influence from US antitrust law and EU competition law. First, in Chapter I, the Model Law aims to control or eliminate restrictive arrangements or agreements, merger and abuse of dominance which limit market access or unduly restrict competition, adversely affect domestic or international trade and economic development.[47] However, the comment in the Chapter goes on to state that the objective of competition law is to achieve consumer benefits and efficiency, though fairness can also be one optional goal to be pursued by competition law.[48] Second, the structure of the Model Law aims to regulate restrictive agreements, abuse of dominance and merger. In particular, it explicitly uses the term 'abuse of dominance', mirroring that in Article 102 TFEU. Furthermore, the Model Law provides to exclude its application to state acts or acts by enterprises or natural persons that are compelled or supervised by the state. This interpretation of the scope of application mirrors that of the state action doctrine under US antitrust law, whereby the US Supreme Court has permitted state agents and certain private actors to show that a state regulatory scheme precludes antitrust liability.[49]

[44] UNCTAD Model Law on Competition, TD/RBP/CONF.7/L1, issued on 30 August 2010. Available at www.unctad.org/en/docs/tdrbpconf7L1_en.pdf.

[45] Ibid.

[46] Ibid.

[47] Chapter I UNCTAD Model Law 2010.

[48] Ibid.

[49] *Parker v Brown*, 317 US 341 (1943).

However, the Model Law is not restricted to a reflection of norms generated by the US antitrust law and EU competition law. Instead, it adopts a pluralist approach by listing, in every chapter, the alternative approaches adopted by all competition regulation regimes of Member States vis-a-vis the approaches provided by the Model Law.[50] For example, in Chapter I on the objectives or purposes of the law, the Model Law has listed 28 competition laws that pursue or pursued goals other than economic efficiency and/or fairness. This approach and the fact that the Model Law is based upon the comments of Member States reinforce the nature of the Model Law, which acts as an open forum for Member States to exchange information on competition law development.

The UN Set and the Model Law on competition have been influenced by the structural features of UNCTAD. First, given the mission of UNCTAD, competition law was, for the first time, officially linked with development in developing countries. Second, in line with UNCTAD practice, the Set emphasizes addressing the social embeddedness of competition regulation in developing countries. Consequently, competition law in developing countries, as suggested by UNCTAD, should pay attention to the lack of equality on the market and the lack of market access in those countries.

D. The WTO and Minimum Harmonization of Competition Law

The end of the Cold War in 1989 saw the hegemonic world pattern replaced by a proliferation of players on the world stage, including the European Community (EC) and Japan, and the embrace of the market economy worldwide. This period also saw the increase of multinational business transactions, foreign investment and further trade liberalization.[51] Consequently, business operators have been increasingly subject to plural forms of laws and regulations, which are generated from state-made laws or non-state-made laws of different jurisdictions.

The unborn ITO left a gap in the institutional framework for trade liberalization. Throughout the years, GATT had achieved success in reducing trade barriers for goods. However, it faced institutional restraints to implementing further liberalization.[52] Members of GATT, headed by the US and the EC, wished to achieve trade liberalization in fields such as services, and took the initiative to open up a Uruguay round of trade liberalization negotiations in 1986. By 1994, ministers from members participating in the negotiations reached agreement in Marrakesh. Based on this, the WTO was created in 1995.

[50] Chapter I UNCTAD Model Law, 4–9.

[51] Joseph Stiglitz, *Globalization and its Discontents* (Penguin, 2002) 4–5.

[52] Peter Van Den Bossche, *The Law and Policy of the World Trade Organization* (Cambridge, 2005) 81.

The EC, encouraged by its own success in economic integration, was interested in establishing competition rules under the multilateral trade organization. In 1992, at the World Competition Forum in Davos, Leon Brittan presented the proposal to set up a multilateral institutional framework for competition rules. In 1995, the EU Commissioner for Competition Karel Van Miert appointed a Group of Experts in Competition Law, whose task was to explore the possibilities for strengthening international cooperation on competition laws.[53] As a result, the EU proposed that a set of substantive international competition rules should be included in the WTO agreements. Member States of the WTO had the option of signing up to the rules. Once the competition rules had been ratified, they were committed to adopting national competition rules, with an effective enforcement mechanism in line with the international competition rules under the WTO framework. By doing so, these Member States agreed to subject their competition law enforcement to the scrutiny of the WTO dispute settlement mechanism.[54]

Upon the proposal from the EU, at the WTO Ministerial Conference in Singapore, a Working Group on the Interaction between Trade and Competition Policy (WGTCP) was set up in 1996.[55]

In the 2001 WTO Doha Ministerial Declaration, it was elaborated that the focus of WGTCP would be to clarify the core principles for WTO competition policy, which included:

— transparency;
— non-discrimination and procedural fairness;
— provisions on hardcore cartels;
— modalities for voluntary cooperation and support for the progressive enforcement of competition institutions in developing countries through capacity building;
— flexibility to developing and least-developed members.[56]

It can be seen that the WTO competition policy has a clear trade liberalization focus, as it placed the emphasis on the convergence of rules on hardcore international cartels. The policy is built upon the norms of non-discrimination and procedural fairness, upheld by substantive and procedural WTO law. More importantly, it responds to the social embeddedness of developing countries and allows for a certain degree of flexibility.

However, the harmonization of competition laws in the WGTCP experienced a deadlock because of the resistance from developing countries and the lukewarm

[53] EC Commission Group of Experts, *Competition Policy in the New Trade Order: Strengthening International Co-operation and Rules* (Office for Official Publications of the European Communities, 1995).

[54] D Grisay, *International Competition Policy from Extra Territoriality to Multilaterality* (Mimeo, 2005).

[55] WTO Ministerial Conference Singapore Declaration, WT/MIN(96)/DEC, para 20.

[56] WTO Ministerial Conference Doha Declaration, WT/MIN(01)/DEC/2 (2001), para 25.

response of the US.[57] When competition policy was put on the agenda under the WGTCP, most developing countries did not have competition laws and were opposed to the harmonized competition rules of the WTO, as they claimed that this would restrict the space for their industrial development and competitiveness building.[58] Similarly, the US was reluctant to welcome the harmonization of competition rules because it was reluctant to subject its robust and well-developed antitrust regime to the harmonized international core principles.[59] In July 2004, the WTO General Council decided that the issue of competition law would not be a part of the programme set out in the WTO Doha Declaration.

E. The ICN

While institutionalized efforts to harmonize competition laws through the WTO did not make substantial progress, the US attempted to promote the convergence of competition laws through informal networks with no strong institutional framework, namely the establishment of the ICN in 2001.[60]

The inception of the ICN was as a result of an initiative by the US ICPAC to the US Department of Justice.[61] The ICN was set up as an informal network of competition authorities from all over the world with the aim of promoting cooperation among these authorities and reducing potential conflicts.[62] In 2000, the US initiative was supported by the EU, and soon after that top officials of the competition authorities, authorized from 14 jurisdictions, launched the ICN. To date, the ICN is a network composed of more than 80 developed or developing economy members. Its membership covers states as well as international institutions, such as the WTO, the OECD and UNCTAD.[63]

With respect to its institutional structure, the ICN is neither based on an international contract nor equipped with administrative budget or staff. Therefore, it calls itself a virtual organization.[64] It comprises a standing steering group of 15 individuals, elected from competition authorities' officials, member

[57] Daniel Gifford and Robert Kurdre, 'Trade and Competition Policy in the Developing World: Is There a Role for WTO' in Chantal Thomas and Joel P Trachtman (eds), *Developing Countries in the WTO Legal System* (Oxford University Press, 2009).

[58] Aditya Bhattacharjea, 'The Case for a Multilateral Agreement on Competition Policy: A Developing Country Perspective' (2006) 9 *Journal of International Economic Law* 293.

[59] Rodney Ludema, 'A WTO Agreement on Competition Policy: Prospects and Pitfalls', *USITC International Economic Review*, USITC Publication 3506, March/April 2002.

[60] Marc Ivaldi and Olivier Bertrand, 'European Competition Policy in International Markets', October 2006. Available at: http://ssrn.com/abstract=951594.

[61] ICPAC, *International Competition Policy Advisory Committee: Final REPORT, Washington, D.C., Department of Justice*, Antitrust Division 2000.

[62] www.internationalcompetitionnetwork.org/about.aspx.

[63] www.internationalcompetitionnetwork.org/members/member-directory.aspx.

[64] Mario Todoino, 'International Competition Network: The State of Play after Naples' (2003) 26(2) *World Competition* 283–302.

organizations or states. It mainly operates at annual conferences and project-based working groups that cover the substantive and procedural aspects of competition regulation. The steering group has the responsibility, among others, of developing consensus-based recommendations for its members.[65] The members of the ICN work on a voluntary basis, with the aim of improving cooperation and reaching consensus on different aspects of competition regulation.[66] However, in practice, the peer pressure emanating from the publication of 'superior antitrust practices', such as US antitrust law, promotes a widespread adoption of ICN best practice recommendations by the member competition authorities.[67]

The above review shows that international organizations have never stopped in seeking convergence and understanding of competition laws since the end of the Second World War. These efforts were made in hard as well as soft law forms, ranging from universal rules on competition law (the ITO) to intergovernmental coordination towards a Model Law on competition law (UNCTAD), to legally binding minimum harmonization of competition rules (the WTO), to informal networks promoting the mutual understanding of competition rules (the OECD or the ICN).

It can be seen that the convergence of competition laws on the part of international organizations has so far relied more on soft law instruments than on hard law instruments. The popularity of the soft law instruments can be partially explained by their more informal, flexible and intergovernmental yet less intrusive nature.[68]

However, the soft law tools also impose constraints to the role played by the OECD, UNCTAD and the ICN in global competition law development. First, the OECD has coverage of mainly industrialized economies and thus has limits in terms of covering the competition development in developing countries.[69] Furthermore, the organizational principle of the OECD is to provide each major area of economic policy with its own autonomous forum for discussion and cooperation. This implies that no single ministry in Member States is responsible for the organization. The soft law on competition law convergence issued by the OECD competition law and policy committee relies on the personal contacts, trust and peer identification among the national regulators for enforcement. Therefore, the OECD's potential in moderating nationalist disagreements over enforcement policies and reducing transaction costs for business is low.[70] Second, UNCTAD has a wider coverage of membership and emphasis on the link between

[65] http://www.internationalcompetitionnetwork.org/uploads/library/doc784.pdf.

[66] www.internationalcompetitionnetwork.org/about.aspx.

[67] Oliver Budazinski, *The Governance of Global Competition: Competence Allocation in International Competition Policy* (Edward Elgar, 2008) 143.

[68] Imelda Maher, 'Competition Law in the International Domain: Networks as a New Form of Governance' (2002) 29(1) *Journal of Law and Society* 111–36.

[69] AD Melamed, 'International Cooperation in Competition Law and Policy: What Can Be Achieved at the Bilateral, Regional and Multilateral Level' (1999) 2(3) *Journal of International Economic Law* 431.

[70] David K Tarullo, 'Norms and Institutions in Global Competition Policy' (2000) 94(3) *American Journal of International Law* 478–504.

competition law and economic development in its convergence efforts. However, its Set and Model Laws are criticized as being ambiguous and lacking enforceability, which reduces their impact as soft laws.[71] For example, the Set provides that countries affected by restrictive practices can deal with disputes in consultation, with no prior commitment to binding arbitration or conciliation.[72] Third, as an informal network, the relationship between the ICN and member authorities is horizontally interwoven rather than hierarchical in nature. When faced with issues such as jurisdiction claiming in antitrust cases or conflict reduction, the ICN faces the challenge of how to solve the competence allocation within its informal framework.[73]

However, among the international organizations players in globalization, the WTO has a well-established institutional framework, a wide coverage of membership and an effective dispute settlement mechanism. Although it has experienced a severe setback in its efforts to achieve minimum harmonization of competition laws, it continues to have the capacity to influence competition law convergence in hard and soft law.[74]

III. THE WTO AND COMPETITION LAW

The WTO's impact on global competition law can be observed from its institutional set-up, normative framework and dispute settlement mechanism.

A. The WTO Institutional and Normative Framework and Competition Law

The institutional framework of the WTO is one of the main justifications for putting the minimum harmonization of competition rules on its mandate.[75] This is because the WTO is an international organization with a wide coverage of membership and a rule-based institutional framework.

The WTO has 159 members, ranging from sovereign states to supranational organizations (for example, the EU), to special administrations (for example, Hong Kong). It has the WTO Ministerial Conference as the top decision-making body, which meets every two years. The WTO General Council is the high decision body, which consists of diplomats from Member States and hold meetings

[71] Joseph Wilson, *Globalization and the Limits of National Merger Control Laws* (Kluwer, 2003) 213.

[72] UNCTAD Docs TD/RBP/CONF/NG/CRP.4, 5 December 1979 and TD/RBP/CONF/ NG/CRP.5/ Rev.1, 6 December 1979.

[73] Budazinski (n 67) 147.

[74] Martyn Taylor, *International Competition Law: A New Dimension for the WTO?* (Cambridge, 2006).

[75] Ibid, 183.

regularly to carry out WTO functions. The General Council is in charge of the Council for Trade in Goods, the Council for Trade in Services and the Council for Trade-Related Intellectual Property, and committees on issues such as Trade and Development and Trade and the Environment. Underneath the councils and committees, the WTO has working parties on specific WTO-related issues such as accession or state trading enterprises. The WTO General Council also sits as the Dispute Settlement Body and the Trade Policy Review Body.

The WTO agreements contain no explicit provision regarding competition regulation. Nevertheless, the WTO normative framework contains the following capacity to influence competition law in Member States.

The non-discrimination principle serves as the theoretical underpinning for the WTO. Under the WTO agreement, the non-discrimination principle contains two aspects, namely, the most favoured nation (MFN) treatment obligation and the national treatment obligation.

The MFN treatment principle is provided in GATT,[76] the General Agreement on Trade and Services (GATS)[77] and the General Agreement on Trade-Related Intellectual Property Rights (TRIPS).[78] Subject to exceptions, the MFN principle requires that any advantage, favour, privilege or immunity granted by any contracting party to any product originating in or destined for any other country shall, immediately and unconditionally, be accorded to the like product originating in or destined for the territories of all other contracting parties. The national treatment principle is also contained in GATT,[79] GATS[80] and TRIPS.[81] Subject to exceptions, it requires each member to accord no less favourable treatment to goods, services and intellectual properties of any other member than it accords to similar products of its own country.

The principle of non-discrimination thus constitutes the main theoretical basis for the WTO and its Member States to examine the domestic competition regulation of members. The main ground for the examination is that restraints of competition on the domestic market may be a result of, or cause for, discriminatory treatment of players on the market, both of which are inconsistent with the WTO objective of ensuring a level playing field in international trade. In particular, government discriminatory regulatory measures that reduce, eliminate or prohibit competition should be subject to the scrutiny of the WTO, as these measures undermine the trade liberalization effort made by the WTO.[82]

GATS and the Annex on Telecommunications touches upon competition regulation in the domestic market of members. Article VIII of GATS provides

[76] Article 1 GATT.
[77] Article 2 GATS.
[78] Article 4 TRIPS.
[79] Article 3 GATT.
[80] Article 17 GATS.
[81] Article 3 TRIPS.
[82] Chairman of WTO Competition Work Group, F Jenny, 'Globalization, Competition and Trade Policy: Issues and Challenges' in J-F Bellis (ed), *The Community Competition Policy in the Face of Globalisation and the Enlargement of the European Union* (Nomos, 2001) 211–40.

regulation in relation to monopolies and exclusive service suppliers. Members of the WTO are required to ascertain that a domestic monopoly supplier of a service complies with the MFN treatment obligation. The member must ensure that the domestic monopoly service supplier does not abuse its monopoly when it competes outside of the scope of its monopoly, either directly or through an affiliated company. In the case of exclusive service suppliers, the member is furthermore prohibited from, either formally or in effect, fixing the number of suppliers or preventing competition among those suppliers. In areas where market access commitments are taken, members are prohibited from taking measures to limit the number of service suppliers, to limit the total value of service transactions and to limit the total number of service operations. Furthermore, the WTO has adopted a Reference Paper on Regulatory Principles of GATS' Basic Telecommunications Agreement in 1997.[83] The regulation mainly proscribes members from engaging in anti-competitive cross subsidization, from using information from competitors to restrain competition and from withholding technical information, for example, essential facilities needed by competitors to provide services.[84]

Article 40 of the TRIPS Agreement provides the control of anti-competitive practices in contractual licences. TRIPS recognizes that some licensing practices, or conditions which restrain competition, may have adverse effects on trade and may impede technology transfer.[85]

The Government Procurement Agreement (GPA) remains one of the plurilateral agreements under the WTO agreements framework and hence is not legally binding on all members.[86] So far, the GPA has 14 contracting parties, most of which are OECD countries.[87] It requires non-discriminatory treatment on tendering, provided by public entities, as far as all members are concerned. In particular, in the tendering procedure, it requires entities not to provide any information on one specific procurement, which would have the effect of precluding competition. The GPA, based on the non-discrimination principle of the WTO agreements, aims to protect a fair market condition in the field of government procurement.[88]

It can be seen that the WTO agreements do exert an influence on competition regulation in Member States. However, the influence of the WTO on competition law is largely construed on its own theoretical underpinning, namely the non-discrimination principle based on the neoliberal ideology. This can be further observed in terms of the WTO dispute settlement mechanism and panel decisions.

[83] Reference Paper on Regulatory Principles of GATS' Basic Telecommunications Agreement available at: www.wto.org/english/tratop_e/serv_e/telecom_e/tel23_e.htm.

[84] Ibid.

[85] Article 40 TRIPS, available at: www.wto.org/english/tratop_e/trips_e/t_agm3_e.htm.

[86] Government Procurement Agreement, available at: www.wto.org/english/docs_e/legal_e/gpr-94_e.pdf.

[87] www.wto.org/english/tratop_E/gproc_e/memobs_e.htm#parties.

[88] Article X WTO Government Procurement Agreement.

B. The WTO Dispute Resolution Mechanism and Competition Law

Unlike other international organizations, the WTO is equipped with an adjudicative organ, namely the Dispute Settlement Mechanism (DSM). The WTO DSM is mainly composed of a two-layered dispute settlement adjudicative system, containing ad hoc WTO dispute settlement panels and the standing WTO Appellate Body. It is driven by members' own initiatives in setting up panels, after exhausting other channels of dispute resolution, such as consultation. The WTO Dispute Settlement Body (DSB), composing all WTO members, is responsible for the administration of the adjudicative dispute settlement system.[89]

The WTO DSM bears the following characteristics. In the first place, it is an integrated mechanism for disputes arising out of any covered WTO agreements. In the second place, it is compulsory and exclusive, which means that the members need not agree to the set-up of a panel, and the launching of the DSM excludes the dispute from the jurisdiction of other international dispute settlement mechanisms.[90]

The WTO DSM provides remedies for the breach of WTO law, which include the withdrawal of measures inconsistent with WTO agreements the compensation and suspension of concessions or other obligations.[91] The compliance with the DSM rulings must be immediate or in reasonable time, otherwise the DSB can authorize the complainant to employ retaliation measures to push the member that breached the WTO agreement to withdraw or amend its inconsistent measures.[92] The WTO DSM is applauded for providing a rule-based adjudicative system for dispute resolution among WTO members, which evolved from the diplomatic negotiation dispute settlement system under GATT.[93]

In the first 10 years after the inception of the WTO DSM, the system has been actively used by members, in particular the US and the EU. More importantly, it has, through its panel decisions, produced rich case law that, together with the WTO agreements, impacts trade liberalization and economic globalization at a normative level. Hence, it is argued that the WTO has achieved constitutional status in governing economic globalization.[94]

The WTO Dispute Settlement Mechanism faces many challenges, however, emanating from the imbalance between political and judicial decision making,

[89] WTO Understanding on Rules and Procedures Governing the Settlement of Disputes, Annex II, WTO Agreements.

[90] Van Den Bossche (n 52) 178–80.

[91] Articles 3.7 and 22 Understanding on Rules and Procedures Governing the Settlement of Disputes, Annex II, WTO Agreements.

[92] Ibid, Article 22.2.

[93] William J Davey, 'The WTO Dispute Settlement: The First Decade' (2005) *Journal of International Economic Law* 17–50.

[94] EU Petersmann, 'Multi-level Judicial Governance of International Trade Requires a Common Conception of the Rule of Law and Justice?' (2007) 10(3) *Journal of International Economic Law* 529–51.

and from its difficult relationship with the domestic courts of members, in particular the US and the EU.[95] The resistance by the EU and the US to incorporating WTO law into their domestic courts has been criticized as the application of double standards.[96] What this shows is that both the US and the EU, leaders in the governance of globalization, are reluctant to concede their governance capacity to other entities, such as the WTO.

Nevertheless, the WTO DSM could be one potential judicial channel for the WTO to pursue competition issues, given the existence of precedents and the broad coverage and popularity of the mechanism, as a forum for international dispute resolution. More importantly, so far there have been two main panel decisions which have touched upon competition law.

i. The Kodak-Fuji *Decision*

Domestic competition regulation was first touched upon in the *Kodak-Fuji* case in 1998.[97] The case involved, at that moment, the Japanese photographic material market, which had two domestic companies (Fuji and Konica) and two foreign companies (Kodak and Agfa). The US claimed that the Japanese government's measures restricted market entry by US consumer photographic materials product manufacturers, including Kodak and Agfa. These measures included distribution counter-measures encouraging the creation of a market structure in which imported products were disadvantaged, the Large Stores Law, which restricted the growth of an alternative distribution channel, and restriction on premium, which restricted sales promotion by imports.[98]

The panel, interpreting Article XXIII:1(b) on non-violation nullification or impairment, established that the US, as the complainant, must prove the existence of measures, the existence of a benefit accruing from the application of the measures, and the causal link between the measures and the nullification or impairment of the benefit. The panel ruled that the US had failed to prove the causal link in all allegations and therefore ruled against it.[99] In particular, in examining whether the US had proved the causal link between the alleged Japanese measures on distribution and the nullification, the panel concluded that the US had failed to prove the causal link between the measures and all alleged upheaval of the conditions of competition.

However, the case established the possibility for the panel to extend WTO scrutiny to domestic market regulation in Member States. In the case, the US alleged that the Japanese distribution measures breached the national treatment principle provided by Article III:4 of GATT. The panel confirmed that the term

[95] Piet Eeckhout, 'Judicial Enforcement of WTO Law in the European Union: Some Further Reflections' (2002) *Journal of International Economic Law* 91–110.

[96] Petersmann (n 940) 85.

[97] Japan-Measures Affecting Consumer Photographic Film and Paper WT/DS44/5 1998.

[98] Ibid.

[99] Ibid.

in Article III:4 has a broad scope of application. In examining the allegation made by the US, the panel emphasized that Article III:4 obliged members of the WTO to provide equality of competitive conditions for imported products in relation to domestic products.[100] Therefore, as proved in WTO case law, members' economic policies, including competition policy, competition laws and regulations, fall within this category and can be subject to scrutiny within the WTO framework.

ii. The US-Mexico *Decision*

The *US-Mexico* case is the first panel proceeding to deal solely with trade in telecommunications services, in which the competition regulation of WTO members is scrutinized.[101] The case involves the liberalization of the telecommunications market in Mexico. Before 1997, long-distance and international telecommunications services had been monopolized by Telefonos de Mexico SA de CV (Telmex). After 1997, the Mexican government liberalized the sector. Consequently, while Telmex remained the dominant player, there were 27 carriers of services in the telecommunication sector, including two American telecommunication service carriers, Avantel (WorldCom) and Alestra (AT&T).

Under the WTO framework, Mexico is bound by the GATS agreement, the Annex on Telecommunications and the Reference Paper on Regulatory Principles of GATS' Basic Telecommunications Agreement. In addition, in the Reference Paper, Mexico made specific commitments to the prevention of anti-competitive practices in telecommunication[102] and to ensuring interconnection with public telecommunication transport network suppliers.[103]

In the panel proceedings, before the DSB of the WTO, the US put forward three main claims: the first was that Mexico had failed to ensure that its major telecommunications supplier provided interconnection at terms and rates reasonable in line with section 2 of the Mexico Reference Paper; the second was that Mexico had not maintained appropriate measures to prevent Telmex from engaging in anti-competitive practices in line with section 1 of the Mexico Reference Paper; and the third was that Mexico had failed to ensure access to and use of its public telecommunications network and services on reasonable and non-discriminatory terms and conditions, in accordance with its obligations under section 5 of the GATS Annex on Telecommunications.[104]

The examination on competition regulation in Mexico is the main issue in the second claim brought by the US. In this respect, Mexico is bound by section 1.1.1

[100] WT/DS44/5 1998, para 10.370-371.

[101] Mexico-Measures Affecting Telecommunication Measures WT/DS204/R, 2 April 2004, para 72.

[102] Section 1, Reference Paper on Regulatory Principles of GATS' Basic Telecommunications Agreement.

[103] Ibid, s 2.

[104] Mexico-Measures Affecting Telecommunication Measures WT/DS204/R, 2 April 2004 VII. A. 7.1 P. 138.

of its Reference Paper as follows: 'Appropriate measures shall be maintained for the purpose of preventing suppliers who, alone or together, are a major supplier from engaging in or continuing anti-competitive practices.'

The US alleged that the Mexican Federal Telecommunication Commission (*Comision Federal De Telecounicaciones*, hereinafter the Commission) issued the International Long-Distance Rules (ILD Rules), which require telecommunication operators to engage in anti-competitive behaviour, given the uniform settlement rate and proportionate return principles contained in the Rules. The ILD Rules require all international gateway operators, including Telmex, to apply a uniform settlement rate. According to rule 13, the operator that has the greatest share of outgoing calls to a particular country in the previous six months has the sole right to negotiate settlement rates with operators of that country. The rate would then be submitted to the Commission for approval and be applied to the rest of the operators on the market. Furthermore, the ILD Rules also require international gateway operators to apply the system of proportionate return so as to distribute among themselves incoming calls from another country, in proportion to the outgoing calls the operator sends to that country.

According to the US allegation, in this case, Telmex became the party which had the sole right to negotiate with operators of another country and initiate, subject to government approval, an anti-competitive price fixing agreement with the rest of the operators on the market. Second, Telmex must give up or accept traffic from other suppliers depending on the proportion of incoming traffic against outgoing traffic, and thus enter into financial compensation agreements with other operators, which consequently constitutes market allocation, restricting competition on the marketplace.

The approach adopted by the panel was: first, to examine whether Telmex was the main supplier; second, whether there had been anti-competitive practices; and, third, whether appropriate measures were maintained. The panel reached the conclusion that Telmex was the main supplier, that the uniform settlement rate and the proportionate return system undertaken by Telmex, although required by Mexican legislation, were de facto anti-competitive agreements which fixed price and allocate markets and were hence anti competitive practices, and that Mexico had failed to maintain appropriate measures to prevent the main supplier from engaging in anti-competitive practices.[105]

The panel argued that removing market access and national treatment barriers was not deemed sufficient to ensure the effective realization of market access commitments in basic telecommunication services. Many members to the WTO agreed to additional commitments to prevent monopoly behaviour or abuse of a dominant position by monopoly operators, with the aim of ensuring that market access and national treatment commitments were not undermined by anti-competitive behaviour by monopolies that are prevalent in the telecommunications sector.[106]

[105] Section C Panel Report US-Mexico.
[106] Ibid, para 7.237.

It has thus been argued that the *US-Mexico* case has provided an opportunity for competition rules to return to the WTO through the backdoor.[107]

However, it is also argued that the panel failed to take the opportunity to establish a conceptual framework on the definition of anti-competitive practices under the WTO or to develop rules as to whether and how economic analysis can be applied in the evaluation of market power in the markets of Member States.[108] Furthermore, the panel failed to clarify the relationship of the sectoral regulation and competition law, of the contracting parties, and thus failed to present satisfactory answers as to the extent of the appropriate measures to be maintained in Mexico.

Both the *Kodak-Fuji* and the *US-Mexico* cases prove that competition regulation in the domestic market of a contracting party, in particular, competition regulation of a service market, can be subject to the scrutiny of the WTO dispute settlement mechanism. Moreover, this scrutiny by the WTO on domestic competition regulation has begun to refer to the prevailing literature on antitrust economic principles.

However, the WTO DSB's examination of domestic competition protection is primarily construed from the angle of the WTO principles, namely the non-discrimination principle and market access. To this end, national treatment, rather than solid economic analysis of market power, is used as the main theoretical framework to evaluate the competition restraints on the markets of Member States.

IV. PURSUIT OF EFFICIENCY AND NON-DISCRIMINATION: CLASH OF NORMS

Based on the discussions in chapters 1 and 2, it can be seen that the US, the EU and international organizations have participated in the development of competition law in the context of the globalization.

Chapter 1 has shown that the EU-US convergence on using competition law to pursue allocative efficiency and maximization of consumer benefits serves to be the raison d'etre for other competition regime to refer to. The pursuit of allocative efficiency by competition law relies on the systematic effects-based economic analysis of market power developed by the jurisprudence of US antitrust law and EU competition law.

Chapter 2 has shown that the efforts of international organizations in harmonizing competition law are embedded within the neoliberal ideology, place

[107] 'The Telmex Dispute at the WTO: Competition Makes a Backdoor', available at: www.cuts-international.org/pdf/Telmex-1-2006.pdf.

[108] Philip Marsden, 'WTO Decides its First Competition Case with Disappointing Results', *Competition Law Insight*, May 2004, available at: www.biicl.org/files/1106_comp_law_insight_-_wto_article.pdf.

emphasis on the social embeddedness of competition regulation regimes and, more importantly, uphold the values of fairness and equality. Whereas the international organizations such as the OECD, UNCTAD and the WTO cross-reference with each other in developing a normative framework of global competition law convergence, the WTO has generated the non-discrimination principle based on its own theoretical underpinning. Therefore, a level playing field with enhanced market access is what international organizations wish to achieve with competition laws in its Member States.

However, differences can be observed between the principle of allocative efficiency and the principle of non-discrimination in terms of their relations to global competition law. First, the non-discrimination principle predominantly emphasizes enhancing market access for international players and domestic disadvantaged players through competition laws. To a certain extent, the non-discrimination principle targeting market access is compatible with the market contestability theory as one economic rationale underpinning competition regulation. A contestable market refers to a market which is free to enter and exit.[109] The non-discrimination principle contributes to the removal of entry barriers to markets and thus improves the contestability of markets. However, market contestability in competition regulation goes beyond market access and requires further the maximization of potential competition on the market.[110]

Nevertheless, the definition of the market entry barrier in antitrust analysis has not achieved consensus.[111] Bain has defined the market entry barrier as an advantage held by established sellers in an industry over potential entrants in the long run, which includes the economy of scale, product differentiation and absolute cost advantages.[112] Stigler argues that the entry barrier is the cost which must be borne by entrants but not by incumbents, which therefore excludes the economy of scale.[113] Ferguson argues that entry barriers refer to factors making entry unprofitable while permitting established firms to set prices above marginal cost.[114] Fisher argues that entry barriers refer to anything which prevents entry when it is socially beneficial.[115]

In the competition analysis, market entry barriers include economic market barriers, but have a broader coverage; for example, these barriers cover the government regulatory barrier. In the evaluation of market power, competition authorities consider factors such as market entry on top of market share analysis based on antitrust market delineation. The fact or likelihood of market entry by

109 Massimo Motta, *Competition Policy: Theory and Practice* (Cambridge University Press, 2004) 73.

110 Ibid.

111 R Preston McAfee, Hugo M Mialon and Michael A Williams, 'What is a Barrier to Entry?', 6 June 2003. Available at http://ssrn.com/abstract=594601.

112 J Bain, *Barriers to New Competition* (Harvard University Press, 1956) 3.

113 George Stigler, *The Organization of Industry* (University of Chicago Press, 1968) 67.

114 James Ferguson, *Advertising and Competition: Theory, Measurement* (Ballinger, 1974).

115 Franklin Fisher, 'Diagnosing Monopoly' (1979) 23 *Quarterly Review of Economics and Businesses* 19.

newcomers to the market would reduce the final evaluation of market power held by the alleged players. In the examination of anti-competitive agreements and the abuse of a dominant position, competition authorities would consider the fact or likelihood of market entry, among many other factors on the conditions of the market, in order to see if the negative impact brought by the anti-competitive restraints can last a long time or can be mitigated by the possibility of new entry. In the examination of mergers, it is argued that a high entry barrier does not necessarily confirm the substantial lessening of competition in the post-merger market. The entry analysis for merger control should be undertaken after the level of competition that would be likely to exist without entry is analysed.[116] Therefore, it is important to note that the presence of market barriers does not mean that the anti-competitive behaviour in question should be caught by law. The restriction should be regulated only when the anti-competitive effects of the restraints outweigh the benefits they bring to social welfare. The examination should be undertaken on a case-by-case basis.[117] In other words, according to the practice of competition authorities, the assessment of market entry barriers is a necessary component of the modern competition evaluation, based on economies analysis, but is not the end of competition regulation.

Second, the fairness value upheld by the non-discrimination principle allows equally bad or good treatment to occur and remains mainly formal in nature. However, some competition regulation regimes, as represented by the EU, have provided positive protection to disadvantaged undertakings on the market, with the aim of preserving rivalry and promoting competition.[118] In this case, whereas the non-discrimination principle emphasizes a more formal realization of the fairness value, practice by competition authorities, as represented by the EU, shows a more substantive way to uphold the fairness value.

Third, as illustrated in the previous chapter, the pursuit of economic efficiency has, throughout the years, produced a conceptual framework for enforcement based on rich case law of US antitrust law and EU competition law. This conceptual framework, greatly influenced by the Chicago School of economic thought, mainly includes the delineation of market power based on supply or demand substitutability, the evaluation of market power and the impact of restraints on competition and efficiencies.[119] However, the latest WTO case law on competition issues has shown that a conceptual framework to link the non-discrimination principle to the enforcement of competition on the market has yet to be developed.

[116] Jeremy K West, 'Barriers to Entry', 2005, OECD Roundtables on Competition Policy Working Paper No 58.

[117] Ibid.

[118] For example, EU competition law provides special responsibilities to dominant players on competition protection, with the aim of protecting rivalry in the marketplace. See Case C 322/81, *Michelin v Commission* [1983] ECR 3461 [57].

[119] See discussion in ch 1.

Hence, in comparison to the principle of the pursuit of allocative efficiency, the non-discrimination principle has neither been built upon detailed economic analysis on market power nor explicitly purported to achieve the maximization of allocative efficiency. Instead, it places the emphasis on creating a level playing field, of which the enhancement of market access by imported goods and services to the targeted market and the improvement of access by disadvantaged players to resources on the domestic market in developing countries serve as the priority goal to be achieved.

V. CONCLUSION

Based on the foregoing, it can be derived that the norm of the pursuit of allocative efficiency generated by convergence between the competition regimes of the EU and the US, and the norm of non-discrimination generated by the WTO are so far the two main soft law norms which exert an influence on the development of competition law around the world. As discussed, this is mainly determined by the weight held by these players in the globalization process and their structural features. However, the two norms are based on fundamentally different theoretical frameworks and serve different goals.

In the face of plural sources of global competition law norms, new competition regimes are under no legal obligations with regard to compliance. In fact, the receiving competition regulation regime largely determines which norm is to be applied in their domestic competition law. It is in this context that the book turns to China and its development of competition regulation for further examination.

Part II

China's Market Governance and the Anti-Monopoly Law

3

Market Governance in China

I. INTRODUCTION

Part II of this book focuses on understanding China's market governance, restraints of competition on the Chinese market and the making of the Anti-Monopoly Law (AML) in the background of China's rise against globalization. Chapter 3 examines the institutional and normative transformations and dispute settlement development in China in line with its reforms. It argues that despite the rationalization of the government's administrative system for market regulation and the formalization of the dispute settlement system, the state structure has remained largely unchanged. The Chinese market governance is subject to a monist market regulatory framework, where the party-state has remained to be a dominant, resilient and strategic actor.

II. INSTITUTIONAL TRANSFORMATION OF MARKET GOVERNANCE

The People's Republic of China (PRC) is comprised of the legislature system headed by the National People's Congress (NPC), the executive system led by the the State Council (the central government), the judiciary headed by the Supreme People's Court (SPC), the Supreme People's Procuratorate (SPP), the Central Military Commission and the President. The State Council is the main state organ responsible for constructing a market economy in China.

The Chinese Communist Party (CCP) functions as a shadowing institution behind the state apparatus and directs decision making by these organs. In the past 60 years, the CCP has remained an organized and stable institution, untouched by China's political movements, market-oriented reform and participation in economic globalization. In the meantime, it has continuously reinvented its ideologies to consolidate legitimacy and adjust capacity, which has had a far-reaching impact on China's market governance.

Hence, the institutional framework of market governance in China needs to be posited from two perspectives, namely the governmental administrative system for its institutional outlook and the CCP for its ideological origins.

A. The Ideological Adaptation of the CCP

As the ruling party in China, the CCP's organizational structure at the central level includes the national CCP Members' Congress of a five-year tenure and the CCP Congress Central Committee created by the Congress. At the plenary session of the CCP Central Committee, the Central Committee Political Bureau (the Politburo) and its Standing Committee is elected. The Politburo Standing Committee elects the Central Committee General Secretary from its own members and the Secretariat of the Central Committee from Central Committee members. The CCP Central Committee General Secretary is in charge of coordinating politburo meetings and directs CCP Central Committee Secretariat, which oversees the administration of the Politburo.[1]

The same organizational structure is replicated at the local CCP branches, corresponding to the local government level. Local CCP branches are directly answerable to the respective organs of the central CCP. Within the CCP organizational structure, the CCP Politburo Standing Committee, composed of individual Chinese leaders, including the President and the Premier of China, remains the main decision-making body.

Since the establishment of the PRC in 1949, the CCP and its Politburo has had five generations of leaders, including Mao Zedong (1949–76), Deng Xiaoping (1978–89), Jiang Zemin (1989–2003), Hu Jingtao (2003–13) and Xi Jingping (2013 onwards). While the CCP in the era of Mao and Deng was characterized by strongman politics, the CCP has been subject to more internal checks and balances and collective decision making in the following leaders' eras.[2]

What the five generations of leaders have in common is their continuous efforts in reinventing the CCP's ideological basis to strengthen its legitimacy and adjust its capacity. The CCP leaders did so by adapting Marxism-Leninism to China's reality, adjusting international governance norms to China's context and rediscovering China's own philosophies and political theories. The Mao Zedong Thoughts, Deng Xiaoping Theory, Three Represents proposed by Jiang Zeming and the Scientific Outlook of Development proposed by Hu Jingtao show consistency in building upon preceding reinventions and adjusting the Party's capacity without abandoning its socialist ideology.

With this background, the development of the Chinese economy has been under the guidance of the CCP through the mechanism of the five-year plan for economic development. The five-year plan is set out by the CCP and is enacted and enforced by the State Council through the government administrative system. From 2011 to 2015, the Chinese economy is under the guidance of CCP's twelfth five-year plan, with the first five-year plan having been enforced in 1953.

[1] www.china.org.cn/english/congress/227030.htm.

[2] Zheng Yongnian, 'Where Does the Chinese Communist Party Go from Here? Challenges and Opportunities' (2012) 10(2) *China: An International Journal* 84–101.

From 1949 to 1976, the CCP was led by Mao's thoughts on development. Embracing Marxism-Leninism ideology, Mao recognized the backwardness of the Chinese economy. He criticized Stalin's complete centralization in economic development, focused on collective rural industrialization and decentralization, motivated the rural population to participate in economic growth through land reform and highlighted egalitarian development in rural and urban areas.[3] However, the collective rural industrialization was unsuccessful and the role of the market was restricted and gradually eliminated. The economic development theme eventually gave way to class struggle-based political movements; for example, the Anti-Rightist Movement (1957–59) and the Cultural Revolution (1966–76). The economy was consequently left in paralysis.

At the Third Plenary Session of the Eleventh Central Committee of the CCP in 1978, Deng Xiaoping as the second-generation CCP leader proposed that the country should refocus on economic growth, and the improvement of living standards and poverty alleviation were key targets. This marked the beginning of China's economic reform. Marxism-Leninism and Mao's thoughts became limited in serving as the ideological basis for the CCP's new economic reform. The CCP began to look for an ideological breakthrough, and its practice under Deng's leadership has since been summarized into the Deng Xiaoping Theory.

Deng's theory upholds the Marxist dialectical and materialist concept of history, with the emphasis on the idea that a socialist China represents an advanced social organization in the evolution of societies. Hence, socialism should not and does not equate to poverty. Referring to the class conflict concept in the Marxist theory of revolution, Deng argued that the main conflict that China faced was no longer the conflict among different classes, but that between low productivity and limited resources for social production.[4] As such, the market mechanism and socialism were not mutually exclusive in a socialist state. This provided the ideological basis for China to return to the market as one engine for economic growth and to install incentives in rural and urban economies.

In the Twelfth CCP Congress in 1982, Deng proposed that China's modernization should be achieved by establishing Socialism with Chinese characteristics, by combining Marxism with China's context. This set the main theme for CCP's subsequent ideological reinventions. However, as Deng's economic development strategies remained primarily pragmatic and experimental, socialism with Chinese characteristics remains an open-ended normative project.

When Jiang Zemin took office as the CCP's leader in 1989, the CCP was faced with the collapse of the USSR, domestic political unrest and sweeping changes to the social and economic structures as a result of reform. The international

[3] Jack Gray, 'Mao in Perspective' (2006) 187 *China Quarterly* 659–79; Mark Selden and Jack Gray, 'Mao Zedong and the Political Economy of Chinese Development' (2006) 187 *China Quarterly* 680–85.

[4] For a summary of the Deng Xiaoping Theory, see http://news.xinhuanet.com/ziliao/2004-10/27/content_2145152.htm.

community, in recognition of China's success in economic development, was watching it closely for pro-democracy political transformation.

Headed by Jiang, the CCP continued the ideological reinvention, centring on socialism with Chinese characteristics proposed by Deng. In 1992, socialism with Chinese characteristics was written into the Amendment of the CCP Constitution at the Fourteenth CCP Congress[5] and a socialist market economy was set as the goal of China's economic reform in 1993.[6]

The socialist market economy as defined by the CCP was to establish a market economy where the market functions as the basic resource allocator, but is subject to the state's macro-adjustment. In order to achieve this, the CCP provides to undertake the following steps: keeping public ownership as the main form of ownership with other forms of ownership coexistent in Chinese economy, reforming the state-owned enterprises through incorporation, building up a united and open national market, transforming government roles, establishing a distribution system prioritizing efficiency while taking equality into consideration and building up a social security system for the rural and urban populations.[7]

In 2000, the CCP's ideological framework was reinvented by Jiang's 'Three Represents Theory'. The Three Represents Theory provides that history has proven that the CCP has the people's support because it has always represented the development trend of advanced productive forces, the orientation of the advanced culture and the fundamental interests of the overwhelming majority of the people in China.[8]

It is argued that Jiang's Three Represents Theory expanded CCP's ideological framework in order to include the Chinese elite. It further showed the CCP's emphasis on development rather than on the conflict between productivity and the resources for production. It also has been argued to have provided an ideological basis and a constitutional foundation for the CCP to stand at the centre of China's state apparatus.[9]

The start of market-oriented reforms stimulated the revival of the Chinese intellectual community. Forbidden Western philosophical and sociological works were translated into Chinese, which triggered a theoretical debate on the ideological basis of China's development. Two main schools of thought, intertwined at certain points, remained the most influential, namely liberalism and the thoughts of the new left.

[5] Amendment to the CCP Constitution adopted at the Fourteenth CCP Congress in 1992.

[6] Decision on Socialist Market Economy Institutions Building adopted at the Third Section of the Fourteenth Congress of the CCP in 1993.

[7] Ibid.

[8] For the Three Represents Theory, see http://news.xinhuanet.com/ziliao/2003-01/21/content_699933.htm.

[9] Larry Catá Backer, 'The Rule of Law, the Chinese Communist Party, and Ideological Campaigns: Sange Daibiao (the "Three Represents"), Socialist Rule of Law, and Modern Chinese Constitutionalism' (2006) 16(1) *Journal of Transnational Law and Contemporary Problems*.

Both liberalism and the thoughts of the new left embrace the reform and opening-up strategies undertaken by the CCP, and are concerned with development strategies for a stronger China. Both have also been critical of the increasing social and economic problems, such as inequality, corruption and the oppression present in Chinese society.[10]

However, the two schools of thought have different opinions on China's domestic governance and international relations. In terms of the challenges of domestic governance, liberalism places a strong emphasis on the market element, liberty and the rule of law,[11] whereas the new left prefers to find solutions through institutional innovation within the current political system.[12]

Whereas liberalism favours the Western style of institutional reshaping compatible with the market economy, the new left views the complete implantation of a Western-style institutional set-up as radical and infeasible—as institutional fetishism.[13] In other words, whereas liberalism in China finds convergence with what is upheld by China's Western counterparts, the new left focuses more on Chinesenization.[14]

The rise of the new left synchronized with the emergence of nationalism in China. Nationalism, as a multifaceted concept, often centres on the nation state and contains institutional identity and international implications. In the Chinese context, nationalism expresses itself in terms of China as a nation state, the Chinese as being of one ethnicity and China as an international player on the world stage.[15] Hence, the new left advocacy on Chinesenization fits in well with the nationalism category. Nationalism began to serve as one of the key elements in the CCP's ideological reinvention.

When Hu Jingtao came into power in 2003, the international pattern facing China had transformed and China has since become more integrated into the international community, as seen in its accession to the World Trade Organization (WTO) in 2001.[16] Internally, China has achieved a continuous and impressive GDP growth. However, economic reform continues to be impeded by the lagging-behind political and social reforms. Chinese society has been troubled with an increasing discrepancy in social stratification, unfair distribution of wealth and an ideological lacuna where Marxism-Leninism is losing its authority.[17]

[10] He Qinglian, *Pitfalls of Modernization* (*Xian dai huai de xian jing*) (Today China Press, 1998); Li Changping, *Telling the Premier the Truth* (*Wo Xiang Zong Li Shuo Shi Hua*) (GuangMing Daily Press, 2002).

[11] Zhu Xueqing, ' Wo Men De Jing Sheng Mo Di Zai Na Li?' (Where is our Spiritual Dock? (2009) 1 Fa Zhi Zi Xun (*Legal Information*) 20–21.

[12] Cui Zhiyuan, 'Liberal Socialism and the Future of China: A Petty Bourgeois Manifesto' in Tianyu Cao (ed), *The Chinese Model of Modern Development* (Routledge, 2005) 157–74.

[13] Ibid.

[14] Zheng Yongnian (n 2) 56.

[15] Ibid, 2–10.

[16] Willy Wo Lap Lam, *Chinese Politics in Hu Jintao Era: New Leaders, New Challenges* (ME Sharpe, 2006).

[17] Wenfang Tang, 'Political and Social Trends in the Post-Deng Urban China: Crisis or Stability?' (2002) *China Quarterly* 890–909.

In 2003, Hu proposed the Scientific Outlook of Development as a further reinvention of CCP's socialism with Chinese characteristics. In developing this theory, the CCP has looked to universal norms and Chinese philosophies for guidance. In 2006, Yu Keping, the leading party theoretician, published a provocative article in the *Beijing Daily* entitled 'Democracy is a Good Thing'.[18] The article advocated that democracy is essential to China's development, but should be developed according to the self-determination of the Chinese people. In the meantime, the CCP leaders proposed that it aimed to build up a socialist, harmonious society in China.[19] Harmony is an important value embedded in Chinese traditional philosophies, mainly represented by Confucianism, which provides that a harmonious relationship among people and between people and the state should be established on the basis of the values of trust and virtue.[20]

The CCP emphasized that founded on the scientific outlook of development theory, a socialist, harmonious society is a society based on, among other things, people.[21] To achieve a socialist, harmonious society, the CCP would promote economic policies to reduce discrepancies and increase employment, increase the social protection of justice by improving democracy and the legal system, build up a virtue-based socialist value system and transform the government into being more service and public governance-oriented.[22]

Given this background, in 2005, the CCP proposed to transform China's development strategy from GDP-oriented economic growth towards new industrialization and sustainable development, focusing on environmental protection, innovation and social equity, and a harmonious society.[23]

In November 2012, Xi Jingping became the latest CCP leader. His legacy on the CPP's ideological reinvention remains to be seen. However, his speech at the conclusion of the Plenary Session of the Eighteenth CCP Congress on 15 November showed clear emphasis on the CCP's responsibility for people's livelihood and determination to combat corruption.[24]

The CCP's continuous transformation of socialism with Chinese characteristics remains open-ended. However, the process has been argued to contain elements of socialism, developmentalism and nationalism, which interact with and restrain each other to shape the ideological basis for CCP as a ruling party.[25] In this process,

[18] Yu Keping, *Democracy is a Good Thing: Essays on Politics, Society and Culture in Contemporary China* (Brookings Institution, 2009) 3.

[19] CCP decision on the construction of a socialist harmonious society, adopted at the sixth plessionary meeting of the sixteenth CCP central committee meeting on 11 October 2006, available at: cpc.people.com.cn/GB/64162/64168/64569/72347/6347991.html.

[20] Tang Yijie, 'The Contemporary Understanding of Confucious Harmonious Society' (2007) 2 *Theory and Reference* 21–23.

[21] CCP decision on the construction of a socialist, harmonious society, adopted at the sixth plessionary meeting of the sixteenth CCP central committee meeting on 11 October 2006, available at: cpc.people.com.cn/GB/64162/64168/64569/72347/6347991.html.

[22] Yu Keping, *Globalization and Changes in China's Governance* (Brill, 2008) 21–63.

[23] http://news.xinhuanet.com/politics/2005-10/18/content_3640318.htm.

[24] http://news.xinhuanet.com/2012-11/19/c_123967017.htm.

[25] Lin Chun, *The Transformation of Chinese Socialism* (Duke University Press, 2006).

the CCP increasingly engages in a consultative process with the public and is more responsive to the wishes of the public in its ideological reformation.[26]

By the same token, the CCP is in the process of developing a socialist market economy with Chinese characteristics. However, the construction of a market economy in China seems to bear a primary goal of utilizing the market's mechanism to serve for the goals resulting from the interaction between socialism, developmentalism and nationalism. Public ownership, as one cornerstone of the socialist ideology, is to be strengthened rather than removed. State-owned enterprises, the main representative of public ownership, will have their competitiveness and efficiency strengthened through the market mechanism and the government's macro-economic policies. In the making of strategies and policies for China's market economy, the CCP has directed the government authorities to be engaged in a consultative process with the Chinese elite and the public, and to communicate more with international actors, such as the US, the EU and international organizations.

B. The Institutional Restructuring of the Government Administrative System

Within the state organization of the PRC, the State Council (central government) is answerable to the NPC and its standing committee, and is supervised by the latter.[27] It is responsible for the administration of political, economic and ideological affairs nationwide, and the administration of international relations. It constitutes four layers of institutions, namely ministries, bureaus, executive offices and affiliated institutions, which are placed in a hierarchical order in terms of status and power.[28]

A similar model is followed at the local level. The Local People's Congress is the organ of the highest state power at the local level, to which local state organs such as local government are accountable. Other than the central government, ie, the State Council, Chinese local governments include governments of municipalities, directly under the State Council, of provinces and autonomous regions, and of cities, counties and towns.[29]

In Deng's China, the Chinese leaders had a cautious and pragmatic attitude towards institutional reform when they were searching for the method as well as the direction of the reform by *crossing the river by touching the stones*. While the Chinese leaders focused on introducing the market element into the economy to

[26] Steve Tsang, 'Consultative Leninism: China's New Political Framework' (2009) 18(62) *Journal of Contemporary China* 865–80.

[27] Art 67.6 and 128 Constitution of the PRC.

[28] For the general institutional structure of the State Council, see http://www.zhb.gov.cn/zhxx/xglj/200911/t20091102_180966.htm.

[29] www.china.org.cn/english/features/43470.htm.

alleviate poverty and increase economic growth, they also attempted to ensure that the introduction of the market element would not affect the stability of the incumbent political system.[30] Hence, the institutional framework of the Chinese administrative system, in particular that of economic and market development, remained largely unchanged during this period.

When the CCP declared the establishment of the socialist market economy in 1993, the Chinese government undertook a series of reforms to institutionalize its market economy construction. From 1993 to 2008, the State Council went through four institutional reforms by deregulation and liberalization of market regulation, with the aim of establishing a modern regulatory framework for the development of a market economy in China.[31]

The incumbent market regulatory framework was mainly established as a result of the central government institutional restructuring in 2003. At the macro-level of regulation, the National Development and Reform Commission (NDRC) was set up to issue economic plans, policies, etc, while the Ministry of Commerce (MOFCOM) was in charge of domestic market development and international trade. At the micro-level, MOFCOM and the State Administration of Industry and Commerce (SAIC) functioned to regulate behaviour on the part of enterprises in the marketplace.

The State Council centralizes regulation of issues of significance to the economic reform whenever necessary. Issues like the reform of state-owned enterprises (SOEs), financial sector reform and the integration of the domestic market remain highly sensitive yet significant. Where no laws have been promulgated on these specific issues, the State Council established a National Office of Rectification and Standardization of Market Economic Order (NORSMEO) in 1998 and the State-owned Asset Supervisions and Administration Commission (SASAC) in 2003, both of which were ad hoc attempts to centralize the regulation, given the urgency and difficulties relating to the issues involved.

The State Council decentralizes the regulation of industries from government ministries to semi-governmental industrial associations. The establishment of these industrial associations are to be set up under the approval of government authorities; the associations are quasi-governmental organizations.[32] They are the main agents that regulate the behaviour of enterprises within each industry.

Within the government market regulatory framework, the NDRC, MOFCOM and the SAIC, which are all answerable to the State Council, are conferred with respective regulatory competence. The NDRC, based on the previous State Development and Planning Commission and State Economic and Trade Commission, is presently one powerful regulator in the Chinese market regulatory

[30] Susan Shirk, *The Political Logic of Economic Reform in China* (University of California Press, 1993) 129–32.

[31] Qianlan Wu, 'The Making of a Market Economy in China: Transformation of Government Regulation of Market Development' (2007) 13(6) *European Law Journal* 750–71.

[32] Arts 9 and 11 Regulation on the Social Association Registration issued by the Ministry of Civil Affairs on 25 October 1998.

framework. Its main responsibilities include setting out long-term and short-term sustainable economic development strategies, and specific economic and development policies, such as industrial, price, foreign investment or regional development policies.[33] Pursuant to the State Council Provisional Regulation on Promoting Industrial Adjustment in 2005, the NDRC issues the Sectoral Investment Catalogue, which sets out guidelines on market entry into sectors of the Chinese economy. The NDRC issues industrial policies and other legislation to lead the structural adjustment of key industries in China, for example, the automobile and steel industries.

MOFCOM is the government authority responsible for the regulation of domestic market development and international trade. It was established on the basis of the previous Ministry of Foreign Trade and Economic Cooperation (MOFTEC), with the competence of the administration of domestic trade having been taken over from the State Economic and Trade Commission (SETC). In recent years, its competence in domestic market regulation has quickly expanded through the setting-up of new departments on Market System Development, Department of Market Operation Regulation and Department of Commercial Reform. Following MOFTEC, its predecessor, MOFCOM is the main government market regulator that is responsible for China's communication and cooperation with international actors on market governance.

The State Administration of Industry and Commerce (SAIC) was upgraded from its bureau level to a ministerial level institution of the State Council. It has been the main government regulator overseeing business registration and business behaviour in the marketplace. The upgrade of the SAIC to the ministerial level shows the State Council's intention to strengthen regulation on the behaviour of companies in China's domestic market.[34]

As a result of institutional reforms, the State Council has set up a market regulatory framework composed of key government authorities, including the NDRC, the Ministry of Finance (MOF), MOFCOM, the SAIC, the SASAC, the State Administration of Taxation (SAT) and the State Administration of Foreign Exchange (SAFE), along with others. These authorities are conferred with different market regulatory competence, are integral parts of the State Council as the central government and are answerable to the latter. Consistent with China's monolithic state structure, regulation of the market in China has not had institutional independence from the executive branch of the state and has long been embedded within the government administrative system.

Different aspects of market governance in China are subject to regulation by the corresponding government authorities. Hence the market governance is segmented. For matters which are in relation to the market as a whole, it requires coordination among the segmented regulators and their joint actions, which is subject to the approval of the central government. In regulating the market,

[33] www.ndrc.gov.cn.
[34] Qianlan Wu (n 31).

the government authorities are keen to maintain and expand their respective regulatory competence, and they have increasingly had pluralistic kinds of strategic interests, which impact on the coordination among the segmented government regulators. As a result, the relationships and interactions among the government market authorities shape the real picture of the enforcement of market regulation in China.

Corresponding to the institutional restructuring of the central government, similar institutional restructuring has taken place at the local government level. Local government at the provincial or city level regulates local markets by relying on its department of reform and development, department of commerce and local bureau of administration of industry and commerce. However, the central-local government relations have been one of the impediments to market regulation in China.

Given the scale of the Chinese market, the central government relies on local governments for the enforcement of central government regulation at the local level and for local economic development. However, local regulators do not necessarily have the same incentives for market regulation as those of the central government.

With the reform of the fiscal system in China in 1994, central and local governments established a shared tax system.[35] Under the shared tax system, the central and local governments defined each other's scope of expenditure and divided the tax revenue into central government tax, local tax and tax shared by central and local governments.[36] The operation of local government relies to a large extent on the local tax revenue. As a result, local business organizations, irrespective of their ownership, can enjoy preferential treatment from local government if they are the main tax payers. Local leaders are motivated to protect local business operators from competition from other provinces in order to keep these tax payers.

Further, leaders in local governments are, on the one hand, provided with wide personal discretion for local development and, on the other hand, subject to the CCP's nomenclature system and its supervision. One of the important criteria for the evaluation and promotion of local officials is the economic growth index of the local economy and the transformation of local state-owned enterprises. Hence, local leaders pay particular attention to the protection of local businesses and market development. As a result, state intervention into the market was often legitimized and disguised in the name of economic development.[37]

[35] State Council Decision on the Shared Tax System, 1993, http://news.xinhuanet.com/ziliao/2005-03/17/content_2709622.htm.

[36] Ibid, s 3.

[37] Jean C Oi, 'Fiscal Reform and the Economic Foundations of Local State Corporatism in China' (1992) 45(1) *World Politics* 99–126.

III. NORMATIVE RATIONALIZATION FOR MARKET GOVERNANCE

China's construction of a socialist market economy with Chinese characteristics saw the transformation of relationships among the state, market and law. When the PRC was established in 1949, the Chinese leaders were determined to break away completely from China's precedent legal systems and develop a legal system of its own. The Chinese legal system is a hybrid of the Soviet Union legal system legacy, which emphasizes social control, of the European continental civil law tradition, which is based on a hierarchy of rules and codification, and of the Chinese practice.[38]

When China started its market-oriented reform in 1978, it speedily enacted laws and regulations to govern contract and business organization. However, at this stage, market regulation in China had been fundamentally based on government red-headed policy papers, which prevailed over the law and regulations when these were in conflict.[39] Laws on market regulation focused more on guaranteeing state control over market development than on protecting individual rights.[40] In 1996, the CCP proposed to develop China into a country ruled by law.[41] With the rapid development of the administrative law system,[42] law began to impose restraints on the power of the state as far as market governance was concerned.

However, despite its rapid development, the Chinese legal system remained largely detached from international norms. Since 1978, China has been a member of over 300 multilateral treaties, with 70 domestic laws touching upon norms provided by these international treaties. The Chinese legal system has the following channels to enforce international law obligations: administrative regulation based on international treaties; the adoption of new legislation in line with international treaties; the amendment of incumbent legislation in line with international obligations; and the direct application of international treaties by judges in a

[38] Jianfu Chen, *Chinese Law: Context and Transformation* (Martinus Nijhoff Publishers, 2008) 36 and 75.

[39] Stanley Lubman, *A Bird in a Cage: Legal Reform in China after Mao* (Stanford University Press, 1999) 4.

[40] Donald Clark, 'Legislating for a Market Economy in China' (2007) 191 *China Quarterly* 567–85.

[41] Jiang Zemin proposed developing China based on the rule by law on the Fifteenth CCP Congress in 2001. See http://cpc.people.com.cn/GB/64156/64157/4418466.html.

[42] Since 1982, the Chinese government has strengthened its administrative law development. In terms of the organization of government, China has adopted the Organization Law of the State Council (1982), the Organization Law of Local Governments (1982) and the Civil Servants Law (2005). Regarding the behaviour on the part of governments, China has adopted the Administrative Penalties Law (1996), the Legislation Law (2003), the Administrative Licenses Law (2003) and a series of State Council regulations. China has also adopted the Administrative Litigation Law (1989), the State Compensation law (1994), the Administrative Supervision Law (1997) and the Administrative Reconsideration Law (1999).

trial process where no relevant domestic law is provided, yet foreign parties are involved.[43]

The relationship between international law and domestic law has remained ambiguous, with no constitutional provision provided. Pursuant to the Civil Procedure Law in 1991, international law prevails over Chinese law unless China has made a reservation to that effect.[44] Nevertheless, in line with China's integration into economic globalization, its attitude towards international law has become more positive and participatory.[45]

With China's WTO membership, it is bound by the WTO general principles and agreements, and is subject to the scrutiny by the WTO dispute settlement mechanism. It is obligated to amend or revoke its incumbent legislation which is inconsistent with the WTO rules and to adopt new laws and legislation to give effect to its WTO obligations. As a result, the Chinese legal system has been reshaped and stimulated, and its communication with international legal norms has been strengthened.[46]

A. Rationalization of the Legal Framework for Market Regulation

With respect to the normative framework for market regulation, multiple actors have the competence to adopt law in China's market regulation. At a central level, these actors include, in a hierarchical order, the NPC and its Standing Committee (the NPCSC), which have the competence to adopt primary legislation, and the State Council, which has the competence to adopt secondary regulation to enforce primary law, and the State Council ministries, which have the competence to adopt rules to enforce primary law and State Council regulations.

Based on this, the local people's congress and local government can issue legally binding decrees and rules that are applicable within local jurisdiction. The local people's congress adopts local decrees to enforce law, State Council regulations or State Council rules, while local government, based on the decree, can adopt local rules for further enforcement within the local jurisdiction. Furthermore, the SPC has the competence to issue legally binding interpretations in relation to issues arising out of the trial process.

As the economic reform continued, the complexity and ambiguity of the normative framework on market regulation began to have an increasing negative impact on China's market governance. First, no clarification had been made

[43] Xue Hanqin and Jin Qian, 'International Treaties in Chinese Domestic Legal System' (2008) 8(2) *Chinese Journal of International Law* 299–322.

[44] Art 236 Civil Procedure Law of the PRC: www.chinacourt.org/flwk/show.php?file_id=122225.

[45] Samuel S Kim, 'The Development of International Law in Post-Mao China: Change and Continuity' (1987) 7 *Journal of Chinese Law* 117.

[46] Julia Ya Qin, 'Trade, Investment and Beyond: The Impact of WTO Accession on China's Legal System' (2007) 191 *China Quarterly* 720–41.

regarding the force, status and relationships of the different instruments used for market governance in Chine, which include laws, regulations, rules, policies or informal rules. Second, no clear procedure had been set out regarding the regulation-making process, including the law-making process by central and local governments. Third, different or even contradictory local regulations were allowed to exist simultaneously within the Chinese administrative system. Therefore, there has been an emerging need to rationalize and unify market regulation on the part of the government administrative system.

The Legislation Law, the first of its kind, was adopted in 2000 as a watershed in the process of the rationalization of the normative framework for market regulation in China.[47] It sets out the legislative competence of each law-making institution within the administrative bureaucratic system, establishes legal procedures for the law-making processes by institutions, clarifies the relationship among different forms of legislation and provides an administrative review mechanism, carried out by the NPCSC, to supervise the legislation adopted by all law-making institutions.[48]

The Legislation Law sets out, for the first time, a boundary of legislative jurisdiction imposed on all law-making institutions. Law must be made by the NPC and the NPCSC when involving issues such as state sovereignty.[49] In general, the State Council issues regulations to enforce laws adopted by the NPC or the NPCSC, or to undertake administration.[50] The local legislature has the competence to issue local decrees to enforce law, State Council administrative regulation or for the purpose of undertaking local administration only.[51] Local governments have the competence to issue local rules to enforce the law, State Council administrative regulation and local decree or for the purpose of undertaking local administration.[52] Local decrees and rules are applicable within the areas in which the issuing local people's congresses or local governments have jurisdiction. State Council ministries, commissions and bureaus have the competence to issue State Council administrative rules to enforce State Council administrative regulations. These administrative rules are binding from the central to the local levels and, exclusively within the field that these ministries are in charge of in terms of China's market governance.[53]

[47] Laura Paler, 'China's Legislation Law and the Making of a More Orderly and Representative Legislative System' (2005) 182 *China Quarterly* 301.

[48] Art 88 Legislation Law.

[49] Art 8 Legislation Law provides that laws must be adopted in relation to the organization of National People's Congress, central and local governments, the People's Court, the People's Procuratorate, the Ethnic Autonomous Area System, the Special Administrative Areas System, the Criminal Law and Penalty System, the Political Freedom of Citizens, the Confiscation of Non-State Owned Assets, the Basic Civil Law System, Basic Economic System and Fiscal, Tax, Customs, Financial and Foreign Trade Systems, Litigation and Arbitration System.

[50] Art 56 Legislation Law and Art 89 Constitution of the PRC.

[51] Art 64 Legislation Law.

[52] Ibid, Art 73.

[53] Ibid, Art 71.

Second, the Legislation Law defines the level of legal binding force held by these different types of legislation. In general, the law adopted by the NPC and the NPCSC provides the legal basis for the rest of the legislation.[54] State Council administrative regulations, State Council administrative rules, local decrees and local rules have a hierarchical legal force, in line with the administrative status of the institutions that issue the legislation.[55] In other words, the State Council administrative regulations prevail over local decrees adopted by the local people's congresses, and the local decrees prevail over local rules adopted by local governments. However, the State Council administrative rules and local government rules have equal legal force.[56]

As a result, the entangled relationship between regulation by local governments and State Council ministries, commissions and bureaus has been clarified by this law. Under the current legal framework, State Council administrative rules are applicable from the central to the local level exclusively in the field of which the issuing institution is in charge. The local decrees and rules are applicable within the local jurisdiction. The State Council has stated that when the matter is of a regional nature, it is subject to regulation by local legislation and State Council rules should not apply. In other words, State Council rules will become applicable only to matters in which the national domestic market is involved.[57]

Furthermore, the discretion of local regulators is restrained and subject to supervision in the following ways. Local legislation, including local decrees and local rules, to enforce incumbent laws and State Council administrative regulations must be recorded at higher people's congress standing committees, and the State Council if applicable. Local legislation, though not challengeable by private parties under current administrative laws, is subject to challenge by other law-making institutions, before the NPCSC under the Legislation Law.

Nevertheless, what should be noted is that the rationalization of government regulation of market development has de facto strengthened the central government's regulatory competence. First, by letting the local regulator deal with routine local administration, it made it possible for the central government to focus on the issues of significance to the development of a market economy.

Second, the State Council is provided with broad legislative competence. The Legislation Law provides that the State Council within its legislative sphere can adopt administrative regulation before the relevant law is promulgated, with the delegation of power from the NPC and NPCSC.[58] Relevant laws can later be promulgated by the NPCSC based on the enforcement of the State Council administrative regulation. The State Council administrative regulations will become void

[54] State Council Regulation on How to Enforce Legislation Law, No 11, issues in 2000.
[55] Arts 78, 79 and 80 Legislation Law.
[56] Ibid, Art 82.
[57] State Council Notice on the Enforcement of Legislation Law, issued in 2003.
[58] Art 56 Legislation Law.

once the relevant law is enacted.[59] Therefore, with the delegation of power from the NPC and NPCSC, the State Council can, of its own accord, adopt administrative regulation in relation to the national economy, tax, finance, international trade and customs administration, all areas which must be regulated by law.[60]

Third, the State Council is conferred with strong powers to interpret administrative regulations and to adjudicate institutional administrative disputes. The Legislation Law provides the NPCSC with the competence to conduct legal interpretation for legislation.[61] However, according to the Decision on Strengthening Legal Interpretation issued by the NPCSC on 10 June 1981, the NPCSC provides interpretation only to the law per se, while legal interpretation in relation to administrative regulations and administrative rules issued by the State Council (central government) and its ministries, and to local rules issued by local governments would be referred back to the State Council. Hence, when conflicts arise between State Council administrative rules and local government rules, the State Council has the competence to make the final ruling.[62]

The rationalization of the normative framework of China's market regulation shows that the state has increasingly relied on the law to protect and support the functioning of the market and to improve regulatory efficiency. However, behind the prolific enactments of laws and regulations and the rationalization of the legal system, a vital point to understand the rapid development of Chinese laws in the past 30 years should be traced back to the society's conception of law, as influenced by China's historical, cultural and ideological legacies.

B. A State Positive Instrumentality View of Law

Chinese society's attitude towards law in the post-1949 period has been predominantly influenced by the Marxist-Leninism ideology upheld by the CCP. Marx recognizes law in its positive forms as a coercive force backed by the state machine. However, Marx's understanding of law focuses on the role of law in society rather than on the analysis of law on its own.[63] Law, according to Marx, is a part of the superstructure of the society that has a dialectical relationship with the economic base, namely the organization of the economy. The dialectical interaction between the superstructure and the economic base constitutes the force that leads social evolutions. In Marx's theory of class struggles, law reflects the will of the ruling class and is an instrument used by it. Hence, Marxism's understanding of the role of law essentially focuses on the instrumentality of law in the evolution of societies.

59 Ibid.
60 Ibid, Art 56.2.
61 Ibid, Art 42.
62 Arts 3 and 4 of the NPCSC Decision on Strengthening Legal Interpretation.
63 Hugh Collins, *Marxism and Law* (Oxford University Press, 1982) 2–14.

When China began its economic reform in 1978, its leaders were motivated to rebuild the Chinese legal system mainly on the ground that law served to facilitate the market-oriented reform under state supervision. In other words, law is a necessary and useful instrument to support the functioning of the emerging market when the party-state started to retreat from the economy; however, law fundamentally serves the strategic goals of the state, which had created and led the construction of a market economy.

This can be well observed in the White Paper on the completion of the construction of a socialist legal system with Chinese characteristics (SLSCC) issued by the NPC in 2011.[64] The White Paper emphasizes China's achievements in enacting new legislation and the rationalization of relationships among laws and regulations. It highlights that the law-making should be based on the demands of socialism with Chinese characteristics and on the reflection of the people's will and long-term interests.

By setting out a normative framework for China's legal development, the White Paper has provided a Chinese definition of social good, namely to pursue socialism with Chinese characteristics and people's long-term interests, though unclear on the relationship between the two. Law clearly has a primary role to play in advancing the social good in Chinese society.

It is not uncommon for a society to view law as an instrument to advance common social good. In fact, the rule of law and the instrumentality of law have long been viewed as being complementary to each other. However, the instrumentality of law contains conflicts over the definition of common social good and the potential risk of being perceived as instruments of power. Further, agents in society may compete to control and manipulate the law as an instrument to advance their respective strategic interests. Hence, it is argued that the instrumentality of law can contain potential damage to the rule of law.[65]

The state positive instrumentality view of law seems to have exceeded in terms of its weight over other understandings of law, such as law as an embodiment of natural principles and social norms, in contemporary Chinese society. The state positive instrumentality view of law helps to explain the role played by law in supporting China's economic and political reforms. However, the excessive emphasis on the state positive instrumentality view of law may create potential tensions with the rule of law in market regulation in China.

IV. DISPUTE SETTLEMENT IN CHINA'S MARKET GOVERNANCE

China's dispute settlement system has become formalized and institutionalized in line with its 30 years of reform. In particular, its formal dispute settlement

[64] www.gov.cn/jrzg/2011-10/27/content_1979498.htm.

[65] Brian Tamanaha, *Law as a Means to an End: Threat to the Rule of Law* (Cambridge University Press, 2006) 2–3.

led by the court system has gone through a process of professionalization and formalization. However, in terms of market governance, the court system continues to serve as an extended state administrative arm and plays a limited role in disputes involving state actors.

In Mao's China, the court system and mediation-based alternative dispute resolutions coexisted alongside each other.[66] Although the people's courts were institutionalized in 1949, they functioned de facto as an instrument for the party-state to solve the class conflicts between people and enemies that could not be mediated.[67] The majority of disputes were deemed to be caused by internal conflict within the working class and were thus solved by alternative resolutions; for example, the People's Mediation Committee (PMC) was set up in local communes with the ability to solve minor civil and criminal disputes.[68] Hence, in Mao's China, both the court and alternative dispute settlement were highly politicalized, with the court playing a limited role.

In line with China's market economy development, the alternative dispute settlement and the court system were separated from each other and were depoliticalized, institutionalized and legalized. With respect to the alternative dispute settlement, the PMC was transformed into justice office *(Si Fa Suo)*.[69] The PMC-turned-justice office is responsible for the mediation of local civil disputes, providing legal aid and facilitating the social rehabilitation of criminals, as one part of the service provided by local government. Furthermore, China has institutionalized and legalized the arbitration and mediation system for dispute resolution in line with international norms.[70]

Similarly, the formal dispute settlement system led by the Chinese court system has become formalized and institutionalized. The legal framework for the court system has been developed, the SPC as the head of the judiciary strengthened, and local courts have played a stronger role in solving civil and commercial disputes.

The state has adopted a series of laws to institutionalize the organization of the court and the administration of judges. In 1979, the NPC issued the Law for the Organization of the People's Courts, which set out the basic rules on the operation of the court system. The Law was later amended in 1982 and 2006.[71] In 1995, the NPC adopted the Judges Law, which set out provisions on both the administration

[66] Philip CC Huang , 'Between Informal Mediation and Formal Adjudication: The Third Realm of Qing Civil Justice' (1993) 19(3) *Modern China* 251–98.

[67] Lubman (n 39) 40.

[68] The People's Mediation Committee (PMC) was institutionalized by the Provisional Regulation on the PMC adopted in 1954. Pursuant to the Regulation, the PMC has the aim of mediating civil disputes and minor criminal offences. See JA Cohen, 'Chinese Mediation on the Eve of Modernization' (1966) 54 *California Law Review* 1201.

[69] The 1989 State Council Regulation on PMC Organization; and the 1990 Ministry of Justice opinions on methods of how to solve civil conflicts.

[70] Tang Hongzhi, 'Arbitration a Method Used by China to Settle Foreign Trade and Economic Disputes' (1984) 4(3) *Pace Law Review* 519; Lubman (n 39) 241–49.

[71] The Law for the Organization of the People's Courts in 1979, amended in 1982 and 2006: www.gov.cn/misc/2005-07/08/content_13200.htm.

of judges and on the procedural requirements for judges to comply with in trials. The Judges Law was amended in 2001.[72]

The Chinese judiciary is composed of the SPC, local courts and special courts, such as the military courts.[73] With the SPC standing at the top of the judiciary, the Chinese court system is composed of the People's High Court, the People's Intermediate Court and the People's Basic Court in cities and provinces. Each court is headed by the adjudicative committee and is organized into divisions according to the nature of the disputes, for example, civil, criminal and administrative dispute divisions. Each court is composed by one president, vice presidents, judges as division heads, and judges and administrative staff.[74]

The Chinese court upholds a two-level system, unless the SPC tries the facts again.[75] In the first instance, the judge can try the case on his or her own in minor civil or criminal cases. However, in most cases, judges must organize themselves into a collegiate panel to try cases in the first instance. Furthermore, each court has an adjudicative committee headed by the president of the court to scrutinize cases of significance or contention.[76] On appeal, the appeal would be examined by a collegiate panel in the higher court, subject to the scrutiny of the adjudicative committee in the higher court. The SPC has the competence to interpret the application of law, to set standards for the application of law in trials, to provide rulings on questions put forward by lower courts and other government departments, and to amend or revoke its own interpretations.[77]

The court system is professionalized. For example, in Mao's China and in the early economic reforms of China, the selection of judges had been based on the candidate's political qualification rather than on his or her legal skills. The 1995 Judges Law set out rules on the qualification requirements in the recruitment of judges, which did not include CCP party membership as a prerequisite.[78] The same requirements have been upheld by the 2001 Judges Law amendment.[79] Furthermore, the amendment of the Judges Law in 2001 added the requirements of the Bar exam for all legal practitioners, including judges and lawyers.[80]

The Supreme Peoples' Court (SPC) has been legalized and strengthened as the head of the judiciary and as the sole element of the judiciary with law-making competence in the Chinese legal system. In 1997, the SPC issued a Regulation on the SPC Legal Interpretation, which was later replaced by its Regulation on

[72] The Judges Law adopted in 1995 amended in 2001: www.gov.cn/banshi/2005-05/26/content_1026.htm.
[73] Art 124 PRC Constitution 1982.
[74] Arts 18–32 Organization Law of People's Court.
[75] Ibid, Art 12.
[76] Ibid, Art 11.
[77] Ibid, Art 14.
[78] Art 9 Judges Law 1995.
[79] Art 9 Judges Law amendment in 2001.
[80] Ibid, Art 51.

Legal Interpretation in 2007.[81] Both Regulations provided that the SPC has the competence to interpret the application of law in the operation of trial[82] and that its interpretation has a legally binding effect.[83]

However, the 2007 Regulation expanded the content of the SPC's legally binding interpretations by providing that its interpretation includes interpretation (*jie shi*), rules (*gui ding*), rulings (*pi fu*) and decisions (*jue ding*), whereas the 1997 Regulation provides only the first three. The 2007 Regulation provides that interpretation includes either the interpretation of the law applied in one specific case or the interpretation on how law should be applied in certain types of cases.[84]

Furthermore, the 2007 Regulation introduced a more legalistic but less administrative approach for the SPC to issue legal interpretation. In contrast, the 1997 regulation defines rules as standards or opinions set out by the SPC, when required, by the necessity of the operation of the trial.[85] Consequently, the SPC was provided with a considerable amount of discretion to set out standards to assist the trial process. In the 2007 Regulation, it is provided that the SPC can set out such rules for trials, but must do so in line with the intention of the relevant laws.[86]

In addition, the 2007 Regulation improved the procedural fairness and transparency of the interpretation adoption process by setting out detailed rules on the initiation, drafting and approval of legal interpretations. In particular, the approval of the SPC interpretation has to clear two hurdles. Whereas each SPC division has the competence to draft legal interpretation, the draft must be scrutinized by the SPC legal research division (*yan jiu shi*), which then examines whether the draft is consistent with the Constitution and the laws, whether the draft was within the SPC's legal interpretation competence, whether it conflicts with previous SPC interpretations and whether the draft was proposed in accordance with procedures, etc.[87] The draft, once cleared by the research division, will then be discussed at the adjudicative committee of the SPC for approval and will be signed either by the President or the Vice President of the SPC for adoption.[88] The SPC has undertaken incremental steps to legalize and expand its competence in law making. By doing so, it has not only improved its efficiency but also, more importantly, its credibility and authority as the head of the judiciary in Chinese society.

Local courts have become increasingly active and strong in the dispute resolution of civil and commercial cases. As a result of thirty years of market oriented reform, the local courts have obtained sufficient experience and skills in dealing with disputes, particularly in the field of civil and commercial disputes. These courts have

[81] 1997 SPC Regulation on legal interpretation: www.chinacourt.org/flwk/show.php?file_id=28433; 2007 Regulation: www.chinacourt.org/flwk/show1.php?file_id=117115.
[82] Art 2 1997 Regulation.
[83] Ibid, Art 4.
[84] Art 6 2007 Regulation.
[85] Art 9 1997 Regulation.
[86] Art 6 2007 Regulation.
[87] Ibid, Art 20.
[88] Ibid, Art 24.

shown an increased ability to decide, with relevant independence, on these cases, as these cases are in general less politically sensitive and less vulnerable to political intervention by the state power, such as the CCP or local governments.[89]

However, in contrast to the dominant and leading roles played by the party-state in China's market governance, the role played by the court system is limited. Pursuant to the Constitution of the PRC, the Chinese judiciary has been made independent of intervention by any administrative organizations, social organizations and individuals.[90] However, in practice, there has been the shadowing influence by the ruling CCP in the operation and administration of the Chinese judiciary through the court adjudicative committee and the CCP nomenclature system.[91]

The Chinese courts, at each level, are faced with the dilemma of a large number of administrative tasks, including CCP-led ideological movements, an increasing caseload and limited personnel and budget resources. Consequently, whereas the court's adjudicative committee and the court appeal system were designed to supervise local courts, they could also serve as administrative channels for political intervention to influence judges in their decision making.[92] The Chinese judiciary is distinctive with its double role as a dispute resolution mechanism and as a state administrative organ.

Although the SPC has been strengthened as the head of the judiciary, and local courts have shown an increased competence in adjudicating civil and commercial cases, the Chinese judiciary faces restraints when handling disputes involving the state. This can be illustrated by the design and enforcement of Chinese administrative law.

Chinese administrative law has imposed restraints on public power. Its development is based on the practice of China's public administrative system and on the principle of the 'law maker explaining its own laws'. Therefore, as discussed before, the SPC's law-making competence is restricted to issuing legally binding interpretations, etc, in relation to issues arising from trials. The competence to interpret primary legislation issued by the NPC lies with the NPC and the NPCSC, and the competence to interpret secondary legislation issued by the State Council lies with the State Council itself.

The process of judicial review for administrative acts in China reflects the same principle. Chinese administrative law provides for the judicial review and

[89] Randall Peerenboom, 'Judicial Independence in China: Common Myths and Unfounded Assumptions', 1 September 2008, La Trobe Law School Legal Studies Research Paper No 2008/11; and Randall Peerenboom, *Judicial Independence in China: Lessons for Global Rule of Law Promotion* (Cambridge University Press, 2009).

[90] Art 126 PRC Constitution 1982.

[91] Zou Keyuan, 'The Party and the Law' in Kjed Erik Brodsgaard and Zheng Yongnian (eds), *The Chinese Communist Party in Reform* (Routledge, 2006) 88–93.

[92] Randall Peerenboom, *China's Long March Toward Rule of Law* (Cambridge University Press, 2002) 283.

administrative review of administrative acts.[93] However, Chinese administrative law provides that administrative acts are divided into two categories: tangible acts, which are specific, concrete and directly affect any legal and natural person; and intangible acts, which are generally applicable and in abstract forms. The Administrative Reconsideration Law has set out that government regulations are generally applicable and thus are intangible.[94] However, intangible administrative acts are subject to supervision by the NPC and the NPCSC or to administrative organs superior to the one in question, and thus falls out of the administrative or judicial review process.[95] Only tangible acts are subject to administrative review by superior administrative organs or to judicial review by the courts, provided that the private parties have satisfied the standing and procedural requirements.[96] It should be noted that as a result of China's WTO membership, China has complied with its WTO commitment to provide access to judicial review for trade-related administrative disputes by setting up specific tribunals for this purpose in the intermediate level of the people's courts.[97] However, this has had little impact on the principle of the Chinese administrative law system or on the court's limited competence to examine government legislation in the trial process.[98]

Nevertheless, in reality, the judicial or administrative review of administrative acts provided by Chinese administrative law can suffer from political intervention, particularly at the local level. This is because although the SPC is the top judiciary, local courts are de facto dependent on local governments for finance and personnel support. This makes them vulnerable to intervention by local regulators.[99]

The Chinese court system thus plays a limited role in dealing with cases where the state is involved. The SPC has its law-making competence limited to the trial process. The judicial review provided by the Chinese court system is only restricted to tangible administrative acts, where the final interpretation of laws as intangible acts lies with law makers themselves. Despite the rise of an increasingly legalized and professionalized court system in China's market governance, the state power largely shuns external scrutiny and is subject to an internal supervision mechanism.[100]

[93] Art 2 Administrative Litigation Law 1989 and Art 2 Administrative Reconsideration Law.

[94] Art 11 Administrative Reconsideration Law.

[95] Art 12 Administrative Litigation Law.

[96] Ibid, Art 11.

[97] Veron Mei-Ying Hung, 'China's WTO Commitment on Independent Judicial Review: Impact on Legal and Political Reform' (2004) 52(1) *American Journal of Comparative Law* 77–132.

[98] M Ulric Killion, 'Post-WTO China and Independent Judicial Review' (2004) 26(3) *Houston Journal of International Law* 507–59.

[99] Peerenboom (n 92) 310–12.

[100] Michael Palmer, 'Controlling the State? Mediation in Administrative Litigation in the People's Republic of China' (2006) 16(1) *Transnational Law & Contemporary Problems* 165–87.

V. CONCLUSION

The examination of China's market governance shows its attempts to converge with international practice. The CCP has continuously adapted its ideology from the one based on class struggle towards a more governance-oriented one. The government administrative system has gone through a series of rationalization and restructuring measures. The dispute settlement system has become legalized and professionalized. The Chinese legal system on market governance has largely been brought into line with international norms, in the context of China's membership of the WTO since 2001. However, the party-state has remained the dominant, strategic and resilient actor in terms of market governance, with enhanced legitimacy, expanded regulatory capacity and more regulatory tools, but limited external supervision. Consequently, these structural features determines China's market regulatory framework as being strongly state-led and unitary.

4

The Market Environment and Restraints of Competition in China

I. INTRODUCTION

This chapter reviews China's economic transformation based on incentives, pricing liberalization and competition promotion. It reveals that business operators face a different market environment, which results from the state control over market entry, financial market and labour market, and from the regional market segmentation in China. Consequently, restrictions of competition can be caused by state distortion of the market element and/or intrinsic market failure.

II. CHINA'S ECONOMIC TRANSFORMATION

It is generally understood that China's success in terms of its economic transformation can be attributed to the leaders' incremental and pragmatic approaches to reforms, China's efforts to attract foreign investment and promote exportation, and its in-time participation in economic globalization. The continuous high growth of the Chinese economy has been explained by state measures, including stimulating incentives, liberalizing pricing and promoting competition and openness in the market.[1]

As a matter of fact, the market-oriented reform started with the state's installation of the incentive mechanism in rural areas. A family responsibility system was applied in rural China to allow for rural households to make profit over crops through trading, after each household satisfies its production goal allocated by the commune. The family responsibility system started from a self-starting initiative by farmers against a failing collective commune economy in the Anhui province and was recognized and developed by the state into a nationwide policy. Similar incentive mechanisms were then gradually introduced into the reform of SOEs and subsequently into all sectors of the economy.[2]

[1] Loren Brandt and Thomas Rawski, *China's Great Economic Transformation* (Cambridge University Press, 2008) 1–22.

[2] Barry Naughton, *The Chinese Economy: Transition and Growth* (MIT Press, 2007) 86–97.

When China began its economic reforms, pricing for products and services were controlled by government planning. The Chinese government adopted a dual-track pricing system (*shuang gui zhi*), composed of market price-based on market signals and state price set out by the economic plan. This means that enterprises could set product prices according to market signals, after satisfying the production requirements set out by the government plan based on state price.[3] In 1997, China declared the establishment of a market-based pricing system, where business operators are provided with the right to determine prices for products and services, according to the market signals,[4] and government guidance price and government price must be restricted to small amounts of products that are crucial to the national economy and public living, scarce products and resources, products subject to a natural monopoly and important products or services provided by public authorities.[5] Following China's joining of the WTO in 2001, the pricing system became more transparent.[6]

The Chinese government opened up its geographical markets based on development concerns and substantially lifted access to product and service markets as a result of its WTO membership. In 1979, the first special economic zone, where experimental policies to attract foreign investment and liberalize the economy were enforced exclusively within the zone, was established in the city of Shen Zhen in southern China. This was followed by a group of special economic zones in the 1980s.[7] The Chinese government has further advocated the opening up of markets in western and central China in 2000[8] and northeastern China in 2003[9] in order to promote regional development.

China's WTO membership has had a profound impact on the openness of its products and service markets. With respect to the products market, China has committed itself to substantially reducing tariffs for industrial products, with the weighted average tariff on the manufacturer reaching as low as 6.9 per cent. China has made a particular tariff reduction in the beverages and tobacco sector, with a 28 per cent reduction, and has undertaken a 15 per cent reduction in the highly protected automobile sector.[10] In addition, it has liberalized the right to trade, has undertaken the phased-in abolition of non-tariff trade barriers and has

[3] Ibid, 91.

[4] Art 10 Price Law.

[5] Ibid, Art 18.

[6] According to China's WTO Accession Protocol, the prices of 46 products are subject to government pricing, those of 30 products are subject to government guidance pricing, those of eight services are subject to government pricing, those of 16 services are subject to government guidance pricing and those of five public utilities are subject to government pricing. Annex 4 Products and Services subject to price control, China's WTO Accession Protocol, 64–65, WT/L/432.

[7] The other four special economic zones are Zhuhai, Xiangmeng, Shantou and Hannan.

[8] State Council Measures on Western China Development: www.china.com.cn/chinese/zhuanti/xbkf5/797214.htm.

[9] The idea was proposed on the State Council Conference on Northeast China Recovery on 10 September 2003: http://chinaneast.xinhuanet.com.

[10] Nicolas Lardy, *Integrating China into the Global Economy* (Brookings Institution Press, 2002) 79–80.

improved the transparency of the regulation on the technical barrier to trade.[11] With respect to services, China has made phased in commitments to open up its telecommunications, financial, insurance, distribution, tourism, education, transport and professional services. China's WTO plus commitment has made its national treatment commitments wider and deeper than any other country.[12] Therefore, its WTO commitment makes its market the most open amongst the large developing countries.[13]

Consequently, ownership of business operators on the market have become diversified. These operators can be categorized into SOEs, foreign invested enterprises (FIEs) and private domestic enterprises (PDEs). However, despite its efforts in installing incentives, liberalizing prices and opening up markets, the state maintains control over market entry, access to the financial market, the labour market and the regional market, as key factors shaping the market environment in China. As a result, SOEs, FIEs and PDEs face drastically different business environments in China.

III. MARKET ENVIRONMENT IN CHINA

A. Government Sectoral Regulation on Market Entry

Government sectoral regulation is the first hurdle for a business to clear in order to enter the Chinese market. A business applicant is required to satisfy all relevant government regulatory requirements before entering the market; however, the NDRC, SASAC and MOFCOM regulatory requirements have a particular impact on market access in China.

The NDRC is responsible for setting out the Sectoral Investment Catalogue, which sets out detailed requirements for market entry into specific sectors. The NDRC Catalogue sets out three types of sector, namely sectors into which entry is encouraged (*gu li lei*), sectors into which entry is restricted (*xian zhi lei*), and sectors into which entry is closed (*tao tai lei*). Based on this, the Ministry of Commerce, the main regulator of foreign investment, issues the Foreign Investment Catalogue in the same style.

Both the NDRC Catalogue and the MOFCOM Catalogue have been formulated in line with China's WTO commitments.[14] In both of these, the sectors that enterprises are encouraged to enter refer to those which China has the capacity to research

[11] WTP Trade Policy Review, *Report by the People's Republic of China*, WT/TPR/G16, 2006, 12.

[12] Aadity Matto, 'The Service Dimension of China's Accession to the WTO' in Deepak Bhattasali, Shangton Li and Will Martin (eds), *China and the WTO: Accession, Policy Reform and Poverty Redution* (World Bank, 2004) 112–41.

[13] Lee Branstetter and Nicholas Lardy, 'China's Embrace of Globalization' in L Rawski (ed), *China's Great Economic Transformation* (Cambridge University Press, 2008) 633.

[14] James Zimmerman, *China Law Deskbook* (ABA Association, 2004) 149.

and develop and which are conducive to technological innovation; in which there is a supply shortage or a high potential market demand either in China or worldwide; which have a high technological content which is beneficial to protect and improve the ecological environment; which make maximum usage of the comparative advantages China has, in particular, which make use of the energy, mineral resources and labour resources in central west and north-east China; and which increase employment or are encouraged by other laws and regulations.[15]

Those wishing to enter these sectors are required, first, to file an application to the investment administration authority, namely to the NDRC if only domestic investment is involved, or to MOFCOM if foreign investment is involved, so as to obtain approval. After obtaining this approval, the operator is required to register with the local government's Industrial and Commercial Administration Bureau. Once the new investment is approved and registered, custom tariff and other import-related Value Added Tax will be waived and the investment will be able to obtain loans from financial institutions.[16]

Sectors into which entry is restricted refer to those in which the new investment does not satisfy the standard set out by the relevant industrial associations; which use backward technology or bring no improvement to the industrial structure; which are not consistent with safe production standards and are not energy efficient and environmentally friendly; which causes low-quality repetitive construction with an abundance of productivity; and which are proscribed by other laws and regulations.

With respect to these sectors, the administrative authority will not approve or register the investment project. The investment project will not be able to obtain a loan from financial institutions. Administration authorities in the fields of land management, urban planning, environmental protection, quality supervision, fire supervision, customs and industrial commercial administration are required not to approve any application from the applicant. Any institution or natural person will face a liability if this requirement is breached.[17]

Sectors into which entry is closed refer to those which endanger production safety, particularly those without safety production protection; which severely pollute the environment or destroy ecology; of which the product is below the minimum standard set by the industrial association or by the state; which cause a severe waste of resources and energy; and which are proscribed by other laws and regulations.[18] Investment is forbidden in the industries listed in this category. Financial institutions are required to cease providing any forms of support and to revoke the loans already given out. The incumbent enterprise in any of these industries should shut down the production lines and a failure to do so will incur a revocation of its licence, administrative fines or personal liabilities.

[15] Art 14 of State Council Provisional Regulation on Promoting Industrial Adjustments, 2005.
[16] Ibid, Art 17.
[17] Ibid, Art 19.
[18] Ibid, Art 16.

Apart from the Catalogue, NDRC industrial policies have a far-reaching impact on market entry in China. For example, the NDRC issued industrial policies for the automobile industry and the steel industry in 2004 and 2005, both of which set out policy, technological and capital requirements for those entering the two industries.[19] These industrial policies aimed to improve the competitiveness of the dominant SOEs in these industries, but are also criticized for protecting SOEs in these industries from competition.[20]

In 2006, the SASAC issued *the guidelines on the adjustment of state-owned capital and reorganization of state-owned enterprises.* These re-emphasized the importance of strengthening state ownership in key sectors of the economy by fostering SOEs with their own intellectual property, brands and strong international competitiveness.[21] The guidelines further provided that the SOEs should maintain their absolute control in key sectors crucial to the national economy and national economic security.[22] The Chinese government has not provided an official definition of key sectors; however, Mr Li Rongrong, by then the head of the SASAC, explicitly indicated that SOEs should have absolute control in seven sectors, namely military engineering, electricity fence and electricity, petroleum and purification, telecommunications, coal, civil aviation and shipping.[23]

MOFCOM is the main regulator for foreign investment in China. Apart from setting out the Foreign Investment Catalogue, together with SASAC, SAIC, the State Administration of Taxation (SAT), the China Securities Regulatory Commission (CSRC) and the State Administration of Foreign Exchange (SAFE), it issued the *Regulation on Merger and Acquisition of Domestic Chinese Enterprises by Foreign Investors* in 2006. Pursuant to the regulation, foreign investors must file notification on the proposed merger to MOFCOM if the merger will enable the foreign investor to acquire controlling rights in one of the key sectors, impair (or have the possibility of impairing) national economic security or cause the transfer of controlling rights of a well-known brand or a well-established traditional Chinese brand.[24]

B. Access to Capital: The Financial System

When China began its economic reform process, its financial system was composed of the People's Bank of China (PBOC) and its local branches. It did

[19] The Steel Industrial Policy was issued by the NDRC in 2005 and the Automobile Industrial Policy was issued in 1994 and then in 2004. For the Automobile Industrial Policy, see: www.ndrc.gov.cn/cyfz/zcfg/t20050711_34962.htm. For the Steel Industrial Policy, see: www.ndrc.gov.cn/gyfz/zcfg/t20050719_37451.htm.

[20] Peter Nolan, 'China and the Global Business Revolution' (2005) 1 *Journal of Cambridge Economics* 119–37.

[21] Guidelines on the adjustment of state-owned capital and reorganization of state-owned enterprises: www.gov.cn/gongbao/content/2007/content_503385.htm.

[22] Ibid, Art 2.3.

[23] www.gov.cn/ztzl/2006-12/18/content_472256.htm.

[24] Art 12 Regulation on Merger and Acquisition of Domestic Chinese Enterprises by Foreign Investors in 2006.

not, however, have any financial markets. To date, the Chinese financial system contains a fast-developing banking sector composed of state-owned commercial banks, city commercial banks, urban credit cooperatives, rural credit cooperatives and foreign banks. The stock market, the bond market, venture capital market and the real estate market began to emerge. China's financial system has also been promoted by the development of a non-standard financial sector, including informal financial institutions and continuous foreign direct investment (FDI) and capital inflow.[25] However, the access of business operators to financial markets in China varies in accordance with their ownership of the operators.

i. The Development of the Banking System

In the early stages of reform, the PBOC served as the regulator as well as the policy bank for the banking system in China.[26] Funds, instead of loans, were directly channelled from state-owned banks to SOEs for the latter's economic activities, as a legacy of China's command economy.

Gradually, the PBOC was separated into the PBOC, as the central bank, and four other state-owned commercial banks (SOCBs). These were the Agricultural Bank of China (ABC), which was responsible for rural finance; the China Construction Bank (CCB), which was responsible for the finance of urban construction projects; the Bank of China (BOC), which was responsible for foreign exchange-related finance; and the Industrial and Commercial Bank of China (ICBC), which was responsible for commercial and industrial finance in urban areas. The four state-owned banks were provided with a complete monopoly in their respective markets, and favoured providing loans to SOEs.[27]

With the inflow of competition from non-state owned players on to the market, SOEs have been faced with increasing competition and have often turned to local governments for support. Consequently, local governments coordinated or pushed local branches of SOCBs into providing loans to help SOEs survive. However, in most cases the SOEs did not have the ability to pay back the loans. Therefore, the SOCB often ended up with soaring amounts of Nonperformaning Loans (NPLs). This, in combination with the underdevelopment of banking skills, caused severe problems to the Chinese banking system in the 1990s.[28] At the same time, the eruption of the East Asian Financial Crisis alarmed the Chinese government into maintaining macro-economy austerity.[29]

The Chinese government took further measures to reform the banking sector, which included the commercialization of state-owned banks and the

[25] Rawski (n 13) 512.

[26] Naughton (n 2).

[27] Shang-Jin Wei and Tao Wang, 'The siamese twins: Do state-owned banks favor state-owned enterprises in China? 'in *China Economic Review*, Volume 8, Issue 1, Spring 1997, Pages 19–29.

[28] Naughton (n 2) 461.

[29] Justin Yifu Lin, Fang Cai, Zhou Li, *The China Miracle: Development Strategy and Economic Reform* (Chinese University of Hong Kong Press, 1996) 132.

centralization and further liberalization of the banking sector. The PBOC set up four asset management companies to pair with each of the four SOCBs in order to tackle each SOCB's soaring NPLs.[30] It removed the policy lending operations from the SOCB to the newly established three policy banks: namely, the China Development Bank, which was responsible for funding large-scale infrastructure projects; the Export-Import Bank, which was responsible for export promotion; and the Agricultural Development Bank, which was responsible for policy-oriented funding in rural areas.[31] The PBOC merged the regional branches of the SOCBs into nine large regional branches and took back the competence of personnel appointment in these branches from local governments.[32]

The banking system has been further liberalized by the introduction of other forms of banks, such as joint stock commercial banks and city banks. These new types of banks are nevertheless closely linked to or controlled by local governments and tend to focus more on specific geographical markets.[33]

Faced with the competition in the financial service market following China's WTO membership, the Chinese government set up the China Banking Regulatory Commission (CBRC) in 2003, which comprised departments responsible for banking supervision previously set up under the PBOC.[34] The CBRC is in charge of the supervision of the operation of Chinese and foreign banks in the Chinese market.[35] Further, the four SOCBs have been transformed into state-controlled publicly listed companies on the domestic and Hong Kong stock markets since 2004. However, as the policy banks are restrained by capital and resources, and the local governments continued to exert pressure on the SOCBs for policy lending to their preferred enterprises, the four SOCBs continue to play an important role in policy lending.[36]

ii. The Development of the Stock Markets

In 1990, the Shanghai and Shenzhen city governments obtained the approval from the Chinese leaders to set up stock markets in these two cities. In 1992, the China Securities Regulatory Commission (CSRC) was set up with the aim of supervising

[30] The Four Asset Management Companies include the China Asset Management Company, the China Great Wall Asset Management Company, Oriental Asset Management and the China Huarong Asset Management Corporation which paired with the CCB, the ABC, the BOC and the ICBC, respectively.

[31] Naughton (n 2) 457.

[32] Nicholas Lardy, 'When Will China's Financial System Meet China's needs?' in Nicholas C Hope, Dennis Tao Yang and Mu Yang Li (eds), *How Far Across the River?: Chinese Policy Reform at the Millennium* (Stanford University Press, 2003) 71–72.

[33] Naughton (n 2) 457.

[34] www.cbrc.gov.cn.

[35] www.cbrc.gov.cn/english/info/yjhjj/index.jspwww.cbrc.gov.cn/showyjhjjindex.do.

[36] Shujie Yao et al, 'WTO Challenges and Efficiency of Chinese Banks' in Chen Jian and Yao Shuijie (eds), *Globalization, Competition and Growth in China* (Routledge, 2006) 59.

the financial markets and public listed companies.[37] To date, the Chinese stock market has overtaken Japan in terms of its value.[38]

However, the development of stock markets in China has been segmented. First, shares are divided into circulating and non-circulating shares. The non-circulating shares include state shares and legal personality shares, and are not transferrable on the stock market, though they can be transferred through private placement. The circulating shares are divided into the following: A shares, denominated in the Chinese currency (RMB); B shares, denominated in foreign currencies; and H shares, listed by Chinese companies on the Hong Kong stock exchange or any other stock markets outside China.[39] For a long time, Chinese residents could only operate on A share markets.[40] The segmentation of shares into circulating and non-circulating shares had been the unique feature of the Chinese stock market.[41]

Second, the operation of stock markets in China suffers from poor regulation and inside manipulation.[42] The listing process of business operators requires coordination among managers, securities companies as intermediate and the CSRC as the regulator. However, state-controlled securities investment companies, as the main underwriters for shares issuing, holds a monopoly over shares trading and listing procedures on the Chinese stock market.[43] The regulator often gives preference to large SOEs, which are treated as the priority to be listed on the stock market. The regulator's intervention in terms of qualification for listing on the Chinese stock market further caused problems of speculation, inside trading and rent-seeking on the financial market.[44] Hence, the role played by the stock market in terms of fundraising for non-state owned enterprises is rather limited.

Nevertheless, the central government attempted to reform its regulation of the non-circulating shares in 2001.[45] The task met with little success until 2007, when the SASAC and the CSRC adopted Provisional Rules on Transfer of Shares of Public Listed Companies by State Share Holders (Provisional Rules).[46] The provisional rule provides that state shareholders can transfer their shares through the stock exchange, agreement or indirect transfer.[47] It requires the transfer of state shares to be transparent and undertaken according to the market signal.[48]

37 www.csrc.gov.cn/pub/csrc_en/.

38 www.chinadaily.com.cn/bizchina/2009-07/20/content_8447558.htm.

39 Naughton (n 2) 469.

40 For a long time, Chinese citizens could only operate on the A share markets. See http://news.xinhuanet.com/fortune/2001-12/19/content_170076.htm.

41 On Kit Tam, 'Capital Market Development in China' (1991) 19(5) *World Development* 511–32.

42 Julan Du and Shang-Jin Wei, 'Does Insider Trading Raise Market Volatility?' (2002) 114(498) *Economic Journal* 916–42.

43 Naughton (n 2) 472.

44 Ibid, 473.

45 The rules on Reducing State Owned Shares and Raise Fund for Social Securities Fund was adopted on 22 June 2001, but was revoked June 2002.

46 www.sasac.gov.cn/n1180/n1566/n258222/n259203/1733853.html.

47 Art 3 Provisional Rules.

48 Ibid, Arts 5 and 11.

However, the state keeps tight control over the transfer of state shares in public listed companies. According to the provisional rules, any party can purchase state-owned shares or legal personality shares only when the purchasing party's size is under a certain scale threshold, the shares transferred by the party within the last three consecutive accounting years have not exceeded five per cent of the total shares and the transfer would not involve the transfer of control of the company.[49] However, the SASAC and corresponding departments in local governments have formed a network of regulators for approving the transfer of state shares in public listed companies.[50] The SASAC has also set up a notification procedure for the transfer of state shares in public listed SOEs.[51] The application of the transfer of state shares must be notified to the central SASAC if the transfer is to have a significant impact on key national economic sectors or on national economic structures, and the local SASAC must be notified if the transfer causes the loss of state control in the company.[52]

C. Labour Market

Prior to the introduction of the contract responsibility farming system in China, the labour market hardly existed. Farmers in rural areas were governed by the people's commune, and workers in the urban areas by the SOEs, as their working unit (*dan wei*). Both farmers and workers were governed by the household registration system (*Hu Kou*), in which individuals must register personal details, city of residence and workplace with the local government. In the early stages of economic reform, food and other resources were rationed by coupons and allocated according to *Hu Kou*. It has been highly difficult to transfer the registration of *Hu kou* between urban and rural areas, rural to rural areas and urban to urban areas.[53]

However, beginning in the 1980s, the CCP and the State Council began to encourage rural labour to seek non-farming employment in the urban areas.[54] In 1985, the CCP permitted farmers to work and establish businesses in towns close to their farms on the condition that the farmers secured financial resources and food to support themselves and did not require resources provided

[49] Ibid, Art 7.

[50] Ibid, Art 8.

[51] Ibid, Art 12. The applicant is required to submit a series of documents, including the feasibility of the transfer.

[52] Art 7 Provisional Rules.

[53] Andrew Walder, *Communist Neo-Traditionalism: Work and Authority in Chinese Industry* (University of California Press, 1988).

[54] Document 1 of the CCP in 1983 encouraged the emergence of specialized households in non-agricultural activities, including long-distance transport and the marketing of commodities and permitting cooperative ventures and employment of labour.

by urban economic planning. Therefore, rural-rural and rural-urban labour mobility has increased.[55]

The urban labour market developed substantially as a result of the reform of SOEs. One of the main reasons why SOEs were poor in terms of economic performance was due to the burden of providing permanent employment and a lifelong pension and retirement benefit package for all employees. One main task that the SOEs faced in the early stages of reform was to lay off employees and reduce the business costs. Furthermore, the downsizing of SOEs on the market increased the number of SOE employees that were laid off. These laid-off workers were given up to three years to find other employment. From 1993 to 2003, it was estimated that at least 28.18 million state enterprises workers were laid off.[56] These workers, freed from their previous employment, have sought jobs based on economic incentives, which has increased the mobility of the labour market.

Hence, the surplus of farmers entering the rural and urban labour markets, and the increase in the number of laid-off workers in the urban market, has provided PDEs and FIEs with rich and low-cost labour resources. This in turn has promoted competition amongst various business operators in the market.

However, the Chinese labour market remains segmented, mainly due to the *Hu Kou* system and an underdeveloped social security system for labour workers. In 1998, the Chinese government loosened the control of *Hu Kou* and made it possible for citizens to transfer *Hu Kou* between rural and urban areas and between cities, provided that they satisfied certain personal or educational conditions.[57] However, the large number of rural workers flowing into the urban market does not satisfy these conditions. Therefore, rural workers tend to stay in employment with no requirement for *Hu Kou* and no social security protection. The mobility of urban laid-off workers within the same city and between firms remained low due to their low education background, age and gender.[58]

Furthermore, as the task of handling laid-off workers was assigned by the central government to local governments, the transformation of the urban labour market has been a very challenging task, not only for SOEs but also for local governments. In many cities, local governments, along with with local reformed SOEs, have set up re-employment centres to provide transitional support to laid-off workers. The completion of the tasks depends on local financial resources and government capacities, and thus the success rates tend to vary from city to city.

The legal protection of labour contracts has progressed in line with China's reforms. China adopted its first Labour Law in 1994. However, with the development of the labour markets, the law begins to show its limits in terms

[55] Fang Cai, Albert Park and Yaohui Zhao, 'The Chinese Labour Market in the Reform Era', in Brandt and Rawski (n 1) 169–75.

[56] Naughton (n 2) 186.

[57] John Knight and Lina Song, *Towards a Labour Market in China* (Oxford University Press, 2005) 87.

[58] S Appleton, J Knight, L Song and Q Xia, 'Labor Retrenchment in China: Determinants and Consequences' (2002) 13(2–3) *China Economic Review* 252–75.

of governing labour relations, as it is ineffective in preventing employers from abusing the labour contract;[59] it focuses primarily on the termination of the labour contract, but provides little on its formation and it provides little regulation on non-standard employment contract, such as casual work.[60]

The New Labour Contract Law was adopted in 2007.[61] It provides detailed regulation on the form and content of all labour contracts and requires contracts to be in written form.[62] It further provides enhanced protection of employee rights by fixing the probation period, imposing mandatory requirements on salary and payment for employees, and restricting employers' use of the non-compete clause in the employment contract.[63]

Although economists have argued that the new labour contract will not reduce employment in law-abiding enterprises in China, the application of the new labour contract law has had a sweeping impact on all business entities in the Chinese labour market.[64] Whereas SOEs and FIEs have enforced relatively more sound human resources management, the PDEs face more challenges in enforcing the law.[65]

Therefore, in an emerging labour market, the *Hu Kou* system, an underdeveloped social security system and the enhanced legal regulation on labour contracts have become the main constraints that have resulted in the segmentation of the labour market.[66]

D. Regional Segmentation of the Market

Local regulators have been provided with wide discretion in local market regulation and have gradually become stakeholders in the economic reforms.[67] Hence, local government regulators have the incentive and regulatory competence to protect local businesses on the local markets, for example, by providing preferential treatment to local business operators in particular local SOEs or preventing competitors from entering the local markets. Further, China's market governance

59 Anita Chan, 'Globalization, China's Free (Read Bonded) Labour Market and the Chinese Trade Unions' (2000) 6(3–4) *Asia Pacific Business Review* 261–68.

60 Ibid 71.

61 Labour Contract Law of the PRC, available at: www.china.com.cn/law/txt/2007-06/30/content_8468871.htm.

62 New Labour Contract Law of the PRC, ch 2.

63 Arts 18, 19, 20 and 21 New Labour Contract Law.

64 YF Chen and M Funke, 'China's New Labour Contract Law: No Harm to Employment?' (2009) 20 *China Economic Review* 558–72.

65 Pan Jie, 'The New Labour Contract Law's Impact on Enterprises' (2010) 6 *Law and Commerce* 296–97.

66 Linda Yueh and John Knight, 'Competition or Segmentation in China's Urban Labour Market?' (2009) 33(1) *Cambridge Journal of Economics* 79–94.

67 David D Li, 'Changing Incentives of the Chinese Bureaucracy' (1988) 88(2) *American Economic Review* 393–97.

framework bears the feature of being led by an overly powerful administrative system subject to internal supervision, with a relatively weaker judiciary. As such, local government regulators intervene in local markets driven by motivations including corruption or rent-seeking behaviour.

Consequently, China's national market remains segmented at a regional level. Fundamentally, the segmentation of regional markets calls for further political reform. However, it has directly impacted on the distribution of goods and services by business operators wishing to enter regional markets.

In China's establishment of a socialist market economy, the state keeps close control over marketization, and the financial, labour and regional markets remain segmented. On the one hand, the state's control over sectoral development has its imperative to maintain state control over key sectors; the state develops the financial markets with a priory goal to facilitate the incorporation of SOEs, and has supported SOEs' transformation to adapt to the emerging labour market. On the other hand, the state is forced to become more responsive to the increasing societal dissatisfaction with government control over market entry; the development of China's market economy in the long run and China's participation in globalization call for a more unified financial market and labour market. The socialist market economy construction is at a crossroads. It is in the context of this background that the SOEs, the FIEs and the PDEs are competing against each other and are facing different challenges in terms of market entry, fundraising, labour costs and distribution.

IV. STATE OWNED ENTERPRISES IN THE CHINESE MARKET

The reform of SOEs has been, and continues to be, at the centre of China's market-oriented reforms. The Chinese central government took incremental measures to transform and modernize SOEs. In the early stages of the reform, SOEs, as *dan wei* (working unit), were the commercial extension of government authorities, which performed business operations under government instructions and provided social and administrative management and services to their employees.[68]

As early as 1984, inspired by the success achieved by the family responsibility system in rural China, the central and local governments introduced the contract responsibilities system into the management of SOEs. Under this system, managers were responsible for the profit making of the enterprises and were rewarded with bonuses based on profits.[69] The government withdrew from the SOEs' daily

[68] Barry Naughton, 'The Economic Foundations of a Unique Institution' in Xiaobu Lu and Elizabeth Perry (eds), *The Changing Chinese Workplace in Historical and Comparative Perspective* (East Gate, 1997) 169–70.

[69] Ross Garnaut, Ligang Song and Yang Yao, 'Impact and Significance of State Owned Enterprises Restructuring in China' in Belton Fleisher, Nicholas Hope, Anti Alves Pena and Dennis Tao Yang (eds), *Policy Reform and Chinese Markets: Progress and Challenges* (Edward Elgar, 2008) 39.

operation. However, the SOEs have remained affiliated to the government, a fact that has helped to maintain social stability.[70] The contract responsibilities system increased the incentives for the managers of SOEs to make profits-oriented decisions. In reality, however, managers of SOEs sometimes enjoyed the economic bonuses brought by good performance, but managed to avoid penalties when SOEs failed to reach their profit targets.[71]

With the deepening of the market-oriented reform, the central government started to tackle the low efficiency of the state-owned sector. The guiding principles for the reform of SOEs were set out by the CCP in 1993 and again in 1997. In 1993, the CCP decided that a modern enterprise system would be established to facilitate the reform of SOEs, which focused on the withdrawal of government from the management of SOEs and the incorporation of SOEs.[72] In 1997, the CCP endorsed the principle of 'letting the small ones go and keeping the big ones' in relation to the reform of SOEs.[73] The reform focused on improving the competitiveness of key SOEs in sectors that were essential to the national economy, and on letting small and medium-sized SOEs in other sectors exit the market, through management buyouts, privatization or shutdowns.[74]

Hence, large-scale enterprises, most of which were owned by the central government, operate in sectors that are important to the Chinese economy and are profit making have gone through the incorporation process. The incorporation provides SOEs with enhanced financial resources, stricter corporate governance and stronger competitiveness.[75]

In the incorporation process of the SOEs, particular attention has been paid in order to ascertain the level of state control of the company. Before 2001, state and legal person shares remained non-circulatable and were insulated from trading. The circulation of state shares became possible when the *Provisional Rules on Transfer of Shares of Public Listed Companies by State Share Holders* was issued in 2001 by the SASAIC and the CSRC.[76] However, the SASAC, by installing a notification system for the transfer of state shares, undertakes particular scrutiny when the transfer may cause the transfer of control of the company and sets a high threshold for exemption from the notification system.[77] The restricted liberalization of the state shares market enables the state to use the

[70] John Hassard, Jonathan Morris, Jackie Sheehan and Xiao Yuxin, 'Downsizing the Danwei: Chinese State-Enterprise Reform and the Surplus Labour Question' (2006) 17(8) *International Journal of Human Resource Management* 1441–55.

[71] Naughton (n 2) 310.

[72] CCP Decisions on Building Socialist Market Economy Institution. Adoped by the Fourteenth CCP Congress in 1993.

[73] The Task was set at the Fifteenth CCP Congress in 1997.

[74] Harry G Broadman, *Meeting the Challenge of Chinese Enterprise Reform* (World Bank, 1995) 6–7.

[75] Qian Sun and Wilson HS Tong, 'China Share Issue Privatization: The Extent of its Success' (2003) 70 *Journal of Financial Economics* 183–222.

[76] www.sasac.gov.cn/n1180/n1566/n258222/n259203/1733853.html.

[77] Art. 8.9.10, ibid.

stock exchange market for fund-raising, while maintaining state control in public listed companies.[78]

A wholly state-owned limited liability company is provided as one particular type of company with limited liability under the Company Law.[79] The wholly state-owned companies have one shareholder, namely the state, represented by the SASAC and its branches, at the local government level.[80] The SASAC appoints the board of directors of the wholly state-owned limited liability companies,[81] supervises the appointments of managers by the board of directors[82] and approves the merger, dissolution and bankruptcy of these companies.[83] The SASAC here serves as both shareholder and regulator, which implies the possibility of administrative intervention in corporate governance and of the politicization of corporate governance. Nevertheless, the wholly state-owned limited liability company provides the Chinese government with a useful vehicle to improve the efficiency of SOEs while keeping close control over them.

In addition to incorporation, the Chinese government has undertaken to form business groups led by corporatized SOEs. Business groups refer to a collection of legally independent firms that are bound by economic and social ties.[84] They were originally regarded as a transitional institution to facilitate China's transition towards market economy. However, since then, the Chinese government has actively promoted the formation of business groups headed or controlled by strong SOEs themselves, or between SOEs and FIEs and domestic private enterprises, with the aim of fostering national champions in China. The government has also consequently instructed merger and acquisition to be used to facilitate the formation of these business groups. With the aim of strengthening the competitiveness of the SOE sector, the government promoted the establishment of business groups led by corporatized SOEs and composed of various types of business organizations, including subsidiaries or joint ventures, with the aim of enjoying benefits produced by different types of business organizations in the Chinese market economy.[85]

Therefore, in terms of market entry, SOEs do not face government regulatory restrictions in entering any sectors of the economy. Rather, the NDRC Catalogue, industrial policies and SASAC policies have made it easier for SOEs to dominate or monopolize key sectors of the economy. These key sectors are not necessarily

[78] Zhou Dao, 'How Would the State Be Willing to Reduce its Shares Easily?', *China Securities Paper* (9 July 2007), available at: http://ifb.cass.cn/show_news.asp?id=13532.

[79] China Company Law, ch 3.

[80] Art 67 Company Law 2005.

[81] Ibid, Art 68.

[82] Ibid, Art 69.

[83] Ibid, Art 67.

[84] Daphne Yiu, Garry D Bruton and Yuan Lu, 'Understanding Business Groups Performance in an Emerging Economy: Acquiring Resources and Capabilities in Order to Prosper' (2005) 42 (10) *Journal of Management Studies* 183–206.

[85] Peter Nolan, 'China and the Global Business Revolution' (2005) 1 *Journal of Cambridge Economics* 119–37.

restricted to public services and allow the SOEs to operate with a profit-making approach. In terms of accessing capital, the SOEs are favoured by the Chinese banking system in relation to policy loans and have privileged access to the financial markets in China. In terms of the labour market, the SOEs have the support of the government through the provision of labour welfare packages. In terms of regional distribution, the incorporated SOEs, especially business groups headed by SOEs, have become highly vertically integrated and have easier access to regional markets because of their close relationship with local governments.

V. DEVELOPMENT OF FOREIGN INVESTED ENTERPRISES

Foreign investment has been one of the key contributors to China's continuous economic growth. The continuous inflow of foreign investment into the Chinese market can be explained by its size, the low cost of labour, preferential treatment by the central and local governments, and China's political stability for the last 30 years.[86] While China's financial market is still under development, foreign investment became the main channel for China to access global capital and foreign technology.[87] With China's membership of the WTO, FDI continues to flow into Chinese markets and has entered the Chinese services sector.[88]

Foreign investors are offered a variety of modes to enter the Chinese market. Foreign investors can choose to set up business organizations with no legal personality—for example, a representative office with no competence in commercial activities or branches acting as a part of the foreign investor established outside China.[89] Since 1979, foreign investors can also enter the Chinese market in the form of equity joint ventures,[90] as well as contractual joint ventures since 1988[91] and wholly foreign-owned enterprises since 1986.[92] Since the adoption of the Company Law in 1993, equity joint ventures and wholly foreign-owned enterprises can be registered as companies, while contractual joint ventures can choose to become a corporation or to remain as a business organization based on a partnership.[93]

In terms of market entry, first, foreign investors must comply with the sectoral regulation set out by the foreign investment catalogue issued by Ministry

[86] Wanda Tseng and Markus Rodlauer, *China Competing in the Global Economy* (IMF, 2003) 73–82.

[87] Naughton (n 2) 401.

[88] Li Yong, 'Extent of Admission of Foreign Investment' in Xiaoli Li (ed), *Assessing the Extent of China's Marketization* (Ashgate, 2006) 232–38.

[89] State Council Provisional Regulation on Representative Office of Foreign Enterprises in China, adopted in 1982 and amended in 2002.

[90] Law on Equity Joint Ventures 1979, amended in 2000.

[91] Law on Contractual Joint Ventures 1988, amended in 2000.

[92] Law on Wholly Foreign Owned Enterprises amended 2001.

[93] Tian, Xiaowen, *Managing International Business in China* (Cambridge University Press, 2007) 77–85.

of Commerce. They must refrain from entering restricted and prohibited sectors and are denied access to the markets which must remain state-controlled.[94] Furthermore, foreign investors that choose to enter the Chinese market by merging with Chinese operators are required to notify MOFCOM as to the impact of the merger on China's economic security and cannot proceed without obtaining the approval of the regulator.

In terms of accessing financial markets, FIE once transformed into companies, have the possibility of raising funds through the Chinese financial market. However, in 2001, the Moftec (the predecessor of MOFCOM) issued the Notice on Foreign Invested Companies Limited with Shares (the Notice),[95] which provided the application procedure for foreign invested companies to be listed on the A or B share markets. MOFCOM and the CSRC subsequently issued opinions on public listed companies and foreign investment (the Opinion), which lowered the threshold of requirement on foreign shares, after the listing, from 25 per cent to 10 per cent.[96] However, it should be noted that the Notice requires that the application must be in line with Foreign Investment Catalogues[97] and the Opinion indicates that foreign invested companies that are required to maintain the state as the majority shareholder must guarantee this after being publicly listed.[98] Furthermore, although the state shares market has been liberalized, the SASAC keeps close control over the acquisition of controlling state shares by foreign investors as discussed earlier.[99] Consequently, FIEs tend to rely substantially on self-financing or financing from non-Chinese financial markets.[100]

Compared with SOEs, FIEs do not have local government support in relation to employee welfare and face higher recruitment costs. However, given the relatively low cost of labour in China, most FIEs, backed by strong financial resources, manage to stay efficient despite the relatively higher costs in providing employee welfare. However, compared with SOEs, FIEs face more challenges in entering local regional markets, given the disintegration of China's domestic market and local protectionism, and tend to stay in areas where they have good connections with local regulators.[101]

[94] Foreign Investment Catalogue 2011, issued by the NDRC and MOFCOM no. 20 order, http://wzs.mofcom.gov.cn/article/n/201112/20111207907751.shtml.

[95] The Notice on Foreign Invested Companies Limited with Shares. See: www.sse.com.cn/cs/zhs/xxfw/flgz/html/t0246.htm.

[96] Art 2.2.3 opinions on public listed companies and foreign investment. See: http://news.xinhuanet.com/fortune/2001-11/14/content_114945.htm.

[97] Art 2.1 notice on foreign invested companies limited with shares: www.sse.com.cn/cs/zhs/xxfw/flgz/html/t0246.htm.

[98] Art 2.2.4 opinions on public listed companies and foreign investment: http://news.xinhuanet.com/fortune/2001-11/14/content_114945.htm.

[99] Please see discussion in III.B.2.

[100] Katherine Connor Linton, 'Access to Capital in China: Competitive Condition for Foreign and Domestic Firms' (2008) 1 *Journal of International Commerce and Economics* 27.

[101] Yadong Luo and Min Chen, 'Does Guanxi Influence Firm Performance?' (1997) 14 *Asia Pacific Journal of Management* 1–16.

VI. DEVELOPMENT OF PRIVATE DOMESTIC ENTERPRISES

The Chinese government strived to foster a business environment which encouraged large SOEs for ideological reasons and was attractive to foreign investment in order to stimulate the country's economic growth. The development of the domestic private sector, however, has so far hardly been at the top of the agenda of government economic development policies. Nevertheless, the domestic private sector has been a highly dynamic and important driving force in the Chinese economy.[102]

However, the development of private domestic business from being a social taboo into a driving force of China's economic development has been subject to government guidance at each step. As a result of China's Cultural Revolution (1966–76), private business had largely been eliminated from the Chinese economy. It was the 1982 Constitutional Amendment which provided that private individual business was a complementary component to socialist public ownership. The state protects the lawful rights of the individual business holder and administers, directs, helps and supervises individual business.[103] Pursuant to the 1988 Constitutional Amendment, the domestic private economy is allowed to exist and develop within permissible spheres. The private economy is a complementary component to socialist public ownership. The state protects the lawful rights and interests of the private economy sector and guides, supervises and administers the private economy.[104] After China declared the establishment of the socialist market economy in 1993, the private sector was given more recognition as an important component of this. It had its remit broadened to cover both individual business and private business organizations in 1999.[105] Pursuant to the 2004 Constitutional Amendment, the state protects the lawful interests and rights of the non-state-owned sector, but the emphasis is placed on encouraging, supporting and supervising the development of this sector. More importantly, the 2004 Constitutional Amendment also protects the right to private property.[106]

Consequently, when China started its economic reform, private business began to emerge. In rural China, the town and village enterprises (TVEs) have been an innovative step taken by the local governments to allow non-state actors to enter the local market. The TVEs are registered in the name of local township and village government agencies, but are controlled by private parties. It has been argued that the support from the town and village authorities provided de facto property protection to the business entity, which promoted the development of this sector.[107]

[102] Baizhu Chen and Yi Feng, 'Determinants of Economic Growth in China: Private Enterprises, Education and Openness' (2000) 11 *China Economic Review* 1–15.

[103] Art 13 Constitution of the PRC.

[104] Art 11 Constitutional Amendment 1988.

[105] Art 11 Constitutional Amendment 1999.

[106] Art 13 Constitutional Amendment 2004.

[107] Martin Weitzman and Chenggang Xu, 'Chinese Township-Village Enterprises as Vaguely Defined Cooepratives' (1994) 18 *Journal of Comparative Economics* 121–45.

However, the ambiguity in relation to the ownership of TVEs has largely restrained their development and efficiency, as the property rights of profit-making TVEs often resulted in disputes between local governments and farmers.[108]

In urban China, domestic enterprises started in the form of family business, which had the advantage of having a good understanding of targeted markets, a vast social network and quick reactions to the market. However, given the limits of household family businesses in terms of management, resources and business strategies, these businesses faced challenges in competing against the business operators of other ownerships.[109]

Although the government promoted the incorporation process in the Chinese market, with the main intention being to facilitate the transformation of SOEs, private enterprises too were provided with the incorporation vehicle. As a result, the Law on Township and Village Enterprises was adopted in 1996.[110] Pursuant to the Law, TVEs are defined as enterprises which are invested in by farmers or rural collective economic organizations, which are located in the village and town areas, and which provide farming-related services.[111] They can be incorporated into a legal person, which must have farmer investors or rural collective economic organizations as the majority shareholders with controlling rights.[112]

In the incorporation process, household family businesses are provided with the opportunity to become established as limited liability companies or companies limited by shares.[113] More importantly, the 2005 Amendment to the Company Law provides for the establishment of a one-person limited liability company.[114] The one-person company provides enhanced vehicles for private business to operate in the market with reduced risk and encourages private companies to enter these markets.

Nevertheless, in comparison to SOEs and foreign enterprises, private enterprises face severe constraints in terms of market entry and access to the financial and labour markets when competing in the Chinese market.

With respect to market entry, the SOEs and the FIEs are given clear guidance on market entry based on the Sectoral Investment Catalogue issued by the NDRC and Foreign Investment Catalogue issued by the MOFCOM, however private enterprises were not provided with similar policy guidance until 2005. In 2005, the State Council adopted *the Opinion on the Encouraging, Supporting and Guiding the Development of Non-State-Owned Economic Sector Including the Individual Private*

108 Jean C Oi , 'Two Decades of Rural Reform in China: An Overview and Assessment' (1999) 159 *China Quarterly* 616–28.

109 Siuyun Wong, 'Chinese Family Business: A Model' (1993) 6(3) *Family Business Review* 327–40.

110 1996 Law on Township and Village Enterprises, available at: www.gov.cn/banshi/2005-06/01/content_3432.htm.

111 Art 2 Law on Township and Village Enterprises 1996.

112 Ibid, Arts 9 and 10.

113 Art 2 Company Law.

114 Ibid, ch 3.

Business.[115] The opinion advocates creating a fairer and more equal environment for private business operators, in particular individual business operators and private companies. It states that private businesses are permitted to enter the natural monopoly sector,[116] the public utilities and infrastructure sector,[117] the financial services sector,[118] national defence, scientific and technological development,[119] and the public service sector, including education, research and development, culture and sports.[120]

The opinion encourages private investors to participate in the reform of SOEs through shareholding or merger or acquisition, and encourage private investment in developing western and north-eastern China.[121] In addition, despite lowered market entry barriers, private businesses are only allowed to acquire ownership or controlling rights in two main sectors: they can enter, in the form of wholly privately owned enterprises, joint ventures or project teams based on partnerships in the sector of general service.[122] Furthermore, private enterprises can acquire ownership or control of the public utility providers in the public utilities and infrastructure sector.[123] In sectors such as those of natural monopoly, financial services, military research and public services, private investment is regarded as an important resource to stimulate development in these sectors, but is not provided with the opportunity to acquire controlling rights. Given the underdevelopment of corporate governance in China, private investors, as minority shareholders in the companies operating in these sectors, may potentially bear higher risks.

The 2005 State Council Opinion states that a fairer environment should be created for private businesses in finance.[124] It provides that the government should undertake to reform the banking sector by introducing private investment in city commercial banks and rural cooperatives, and by ensuring increased loans to the private sector.[125] The Opinion states that the Chinese government should further develop its banking credit and guarantee system, catering to the financial demands of the private sector, and should provide equal treatment to the listing of private or state-owned enterprises on the domestic stock markets.[126]

The reason that this is proposed by the government is that many private businesses started with family savings and private loans and had limited access to the Chinese financial markets. This is partially explained by the Chinese business

115 State Council Opinion No 3 2005, available at: www.sme.gov.cn/web/assembly/action/browsePage.do?channelID=10089&contentID=1109154467881.
116 Ibid, Art 1.2 Opinions.
117 Ibid, Art 1.3.
118 Ibid, Art 1.5.
119 Ibid, Art 1.6.
120 Ibid, Art 1.4.
121 Ibid, Arts 1.7. and 1.8.
122 Ibid, Art 1.2.
123 Ibid, Art 1.3.
124 State Opinion, s 2.
125 Ibid, Art 13.
126 Ibid, Art 11.

culture and partially by the underdevelopment of China's banking and financial markets, and the latter's priority to reform of the SOEs.[127] The scenario is further aggregated by the underdevelopment of financial service provider, in particular financial intermediaries, for small and medium-sized enterprises in local regional markets.[128] Hence, an informal financial channel for private business has been developed and actively fuels the development of private business in China.[129]

Given the underdevelopment of China's stock markets, the majority of domestic private companies have remained highly cautious of being listed on the Chinese stock markets. It is not rare for domestic private companies to leave China or attempt to be listed on the international stock markets and, consequently, becoming FIEs. As a result, these companies can benefit from higher protection of shareholders provided by the international financial markets and the preferential treatment provided to FIEs by the Chinese government.[130]

With respect to the labour market, one of the main constraints that the private domestic enterprises face in its development on the Chinese market is human resources management.[131] In the incorporation process, PDEs have been particularly disadvantaged as most of the businesses started as family businesses or TVEs and had scant human resources management experience and skills. Thus, there was a lack of knowledge or expertise on corporate governance and business strategies.[132] With a national social security system far from being established in China, PDEs are disadvantaged in terms of attracting human resources for management or research development when the state-owned sector can provide better welfare packages and the foreign sector can make more lucrative offers to candidates. Furthermore, until 2008, many small and medium-sized private enterprises in China have exploited the underdeveloped labour protection system though abusive behaviour, eg, hiring without contracts or delaying the payment of salary to employees, with the aim of seeking economic benefits or to survive market competition.[133] Under the new Labour Contract Law, these players are faced with higher compliance costs in terms of human resources management than was previously the case.[134]

Therefore, it can be seen that domestic private business operators have faced higher market entry policy barriers, have limited access to domestic financial

[127] Yaseng Huang, *Capitalism with Chinese Characteristics: Entrepreneurship and the State* (Cambridge University Press, 2008) 138.

[128] Stephan Haggard and Yaseng Huang, 'The Political Economy of Private Sector Development in China', in Rawski (n 13) 337–75.

[129] Ibid.

[130] Yaseng Huang, 'Just how Capitalist is China?', 4 April 2008, MIT Sloan Research Paper No 4699-08, available at: http://ssrn.com/abstract=1118019.

[131] Ibid.

[132] Malcolm Warner, *Human Resource Management in China Revisited* (Routledge, 2005) 226–27.

[133] Virginia Ho, 'From Contracts to Compliance? An Early Look at Implementation Under China's New Labour Legislation' 23 *Columbia Journal of Asian Law* 35.

[134] Pan Jie, 'The New Labour Contract Law's Impact on Enterprises' (2010) 6 *Law and Commerce* 296–97.

markets and the banking system, and are disadvantaged in terms of human resources management. Although the Chinese government has attempted to create a more fair business environment for domestic private business, by increasing market access and providing more access to the financial markets, the effect of the policies remains to be tested. Moreover, the policy measures taken by the Chinese government to increase fairness in the market do not undermine the government's policy of providing priority treatment to the state-owned sectors. In conclusion, it can be seen that in comparison to SOEs, FIEs and domestic private businesses operate in a market environment where constraints persist due to the nature of ownership of these operators.

The constraints faced by non-state-owned business operators can be explained by the lagging behind of institutional building to support the functioning of a market economy, such as the rule of law, and the incomplete construction of a factors market including the financial and labour markets. It further reflects the fact that in China's market economy construction, fairness and social equity have not, at least in the recent decades of reforms, been rated as important values in its market governance.

VII. RESTRAINTS ON COMPETITION IN CHINA

The above analysis shows that although China has adopted a gradual and incentive-based economic transformation, it is constrained by its own social embeddedness. Hence, whereas it has successfully introduced the market element into its economy construction (for example, the pricing system), the role of the state in some aspects of the development of a market economy has been maintained or strengthened—for example, state control over market entry, financial systems and the labour markets, and the disintegration of national markets.

Consequently, the relationship between the state and the market in contemporary China has become extremely difficult to measure when taking into account the various factors including market entry, the financial market, the labour market and the operations carried out by different players in the market. In turn, the level to which the market plays a leading role in resource allocation is variable and is therefore, hard to quantify.

Nevertheless, a common feature in the various levels of marketization is the clash between the state and the market. Where an environment provides little or no state distortion of the different aspects of the markets, but relies largely on market rules, it enjoys a high level of marketization. Where an environment functions on basic market mechanisms such as price signals, but provides the possibility for discretionary intervention by the state in the market, the marketization level remains relatively low. Where an environment, justified on public policy grounds, ensures that state intervention in the form of government regulation prevails over the market mechanism, the marketization level remains limited.

The three levels of marketization can exist in the same sector or the same geographical market in China, which further complicates matters.

When both the state and the market may act as resource allocators in the economy, the restraints on competition can stem from both private and public parties. Hence, both the state distortion of the market and market failure can provide the restriction on or prohibition of competition on the Chinese market.[135] Where marketization remains higher, the restraints on competition are more likely to be caused by private restraints on competition; where marketization remains lower, the restraints of competition are more likely to be caused by distortion of the market by the state. However, it should be noted that private and public restraints on competition are not mutually exclusive and can coexist at the same time. Furthermore, given the dominant role played by the administrative system in China, the possibility of distortion by the state occurring in environments with higher levels of marketization should not be completely excluded.

A. Private Restraints on Competition

In the business environment with higher marketization levels, private activities with the aim or effect of restraining competition have existed since the beginning of the reform process, eg, the predatory price war which broke out among TV manufacturers in the 1990s.[136]

One of the clear examples of this is the price cartel formed among manufacturers of instant noodles in China in 2004. The market for instant noodles has a high level of marketization. Except for government regulation in terms of food safety,[137] the market has a low market entry requirement, a variety of players and low exit barriers.[138] The competition in the market has been fierce and by 2002 there were 292 manufacturers, which had received annual revenue of more than 5 million RMB.[139]

In February 2004, several instant noodle manufacturers signed an agreement called the China Instant Noodle Self-Disciplinary Alliance. According to the agreement, given the price increase in palm oil and powder as the main raw materials for instant noodles, the manufacturers would raise the retail price for

[135] Jijian Yang, 'Market Power in China: Manifestations, Effects and Legislations' (2003) 21 *Review of Industrial Organization* 167–83.

[136] See http://finance.sina.com.cn/2000-08-21/7521.html.

[137] From the 1980s to 2006, the government undertook to regulate the production of instant noodles on the market. The government regulator, the General Administration of Quality Supervision, Inspection and Quarantine of the PRC, has tightened its regulation of instant food production by setting out detailed requirements regarding the production process.

[138] In 1989, China had around 350 production lines for instant noodles and by 2001, it had around 1,800. According to the database provided by the regulator, there are 371 incumbent instant noodle manufactures, covering 28 provinces in China.

[139] Market analysis report on instant noodles market in China: www.tech-food.com/news/2002-7-30/n0008981.html.

instant noodles in three phases by 8 April 2004. First, the retail price for instant noodles, at 0.5 RMB per bag, would be raised by six per cent, and 1.00 RMB per bag by 10 per cent. Second, the price rise would be executed three times: on 26 February 2004, 10 March 2004 and 8 April 2004. Third, on the precondition that consumers were happy with the results, manufactures could adjust the size of their products to achieve the same effect as would be created by raising their prices.[140] However, the price cartel broke down when some of the parties backed out at the last minute.

In March 1997, the International Ramen Manufacturers Association (IRMA), a non-governmental industrial association for instant noodle manufacturers worldwide, was set up in Japan. In September 2004, a Chinese sub-association, the Chinese Association of Instant Noodle Manufacturers, was set up under the IRMA.

The Chinese sub-association has convened three meetings since its installation. On 26 December 2006, it had a meeting in Beijing, during which members set the price for high-quality, medium-quality and low-quality instant noodles, and set the time schedule for the price rise. On 21 April 2007, it met in Hang Zhou, during which the price rise ratio was fixed.[141] On 5 July 2007, it convened a meeting in Beijing, during which some of the members decided to enforce the price rise from 26 July.[142] In the summer of 2007, consumers found that instant noodle prices had been raised overnight.

The above example shows that hardcore, private competition restrictions have existed in the Chinese market throughout the reform process. It proves that with the introduction of the invisible hand into the Chinese markets, the market players have a tendency towards creating a monopoly so as to maximize their individual economic interests.

It should be noted that in these sectors, non-state sector business operators, in particular foreign business operators, backed by their financial and technological resources, may often become the main players in the market as a result of competition. However, whereas these non-state sectors started to gain a growing market share in these markets, they have become active in anti-competitive behaviour, with the aim of maintaining their market position and boosting their profits. In fact, with no comprehensive competition regulation in place, the abuse of market power by FIEs has grown considerably and has caught the attention of the Chinese government.[143]

[140] *Ill fate of price fixing agreement and new development of price wars—instant noodle market development in 2004*, Tobacco and Alcohol Market Weekly 2004, http://www.emkt.com.cn/article/148/14844.html

[141] The price for high-quality instant noodles would be raised from 1.5 RMB per bag to 1.7 RMB per bag. More importantly, under the framework of the association, the meeting set out that the price rise would take effect across the whole instant noodle manufacturing industry on 1 June 2007 and that all instant noodle manufacture members of the association had to comply with the decision.

[142] *First Finance Daily* (*Di Yi Cai Jin Ri Bao*), 21 August 2007.

[143] Fair Transaction Bureau of the State Administration of Industry and Commerce (SAIC), 'Report on Anti-competitive Behaviour by Multinational Companies and Policies to be Taken', *Biweekly of Administration for Industry and Commerce*, published by the SAIC in May 2004, 42.

B. Restraints on Competition Caused by Public Power

In an environment where the marketization level is low, it is more likely for state intervention in the market to produce restraints on or prohibition of competition.

The excessive price competition in some markets in China serves as a good example of this. Excessive price competition is defined as a situation where in industries with a low concentration ratio, enterprises, in most cases SOEs, compete excessively on price or even on price below cost, but could not exit the industry easily.[144] In mature market economies, business operators may be stuck in excessive price competition in these markets because of the high sunk costs. However, they can eventually exit the market legally through the insolvency procedure.

This is not necessarily the case as far as the reform of SOEs in China is concerned. A number of SOEs at the local government level, though in deficit, continue to stay in the market. First, this is mainly because SOEs, as explained above, have been the main revenue contributor to the local government's budget and are closely linked with the political and economic performance evaluation of local officials. The local government is therefore reluctant to see local SOEs lose their market share and the potential associated profit.[145] Second, local government tend to prevent SOEs from exiting the market through bankruptcy so as to avoid having to taking over the responsibility of providing social welfare to the current and retired employees of the SOEs. Furthermore, given the large amount of financial assistance provided by the local banks to SOEs, the local national banks are reluctant to see SOEs go bankrupt and would prefer to strengthen the financial assistance given to them, in the hope that the loans can be repaid in the future.

It can be seen that in this type of market, the state distortion of the market mechanism has become the main barrier prohibiting these markets from giving full rein to competition, based on the market mechanism. Many Chinese scholars argue that restriction on competition in the Chinese market is mainly due to the abuse of administrative power on the part of the state.[146]

C. Restraints on Competition and Sectoral Regulation

In 2006, the SASAC declared that the following key industries would be subject to state regulation: industries involved in national security, infrastructure and

[144] Jie Ma and Weiying Zhang, 'Ownership Distortion as a Cause for Excessive Competition' (1999) *Economic Research Journal* 11–20.

[145] Please see discussion in III.D.

[146] Xiaoye Wang, 'The Biggest Problem in the Antimonopoly Law Draft' (2007) 3 *Xue Xi Yue Kan*, available at: http://china.eastview.com/kns50/detail.aspx?QueryID=101&CurRec=23.

mineral resources, those providing important public services and key hi-tech industries.[147] It should be noted that the development of these sectors is completely subject to state regulation in terms of market entry and business strategies in the market.

For example, in the petroleum and oil industry, the national market is controlled by the China Petroleum and Gas Corporation, the China Petroleum Chemical Corporation and the China Ocean Petroleum Corporation, which are large incorporated SOEs. The business organizations, though incorporated, function on a de facto bureaucratic basis and benefit from close links with government agencies. They enjoy further privileges including operating on the market based on government guidance prices and having preferential access to China's financial systems. However, they avoid competition, as market entry is forbidden to other business organizations.[148] Nevertheless, as indicated before, Chinese SOEs in these sectors, although state-owned, operate with the primary goal of profit making rather than providing non-profit-making services to the public.[149]

The fact that sectors that are significant to the Chinese economy, in particular the energy sector, are subject to government regulation, which excludes the entry of other players, has aroused concerns among the public and business operators dependent on or linked to these sectors. Consumers and business operators mainly feel that they have been exploited by the pricing behaviour of the state-backed monopolies or oligopolies. Public opinion holds that the state regulations fostering the SOEs undermine fairness in the marketplace by conferring purely commercial goals upon them and providing them with a legally monopolistic status. It further holds that the SOEs are insulated by state regulation and should be the primary target to be tackled by China's hotly debated AML.[150]

VIII. CONCLUSION

During the preparation for a competition law in China, much of the debate has centred upon the issue of whether China needs a competition law. There has been the view that given the predominant role played by the state in the creation and development of the market economy, and the fact that the Chinese economy has

[147] SASC Opinions on Adjustment of State-Owned Shares and State-Owned Enterprises: www.sasac.gov.cn/gzjg/xcgz/200612180138.htm.

[148] Shaofeng Chen, 'State Regulated Marketization: China's Oil Pricing Regime' (2006) 7(3) *Perspectives* 151–72.

[149] Xiaobo Hu, 'The State, Enterprises, and Society in Post-Deng China: Impact of the New Round of SOE Reform' (2000) 40(4) *Asian Survey* 641.

[150] 'Why Sino-Petroleum sell oil product at 80 dollars with cost at 8 dollars?', 5 July 2009. http://business.sohu.com/20090705/n264985795.shtml

been viewed as highly concentrated with state-owned players and is far from being competitive, there is little space for competition law to play a role.[151]

However, the analysis above has shown that although the state plays a leading role in China's market economy development, the majority of markets in China have become highly competitive to serve as the driving force for the country's economic growth.[152] Nevertheless, the marketization level of China's economic transformation is reliant on the functioning of variable factors, and its exploration requires the examination of individual cases.

In China's market environment, private restraints on competition are much more likely to occur where the marketization level is high, while the restraints on competition caused by the intervention of the state in the market are more likely to emerge where the marketization level is low.

Therefore, the restraints on competition, which reduce efficiency and undermine social equity, coexist in the Chinese market. The restraints can be caused by both state interventions in the market and intrinsic market failure. It remains to be seen how the Chinese government would tackle the challenges lying ahead, with its much-anticipated AML.

[151] For example, Chen Qinlan, 'Antitrust is Injurious', 16 August 2006, http://finance.sina.com.cn/review/zlhd/20060811/09422813304.shtml.

[152] Brandt and Rawski (n 1) 21; Naughton (n 2); Peter Nolan, *Crossroads: The End of Wild Capitalism and the Future of Humanity* (Marshall Cavendish, 2009) 130.

5

The Making of the Anti-Monopoly Law

I. INTRODUCTION

Following the discussions on the characteristics of market governance and the complexity of the restraints upon competition in China, this chapter reviews the process in which its first comprehensive competition law, the Anti-Monopoly Law (AML), came into being. It shows how China, on the one hand, strives to fit into the global competition law community and, on the other hand, makes continuous efforts to adjust international competition law norms in order to achieve its own strategic goals and to preserve the incumbent market regulation framework in the context of globalization. To this extent, the embeddedness of China's market governance, the law-making process and the interaction with international competition law norms have contributed to the outcome of the AML.

II. PRODUCTION OF THE ANTI-MONOPOLY BILL

China planned to enact legislation as early as 1987 to protect competition as one part of its legal reforms to support the construction of a market economy. The enactment of the AML was listed on the legislative agenda of the Eighth, Ninth and Tenth NPCSCs in 1993, 1998 and 2003, respectively.

Pursuant to the Legislation Law, apart from the deputies of the NPC, the NPC Presidium, the NPCSC, the State Council, the Central Military Committee, the Supreme People's Court, the People's Procuratorate and the NPC committees have the competence to submit legislative bills to the NPC and the NPCSC.[1] The State Council, the main agent responsible for economic regulation in China, was responsible for submitting the legislative bill on the AML to be enacted by the NPCSC.

[1] Art 12 Legislation Law.

A. The State Council's Making of Legislative Bills

The procedures for the making of legislative bills by the State Council have been formalized with the enactment of the Regulation for the Procedures of Administrative Regulation issued by the State Council on 16 November 2011, which came into effect on 1 January 2012.[2] The making of a legislative bill by the State Council includes the stages of proposal, drafting, scrutiny, decision, publication and explanation.[3] The State Council Legislative Affairs Office (LAO) is in charge of setting out the annual legislative plan, which includes the planning for legislative bills, the enactment of the State Council regulations and rules, etc. The State Council ministries and commissions have the competence to submit proposals for legislative bills. The LAO decides whether to include the proposals into its annual legislative plan based on the following principles: the proposal should respond to the needs of reform, development and stability; China should have obtained relevant experience at a mature level in relation to the proposal; and the proposal should fall within the competence of the State Council.[4]

Once the LAO lists the proposal on its annual legislative plan, the legislative bill can be drafted by the LAO itself or by one or more State Council ministries jointly.[5] The regulation has not been clear on the criterion for the allocation of drafting responsibilities among the LAO and the ministries. It sets out that the drafting should be consistent with the general principles of the Legislation Law, the Constitution and other laws. In particular, the draft should reflect China's reform spirit and should facilitate the transformation of the government's role in terms of economic coordination, management and public service. In addition, the legislative bill should aim to provide simplified, uniform and efficient regulation (and this regulation should be enforced by a single government authority), it should protect the lawful interests of citizens, legal persons and other organizations, and it should not only confer regulatory power on government authorities, but also set out the conditions, procedures and responsibilities of this power.[6]

During the drafting process, the authority responsible should conduct field trip research with the relevant organizations or individuals, in the form of hearings or meetings.[7] When the drafted bill touches upon the regulatory competence held by other state organs, the authority should coordinate with these organs to reach an agreement. Where an agreement cannot be reached, the authority responsible

[2] Regulation on the Procedures of Administrative Regulation Making issued by the State Council on 16 November 2011 and effected on 1 January 2002 (hereinafter 'the Regulation'). Art 34 of the Regulation provides that the State Council can refer to the same rules of procedure in making legislative bills submitted to the NPC and NPCSC.

[3] Ibid, Art 2.

[4] Ibid, Art 10.

[5] Ibid, Art 10.

[6] Ibid, Art 11.

[7] Ibid, Art 12.

for drafting should produce a statement for the reasons of the failure.[8] When the proposal involves an issue of significance in relation to national policy or institutional setting, the drafting authority should make recommendations which will be decided upon by the State Council LAO.[9] Based on this, the drafting authority (or authorities) needs to submit the following documents: the draft for the legislative bill; a statement on the justification for the proposed bill; the institutional arrangement for enforcement; feedback and comment from stakeholders, and consultation with the relevant authorities, organizations and citizens; and supplementary documents regarding the relevant domestic legislation and similar legislation of foreign jurisdictions, as well as research and working reports.

The State Council LAO scrutinizes the drafted legislative bill and can either decide to withhold the bill-making process or to return the draft back to the authority if it feels that the following conditions have not been met: the general conditions for the enactment of a draft bill have not been met; the relevant authorities have significant concerns over the draft and the drafting authority has not coordinated with the relevant authorities; the draft bill has not been signed by the head(s) of the proposing authorities; and the draft bill has not been accompanied by the statements and supplementary documents as requested.[10]

In order to complete the scrutiny over the drafted legislative bill, the LAO will, at this stage, carry out the second round of field research, hearings and meetings. It will distribute the draft among the State Council organs, the local government institutions, and the relevant organizations and experts, inviting comments and opinions.[11] With the approval of the State Council, the draft can be presented to the public for comment.[12] It should be noted that when the drafted bill involves a significant or difficult issue, the LAO should hold meetings with the relevant authorities and experts to seek a solution. When the drafted bill faces severe disagreement over the general policy guiding the bill, the setting-up of the enforcement framework or the allocation of a regulatory sphere among State Council authorities, the LAO should coordinate with the authorities in order to facilitate agreement. Where such agreement fails to be achieved, the LAO should report to the State Council on the issue involved, along with the opinions of the authorities involved and its own opinion, and should ask for a final decision.[13] The legislative bill, once scrutinized by the LAO, will be subject to the executive meeting of the State Council for approval. The drafting authorities and the LAO will be required to attend the meeting to make statements.[14]

The State Council executive meeting provides comments on the draft of a bill. The LAO will revise the draft based on these comments. Once the LAO completes

[8] Ibid, Art 13.
[9] Ibid, Art 14.
[10] Ibid, Art 17.
[11] Ibid, Art 19.
[12] Ibid.
[13] Ibid, Art 23.
[14] Ibid, Art 26.

the revision, the draft will be submitted to the premier of the State Council to be signed off.[15] The bill will then be submitted to the NPCSC for deliberation and enactment.

In line with the institutional readjustments undertaken by the State Council administrative system, the State Council ministries and commissions have become leading agents which oversee different aspects of China's market development. Over the years, the division of regulatory competence held by the ministries and commissions has become concretised and, consequently, market regulation is segmented into the respective ministerial competences subject to State Council coordination. During the process, the State Council authorities engage in the negotiations, cooperation and competitions with each other with the aim of curbing and expanding their respective regulatory competence. The state instrumentality view of the law enables these organs to seek the expansion of their regulatory competence through the enactment of laws and regulations.

Consequently, coordination among relevant regulators becomes one of the main hurdles to be cleared in the production of a legislative bill. This can be confirmed by the levels of coordination in the bill-making process required by the State Council LAO. First, during the drafting stage, if the bill is likely to touch upon the competence of other regulators, the drafting authority is required to consult with and obtain agreement from these relevant authorities, which is then reflected in the documents supporting the draft bill. Second, during the scrutiny stage, the State Council LAO not only examines the legality of the draft with respect to substance and procedure, but also functions as a mediator to facilitate the reaching of an agreement by the authorities on the design and the enforcement of the bill. Third, during the approval stage, the State Council executive meeting delivers its comments on the drafted bill. However, these take into consideration the statements made by the drafting authority and the LAO, which provides a further opportunity for the State Council executive meeting to coordinate its subordinate organs. This coordination can be based on law, but can go beyond the law to reach political compromises with relevant regulators. As the State Council has not provided a specific timeframe with respect to the different stages in the process of making legislative bills, coordination can be a lengthy and complicated process that prolongs the enactment of the law.

However, the fact that the drafting authority must provide supplementary documents which include information on similar laws in foreign jurisdictions and on the authority's working reports on the law's relevance to China shows that the State Council and the LAO have paid increasing attention to international practices on economic regulation. In this process, the drafting authorities can be incentivized to refer to international legal norms with the aim of justifying the design of the drafted bill and curbing respective regulatory competence.

[15] Ibid, Art 27.

It nevertheless demonstrates that the reference to international legal practice has been institutionalized in the law-making process in China.

B. The Making of the AML

The making of the draft bill of the AML posed new challenges to China's market regulatory framework, not only due to the technicality of the law but also to the fact that the envisaged law did not fit in with the regulatory sphere of any single government authority.

The State Council LAO delegated MOFCOM and SAIC to be jointly responsible for drafting the bill. Both MOFCOM and the SAIC undertook extensive research on the preparation for the draft and extensive consultation with government authorities within the administrative system on the bill for the AML. In China's design of the enforcement framework of the law, the NDRC, MOFCOM and the SAIC competed to become the main authority under the AML.

MOFCOM produced and publicized a draft of the AML in 2003. In 2004, it set up a competition dialogue with the EU. In the same year, it also set up its own Anti-Monopoly Investigation Bureau. Moreover, it has been the main enforcer of the regulation on mergers by foreign investors of Chinese enterprises, jointly issued by six State Council ministries to regulate mergers and acquisitions on the part of foreign investors since 2006.[16] It further pointed out that China had, up to that point, no competition authorities to enforce competition regulation.[17]

The SAIC emphasized that it was by far the most experienced authority in relation to competition regulation.[18] This was because since 1993, it has been the sole agency enforcing the Anti-Unfair Competition Law. The Anti-Unfair Competition Law goes beyond regulating dishonest practice in competition in relation to industrial or commercial matters and includes regulation against the abuse of dominant positions by public and other enterprises, which have acquired their dominant positions in a lawful way. It also regulates restrictions on competition imposed by governments and affiliated agents. For the enforcement of competition regulation, the SAIC indicates that it has a well-organized institutional framework in place, and has a team of staff with the requisite knowledge and skills in competition investigation and enforcement. During the consultation on the AML draft, the SAIC commented that competition regulation is a formidable task that cannot easily be completed by merely setting up a new office or bureau.[19]

[16] Art 32 of the Regulation on Mergers and Acquisitions by Foreign Enterprises on the Chinese Market, issued jointly issued by MOFCOM, the SASAC, the State Tax Administration, the SAIC, the China Securities Commission and the State Administration of Foreign Exchange in 2006.

[17] http://business.sohu.com/20090826/n266236732.shtml.

[18] www.saic.gov.cn/fldyfbzdjz/gzdt/200909/t20090927_71230.html.

[19] Ibid.

The NDRC, as the key authority in the government administrative system, has been the sole authority enforcing the Price Law since 1997. The Price Law regulates the pricing behaviour of business operators in the market and proscribes business operators from engaging in price fixing and conspiracy. This ranges from predatory pricing with the aim of creating a monopoly in the market to disseminating fraudulent information, to raise pricing and to using fraudulent pricing measures to deal with consumers, as well as conducting price discrimination.[20] The NDRC is well supported by its strong institutional framework and resources at central and local government levels.

Given the significance of the draft bill to China's market regulation, the State Council LAO set up a working group to scrutinize the draft of the AML bill. The working group was composed of representatives from the NPC Financial and Economics Committee, the NPC Law Committee, the Supreme People's Court, the NDRC, MOFCOM, the SAIC, the Development Research Center of the State Council and the Chinese Academy of Social Sciences. In addition, the LAO set up an expert group composed of 24 lawyers, economists and other scholars from leading universities in China. It extensively consulted other State Council authorities, local governments, enterprises, relevant industrial associations, Chinese and international scholars, and international competition regimes and international organizations on the drafted bill.[21] Based on this, it took over a year to further develop the draft bill. Before it submitted the draft to the State Council executive committee for comment, it reported on its draft to the NPC Financial and Economics Committee, the NPC Law Committee and the NPCSC legislative affairs commission. The draft was approved by the State Council executive meeting on 7 June 2006 and was signed off to be submitted to the NPCSC on 16 June 2006.[22]

The making of the AML bill by the State Council confirms that there has been a rising diversity of interests among State Council organs in terms of market governance. The State Council's coordination among these organs undoubtedly had an impact on the outcome of the bill. However, with China's rise on the global stage, its market governance is no longer merely one of domestic concern. International actors, including international organizations and competition authorities, are enthusiastic in terms of communicating and exporting competition law norms to China, given China's weight in the global market. In turn, China's communication with pluralist sources of competition law norms has influenced its competition law choice.

[20] Art 14 the Price Law.
[21] An, Jian, *Interpretation of the Antimonopoly Law of the P.R.China* (Law Press China, 2007) 138.
[22] Ibid, 2 and 138.

III. CHINA'S COMMUNICATION WITH COMPETITION LAW NORMS

In the development of a competition regulation regime, China has undertaken an unprecedented level of communication with international actors on competition law. Faced with a world containing plural forms of competition law norms, it proactively engaged in communication with international organizations, leading competition regimes such as EU competition law and US antitrust law, the competition law regimes with similar cultural backgrounds, such as competition regimes of other East Asian countries, and competition regimes where it had a geopolitical connection, such as the Australian competition regime. The communication became the main channel through which China could understand and learn about competition regulation. Consequently, as a new competition regulation regime, it benefited from being a latecomer to competition regulation and based the design of its AML on international legal norms in practice.

China's approach in communicating with international actors on competition law has not been institutionalized. Nevertheless, characteristics of the approach can be observed as follows. In selecting the actors to communicate with, China became increasingly open to all forms of international actors in communication, with the aim of understanding and assimilating the strength of various types of norms to help it develop its AML. In other words, it did not necessarily undertake in-depth research beforehand; hence, it did not necessarily target one particular actor to begin with. During the communication process, it remained passive and quiet in the early stages by focusing on the technicality of the AML and was often results-oriented in seeking solutions. Further, in preparing the draft bill of the AML, it subconsciously sought approval from peer competition authorities in developing the substance of its competition rules.

However, China was by no means passive in receiving norms in this process. In socializing the international competition law norms, it adhered to the instrumental view of international legal norms. In other words, learning about the strength and limits of various norms on competition regulation was conditioned by the issue of whether the norms could serve China's own strategic interests and could be enforced by the incumbent market regulatory framework at minimum cost. Where the international legal norms could not serve China's strategic interests, China did not succumb to international legal norms. Instead, it often looked for creative normative solutions by resorting to its own legal normative framework.

It is with this background in mind that China's communications with international actors on competition law needs to be examined at the multilateral and bilateral levels. At the multilateral level, the WTO, the OECD and UNCTAD are the three main actors that China communicated with on the development of its AML.

China acceded to the WTO in 2001 and has since been bound by the WTO general principle, including the non-discrimination principle, the WTO agreements and the WTO dispute settlement mechanism. China's WTO Accession Protocol has not provided it with the obligation to adopt a law to protect competition.[23] However, China has pledged to enact a fairness-based competition law since its pre-accession working group meetings:

> The representative of China noted that the Government of China encouraged fair competition and was against acts of unfair competition of all kinds. The Law of the People's Republic of China on Combating Unfair Competition, promulgated on 2 September 1993 and implemented on 1 December 1993, was the basic law to maintain the order of competition in the market. In addition, the Price Law, the Law on Tendering and Bidding, the Criminal Law and other relevant laws also contained provisions on anti-monopoly and unfair competition. China was now formulating the Law on Anti-Monopoly.[24]

By committing to a fairness-based competition law, the Chinese government showed its determination to create a level playing field in its domestic market, which may have lent it political support and bargaining power in its pre-accession negotiations.[25]

In the meantime, the WTO continued to influence China's AML preparation through non-legally binding mechanisms. As a part of its WTO plus package, China was subject to the transitional review mechanism by the WTO General Council.[26] The 2006 WTO Trade Policy Review for China provided that China's AML needed to set its regulatory target on a non-discriminatory basis: namely, that all undertakings, whether private or public, should fall under the regulation of the law and that the enforcement of the competition law should be undertaken in an equal and non-discriminatory way.[27] In other words, competition law in China should not constitute a hidden protection for the domestic market. While the WTO trade policy review was not legally binding on China, its comments contained attempts of political persuasion as far as China's design of competition regulation was concerned.

China's reference to the competition law norms generated by the WTO has served the government's strategic developmental purposes. Before the enactment of the AML, some Chinese scholars argued that it is the abuse of administrative power conferred upon public authorities rather than private restrictions that constitute the main restraint on competition in the marketplace, and that such restraints require fundamental political reforms that go beyond the scope of competition law.[28] Indeed, the restraint upon competition caused by the abuse of

[23] Accession Protocol of the People's Republic of China, WT/L/432, 23 November 2001.

[24] Report of the Working Party on the Accession of China, WT/MIN/(01)3, November 2001, para 65, p 12.

[25] Qianlan Wu, 'Harmonization of Competition Laws under Multilateral Trade Framework: China's WTO Membership and its Anti-Monopoly Law', in Andenas, M and Andersen, C, *Theory and Practice of Harmonization* (Cheltenham, Edward Elgar, 2012).

[26] Art 18 Accession Protocol of the P.R.China, WT/L.

[27] WTO Secretariat Report on Trade Policy Review for China, WT/TPR/S/161, paras 44 and 243, pp 22 and 139.

[28] Li Changqing and Ma Hongmei, 'Anti-monopoly Law Should Be Delayed', *Legal Daily* (*Fazhi Ribao*), 6 March 2002.

power by public authorities has not been a new problem faced by China. Since the beginning of the reform, the Chinese government has more than once attempted to tackle the abuse of public power in the market, but with limited effect.[29] In this scenario, the Chinese government, on many occasions, emphasized that China needs to adopt the AML after its WTO membership, implying that the Law was required as one part of China's WTO obligations. One such example was when the Spokesman Zeng Jianhui of the NPC stated on 4 March 2002 that after its accession to the WTO, China would comply with its WTO commitment to bring its laws into line with the WTO principles and would adopt new laws, including the AML.[30] However, the inclusion of regulation on public restraints on competition law has been a highly contentious topic in the adoption process of China's AML, to the extent that the regulation was included and then removed from the drafts, but was eventually included in the final version for adoption.[31] By justifying the adoption of the AML on the grounds of its WTO obligations, the Chinese government seized the opportunity to push forward some of its deadlocked domestic reforms. This shows how it strategically used the WTO general principles on non-discrimination and the WTO trade policy review as the basis to legitimize the inclusion of regulation on public authorities into the AML draft.

Although not an OECD member, China signed the China-OECD Cooperation and Dialogue Programme in 1995.[32] Under the framework of the Dialogue Programme, the OECD members contribute to policy reforms in China; in turn, China presents the results of its policy reform to be scrutinized by the members of the OECD. Thus, the OECD has provided support to China's economic policy formulation, including that on the competition policy and law. During the process, MOFCOM and the SAIC requested OECD support in designing China's competition policy and law. In response, the OECD signed a Memorandum of Understanding (MOU) with the Asian Development Bank (ADB) in order to support its competition policy and law development.[33] In 2005, China's State Council LAO circulated the draft of the AML bill to the OECD for comments. In 2005, the SAIC and MOFCOM each held a joint conference with the OECD and the ADB on the design of the AML in June and November, respectively.[34] In 2007, China became one of the five key partners of the OECD.[35] The OECD has regularly organized a Global Forum on Competition since 2001, which is attended by China. Chinese officials find communication with the OECD resourceful and helpful for the country's AML development. This is mainly because China

[29] Interim State Council Regulation on Fostering and Protecting Socialist Competition 1988; Art 7 Unfair Competition Law.

[30] www.people.com.cn/GB/shizheng/7501/7507/20020304/678785.html.

[31] Huang, Yong, 'Pursuing the Second Best: The History, Momentum, and Remaining Issues of China's Anti-Monopoly Law' (2008) 75 *Antitrust Law Journal* 117.

[32] www.oecd.org/china/chinaandtheoecd.htm.

[33] *OECD-CHINA Cooperation: The First Ten Years*, November 2005, 13.

[34] Ibid.

[35] OECD Council Resolution on Enlargement and Enhanced Engagement, adopted on 26 May 2007.

is able to seek comments and technical solutions regarding specific aspects of its competition regulation from experienced competition authorities of mature market economies.

China became one of the G77 members of UNCTAD in 1964. In its communication with China, UNCTAD advocates the possible role that can be played by the AML for China as a developmental state, such as using the AML to tackle distortion of the market by the abuse of public power. Chinese officials were in contact with UNCTAD regarding the preparation of the AML bill and regularly attended the UNCTAD Intergovernmental Group of Experts Meeting on Competition Policy and Law from 2008, where the competition authorities of developing countries engage in voluntary peer review on competition law. China's participation, however, has remained cautious and less visible than the competition authorities of other large developing economies.

The communication with international organizations on the development of the AML provided China with the opportunity to understand the role of competition law in macro-economic development and in the context of globalization. In order to develop the AML in a concrete form, China was keen to communicate with leading competition authorities at the bilateral level. At this level, the EU and the US competition authorities are the main counterparts that China has communicated with.

China established diplomatic relations with the European Economic Community in 1975. The EU-China relationship was quickly upgraded into a comprehensive relationship, with the economic relationship remaining the central focus. Given this background, the EU and China have set up 24 sectoral dialogues and agreements, ranging from environmental protection to industrial policy, to education and culture. The EU-China Competition Dialogue was one such dialogue set up in 2004, following the initiative of the EU-China Summit in 2001. The EU-China Competition Dialogue is a permanent, institutionalized set-up based on an equal footing, with no legally binding obligations on either side. It is a dialogue exclusively between the EU and the Chinese competition authorities, and is built upon workshops and conferences attended by officials from the EU and the Chinese competition authorities. The content of these activities has so far remained focused on competition issues.[36]

Chinese officials have confirmed that the EU-China Competition Dialogue directly impacted the development of the AML.[37] The EU has been a protagonist in advocating the internationalization of its competition law norms worldwide.[38] Under the Competition Dialogue with China, the EU, with the facilitation of the European Commission Delegation in China, provided technical assistance

[36] *Terms of Reference of the EU-China Competition Dialogue*, available at: http://ec.europa.eu/competition/international/bilateral/cn2b_en.pdf.

[37] Francis Snyder, *The European Union and China: 1949–2008: Basic Documents and Commentary* (Hart Publishing, 2010) 807.

[38] Anestis S Papadopoulos, *The International Dimension of EU Competition Law and Policy* (Cambridge University Press, 2010) 264–65.

to China in its preparation of the AML. This was done through institutionalized communication and routinized conferences, workshops and meetings with Chinese government authorities. In communicating with China, the EU adopted a Chinese-oriented approach and tailored its own competition law normative framework to suit China's needs in the development of the AML.[39]

China began to favour the EU competition law model, partially due to the EU's systematic technical assistance and its China-oriented approach, as well as EU competition law's civil law influence and its reliance on public administrative enforcement, elements that are compatible with China's legal system and market regulatory framework. Consequently, the EU competition law model established itself as the main reference point for China in developing its own competition regulation model in the preparation stage.[40]

China and the US established diplomatic relations in 1979. In preparing for the AML bill, the State Council LAO circulated the draft bill to the US for comment. The US Antitrust authorities expressed concern over the draft circulated by the Chinese government and the American Bar Association (ABA) commented on the AML drafts in 2003 and 2005.[41] The ABA pointed out the ambiguities and the inconsistencies of the AML draft by comparing the draft with US and EU practice. It strongly welcomed the law's application to the abuse of public power that restricts competition and requested that the SOEs be expressly subject to the AML.[42] It further indicated that an independent enforcement agency under the direct control of the State Council would be helpful in order to achieve the optimal effect of the AML.[43] However, in comparison with China's communication with the EU, the US and China did not engage in institutionalized communication and cooperation before the enactment of the AML. China was reluctant to follow the US antitrust law model, partially because of the US antitrust law's common law influence and its reliance on private enforcement, which are difficult for China, given the nature of its market regulatory framework and its legal system.

In 2011, the US Department of Justice (DOJ) and Federal Trade Commission (FTC) signed an MOU on Antitrust and Antimonopoly Cooperation with China.[44] In terms of the framework of the MOU, a joint dialogue on antitrust and anti-monopoly issues is held at the senior official level between the US and

[39] Qianlan Wu, 'EU-China Competition Dialogue: A New Step in the Internationalisation of EU Competition Law?' (2012) 18(3) *European Law Journal* 461–77.

[40] Ibid.

[41] Joint comment on China's Anti-Monopoly Law Draft by the American Bar Association Section of Antitrust, Intellectual Property and International Law in 2005, available at: http://meetings.abanet.org/webupload/commupload/IC990000/newsletterpubs/abaprc2005fin.pdf.

[42] Ibid, 4.

[43] Ibid.

[44] Memorandum of Understanding on Antitrust and Antimonopoly Cooperation between the United States Department of Justice and Federal Trade Commission, on the One Hand, and the People's Republic of China National Development and Reform Commission, Ministry of Commerce, and State Administration for Industry and Commerce, on the Other Hand, available at www.justice.gov/atr/public/international/docs/273310a.pdf.

China once a year, with the venue alternating between the two countries. There is communication and cooperation between the antitrust agencies and the anti-monopoly agencies, including the exchange of information and cooperation in investigations.[45] Although China has chosen to converge with the EU competition law model in terms of the structure of the AML, Chinese officials are aware of the role played by US antitrust law in leading or shaping the economic underpinnings for competition laws globally. China has paid close attention to the US antitrust economic theories and procedural rules. The MOU sets out a formal institutional framework for China in communicating with the US on this aspect.

Communication with international actors at the multilateral and bilateral levels was an indispensable step taken by China in the development of its own competition regulation regime. During this process, it demonstrated an unprecedented and proactive effort in seeking comments from international actors in order to learn and absorb the knowledge and the technicalities of the law. However, China's attitude towards international competition law norms has remained instrumental and China-centred. The enactment of the AML in China was fundamentally influenced and shaped by the power relations in the domestic law-making process and the embeddedness of the market regulatory framework in China.

IV. ENACTMENT OF THE AML

Upon receiving the draft submitted by the State Council, the NPCSC spent another year conducting further research and consultation. The NPC Law Committee and the NPCSC Legislative Affairs Commission distributed the draft amongst the relevant state organs, local government institutions and research institutes for comment. It also conducted field research in order to gain feedback from industrial associations, enterprises and scholars. Based on the collective feedback as well as its own comments, the Commission produced a revised bill,[46] which was deliberated at the NPCSC three times. The first deliberation was presided over by the NPC Legislative Committee on 12 June 2007, which was attended by the NPC Financial and Economic Committee, the State Council LAO, MOFCOM and the SAIC as observers. It also included the deliberation presided over by the NPC Legislative Committee on 19 June to provide comment on the further revision of the revised bill based on the deliberation results of 12 June. The same procedure was repeated at the second round of deliberation which took place on 9 and 12 August and at the third deliberation on 24 and 26 August. As a result of these deliberations, the NPC Legislative Committee provided final comments on the revised AML before the AML bill was voted upon at the NPCSC.

[45] Ibid, 2.
[46] Ibid, 3.

In the practice of law making, the State Council and the NPC are in extensive consultation and coordination with each other, both during the stages of producing the bill and of deliberation. Furthermore, it should be noted that while members of the NPCSC are elected from the NPC, many are retired senior officials or ministers of the State Council ministries and commission, and have vested interests in promoting the interests of individual ministries in the course of their participation in the law-making process. Consequently, the deliberations shaped the outcome of the making of the AML.

First, the NPC Legislative Committee in its final comment strengthened the role of the State Council in terms of setting out the enforcement framework of the AML and in terms of handling relations between anti-monopoly authorities and sectoral regulators. In reaction to the feedback to strengthen the role of the State Council Anti-Monopoly Commission, the NPC Legislative Committee clarified that the Anti-Monopoly Commission acts as a coordinating institution with no capacity to make administrative decisions and that the enforcement of the AML will be undertaken by authorities appointed by the State Council.[47] Further, in the second deliberation, Article 56 of the AML bill provided that when restraints on competition occur in sectors, they should be subject to regulation by the sectoral regulators where the laws and regulations provided so. The sectoral regulators should report to the Anti-Monopoly Commission on their decisions. The NPC Legislative Committee decided to delete this article, as some NPCSC members indicated that the AML general principle provides that the AML authorities appointed by the State Council will regulate competition restraints on the market. The NPC Legislative Committee left it to the State Council to coordinate the relationship between the AML authorities and sectoral regulators.[48]

Second, the NPC Legislative Committee's revision of the AML focused on further developing the general principles of the AML bill. Article 4 was added to ensure that the state would make and enforce competition rules that were compatible with China's socialist market economy, strengthening and improving macro-adjustment and guaranteeing a unified, open, competitive and orderly market system. This was added because the NPCSC members, local government institutions and NPC deputies indicated that the AML should be based on China's reality and should serve the socialist market economy, and that it should be guided by the state's macro-adjustment, which coordinates industrial and competition policies.[49] Article 5 was added to ensure that business operators could form concentrations lawfully in order to expand their scale and improve competitiveness based on the principles of fair competition and voluntariness. This is mainly because China's industrial policies encourage Chinese enterprises to increase competitiveness and scale through mergers and acquisitions. Article 6 was

[47] Report on the Revision of the AML, 29 August 2007, Tenth Meeting, Twenty-Ninth Plenary Session of the NPCSC.

[48] Ibid.

[49] Report on the Revision of the AML 24 June 2007, Tenth Meeting of the NPCSC.

added to ensure that dominant business operators should not restrict or exclude competition by abusing their dominance, as this is consistent with international competition law norms. However, members of the NPCSC and NPC deputies argued that industries crucial to the national economy and national economic security should be protected for their lawful business activities. In the meantime, the state should strengthen its regulation of the pricing behaviour of business operators in these industries to protect consumers and promote technological development. Consequently, Article 7 was added to ensure that the industries which are dominated by SOEs and are crucial to the national economy and national economic security are protected by the state for their lawful activities.[50]

The deliberation further developed the AML by identifying loopholes and seeking creative solutions for thorny issues in the design of the law. For example, Article 33 of the bill, which covered the restraints on competition caused by the abuse of administrative power on the part of public authorities, was expanded to include behaviour that hinders the free movement of products amongst the regions of China. Furthermore, given China's market regulatory framework, how should anti-monopoly authorities handle the abuse of administrative power that restrains competition once such restraint is established? Article 51 was expanded to confer upon AML authorities the competence to make recommendations to public authorities superior to the authorities in question in terms of how to correct the abuse of administrative monopoly.[51]

With the conclusion of the deliberations, the AML bill in its final revised version was voted upon at the twenty-ninth plenary session of the Tenth NPCSC meeting, where 150 out of the 153 NPCSC members voted for the bill. The AML was enacted on 30 August 2007 and came into effect on 1 August 2008.[52]

V. THE ENACTED AML

A. Substance of the AML

The enacted AML is the first comprehensive legislation which aims to regulate competition in China and constitutes the cornerstone of the legal framework of China's competition regime. In this process, the emergence of the pluralized interests of market regulators in China, the characteristics of China's law-making process and its approach to communication with international competition law norms contributed to the outcome of the AML. The understanding of these

[50] Report on the Revision of the AML, 29 August 2007, Tenth Meeting, Twenty-Ninth Plenary Session of the NPCSC.
[51] Ibid.
[52] An, Jian (n 21) 3.

factors is important, if not crucial, in elucidating the origins of the design of the AML.

The AML contains the following sections:

- General Provision (Articles 1–12).
- Regulation on Anti-Competitive Agreements (Articles 13–16).
- Regulation on Abuse of Dominance (Articles 17–18).
- Regulation on Concentration (Articles 20–31).
- Regulation on Administrative Abuse (Articles 31–37).
- Investigation into Suspicious Monopolistic Conducts (Articles 38–45).
- Legal Liability (Articles 46–54).
- Supplementary Provisions (Articles 55–57).

Article 1 of the AML sets out its goals regarding the prevention and prohibition of monopolistic behaviour, the protection of fair competition, the improvement of market efficiency, the protection of consumer interests and public interests, and the promotion of the healthy development of China's socialist market economy.[53] The goals to be pursued are not necessarily compatible with each other and may conflict in the process of enforcement. However, the goals are not chosen on a random basis.

The goals show the law makers' efforts, on the one hand, to converge with the pluralistic international competition law norms and, on the other hand, to adjust the AML to pursue the public interest and promote the socialist market economy. Nevertheless, the diversity of the goals reveals China's awareness of the coexistence of restraints on competition that impair consumer benefits and undermine fairness in the market. It also reveals the difficulty for China, as a new competition law regime, in locating a systematic theoretical underpinning for the AML in the face of pluralistic legal norms. More importantly, the emphasis on the role of the AML in promoting the public interest and the healthy development of the socialist market economy reveals the compromises made by law makers in the process of producing the AML, which is marked by coordination among stakeholders in the drafting and deliberation stages.

In terms of the regulation of anti-competitive agreements, the AML mirrors Article 101 of the TFEU in substance but is also designed to promote China's developmental needs. First, the AML has borrowed legal terms and norms, extensively, from Article 101.1 of the TFEU. For example, the anti-competitive agreement is broadly defined to include agreements, decisions or other concerted actions that eliminate or restrict competition, which mirrors the language used by Article 101.1 word by word. Article 15 of the AML is an exemption clause which is similar to Article 101.3 of the TFEU.

However, the AML regulation on anti-competitive agreements provides broader and more fluid grounds for exemption. The AML exemption clause

[53] The General Provision of the AML.

provides more public policy grounds, including the protection of small and medium-sized enterprises, the protection of the environment, the protection of China's justifiable interests in international trade and international economic cooperation, and the alleviation of reduced production caused by the economic slump.[54] It further ensures that the agreement in question can be exempted on other grounds provided by law and other State Council regulations and rules.[55] The threshold for satisfying exemption is lowered. The AML guarantees that anti-competitive agreements can be exempted as long as the business operators can prove that it satisfies either the ground on justifiable interests in international trade or other grounds provided by other laws.[56] For grounds other than the two mentioned above, business operators are required to ensure, at the same time, that the agreement does not severely restrict competition in the related market and enables consumers to benefit from the agreement cumulatively.[57]

The AML regulation on the abuse of dominance mirrors Article 102 of the TFEU. Article 17 of the AML attempts to regulate the abuse of dominance, but not dominance per se. The AML regulates both exclusive and exploitative abuse of a dominant position, including predatory pricing, refusal to deal, tie-in sales, discriminatory pricing and other abuses defined by the competition authority.[58] Articles 18 and 19 of the AML emphasize that dominance should be established based on the analysis of the market share and other factors, and lists the threshold for the assumption of dominance based on the market share.[59]

The regulation of the abuse of dominance remains a sensitive field in China's market regulation due to the dominant roles played by the SOEs in the economy. Resulting from the coordination amongst anti-monopoly authorities and sectoral regulators in the process of creating the AML, a certain leeway is provided for dominant players. Article 19 of the AML ensures that dominant positions, based on market share analysis, can be treated as not dominant if the undertaking in question can prove otherwise.[60]

Furthermore, Article 7 was added to the general principles of the AML as a result of the NPCSC deliberation. It states that:

> With respect to the industries controlled by the state-owned economy and concerning the lifeline of the national economy and national security or the industries implementing exclusive operation and sales according to law, the state protects the lawful business operations conducted by the business operators therein. The state also lawfully regulates and controls their business operations and the prices of their commodities and services so as to safeguard the interests of consumers and promote technical progresses.

[54] Art 15.6 AML.
[55] Ibid, Art 15.7.
[56] Ibid, Art 15.
[57] Ibid, Art 15.
[58] Ibid, Art 17.
[59] Ibid, Art 19.
[60] Ibid.

The addition of Article 7 reveals the conflicts of interest between SOEs, regulators and anti-monopoly authorities, in the process of creating the AML. It shows that as a result of coordination during the deliberation stage, the law makers intended to protect the competition-restricting behaviour of the SOEs in the marketplace when the behaviour is backed by dominance conferred by the government based on other laws and regulations.

The regulation of concentration is provided by Articles 20–31 of the AML. The AML cross-referenced the ECMR in both substantive and procedural aspects. The term 'concentration' is used and defined as a merger, acquisition and joint venture.[61] With respect to substantive analysis, the AML cross-referenced the substantive analysis criteria of the ECMR and aims to examine the market power of undertakings to the merger, the market concentration ratio, the impact of the merger on market access and technological progress, the impact of the merger on the consumer and the impact of the merger on the national economy.[62] A notification system based on the threshold of the turnover of business operators involved, both on the Chinese and the global markets, is set up by the AML.[63]

The AML's regulation of administrative monopoly, namely the public restraint of competition on the Chinese market, shows its compliance with the WTO Trade Policy Review Recommendations in 2006 and the State Council's renewed efforts to tackle the long-term restraints on its market economy development. The regulation on administrative monopoly targets two kinds of public authorities within the Chinese administration system, namely the administrative organs and the organizations conferred with public administration functions provided by laws and rules.[64]

Both categories of public authorities are prohibited from abusing their power to conduct the following: to require working units or individuals to operate, purchase or use products provided by specific economic operators on the market;[65] to restrict the free movement of products on the Chinese market;[66] to restrict or prevent non-local economic operators from participating in local bidding by setting out discriminatory qualification requirements;[67] to restrict or prevent economic operators investing or setting up branches in the local market by setting out discriminatory treatment to local and non-local economic players;[68] and to require economic operators to engage in the economic activities prohibited by the AML.[69] Furthermore, government authorities are prohibited from setting out

[61] Ibid, Art 20.
[62] Ibid, Art 27.
[63] For discussion on the threshold for notification under China's merger control, see ch 7.
[64] Art 32 AML.
[65] Ibid.
[66] Ibid, Art 33.
[67] Ibid, Art 34.
[68] Ibid, Art 35.
[69] Ibid, Art 36.

legally binding rules which prevent or restrict competition.[70] Under the regulation of anti-competitive agreements, in terms of the AML, industrial associations are prohibited from organizing their members into anti-competitive agreements.[71]

Following the principles of administrative law in China, when the administrative organs or organizations are found to be guilty of administrative monopoly, in terms of the AML, the superior authority should set out an order for the organs in question to correct their behaviour. In this case, the anti-monopoly authorities can put forward recommendations to the superior authority on how to handle the case according to the law, as suggested in the NPCSC deliberation.[72]

B. Enforcement Framework of the AML

The AML provides public enforcement by its government administrative system and private enforcement by the Chinese court system. In its communication with international actors regarding the development of the AML, China has been well informed about the importance of the independence of the anti-monopoly authority. Chinese scholars have frequently urged the government to pay attention to the independence of the authority that is in charge of the AML enforcement.[73]

As shown in the process of creating the AML, MOFCOM, the SAIC and the NDRC were in competition during the drafting of the bill. As a result of coordination within the State Council organs during the preparation of the bill, MOFCOM and the SAIC proposed a two-tier public enforcement framework as a compromise. The two-tier public enforcement of the AML is as follows. At the top tier, the State Anti-Monopoly Commission is set up as an ad hoc institution under the State Council. Its competence includes setting out competition policy, organizing the investigation and evaluation of competition in the market and issuing competition evaluation reports, setting out anti-monopoly policies, coordinating the enforcement of anti-monopoly law and enforcing other competences conferred by the State Council. At the bottom tier, the NDRC enforces the AML against price-related restraints on competition, the SAIC enforces the AML against non-price-related anti-competitive agreements, and non-price-related abuses of dominance and non-price-related administrative monopoly, and MOFCOM enforces the AML against concentration.[74]

During the deliberation process, the NPCSC's suggestion that the State Council should decide on the public enforcement framework facilitated the legalization of the proposed enforcement framework under the AML. Consequently, Article 9

[70] Ibid, Art 37.

[71] Ibid, Art 16.

[72] Ibid, Art 51.

[73] Wang Xiaoye, *On Antitrust Law* (China Social Sciences Press, 2010) 412.

[74] State Council Regulation on the Antimonopoly Commission Working Methods, issued in September 2008.

of the AML guarantees that the enforcement of the AML is to be coordinated by the State Council Anti-Monopoly Commission and that the composition and detailed enforcement framework is to be decided by the State Council.[75] In September 2008, the State Council issued the Regulation on the Anti-Monopoly Commission Working Methods, which completes the legalization of the two-tier public enforcement framework proposed by MOFCOM and the SAIC.[76] Hence, instead of losing out regulatory competence to one individual authority, MOFCOM, the SAIC and the NDRC have their respective regulatory competences strengthened based on the AML.

In the process of creating the AML, the SPC was involved in the consultation and coordination process during both the drafting and deliberation stages of the AML. At the same time, it has been in close communication with the US government, the ABA, the EU-China Commerce Chamber, the China-Japan Commerce Chamber and the Competition Policy and Law Commission of the China-WTO Studies Association regarding the making of private enforcement rules of the AML.[77] Article 50 of the AML ensures that the business operator bears civil liability for the loss caused by its monopolistic behaviour.[78] On 30 January 2012, the SPC issued the legal Interpretation on the Rules of the Application of Law on Civil Dispute Cases Caused by Monopolistic Behaviour, which sets out the detailed regulation of the private enforcement of the AML.[79] Pursuant to the SPC interpretation, any party can file a suit on a civil dispute based on Article 50 of the AML to the relevant Chinese courts without filing a complaint on the restriction on competition at the anti-monopoly authorities as a prerequisite.[80] Furthermore, consistent with China's administrative law doctrines, Article 53 of the AML guarantees that the decisions of the anti-monopoly authorities are subject to both administrative review and judicial review.[81] However, given the technicality involved in the decisions on concentration, the AML ensures that the claimant should apply for administrative review of the decision prior to bringing action against the decision in the courts.[82]

In building up the enforcement framework for the AML, Chinese law makers have provided public and private enforcement parallel to each other, and have subjected the anti-monopoly authorities to administrative and judicial review. However, the public enforcement of the AML has been designed to preserve and strengthen the incumbent market regulatory framework.

[75] Art 9 AML.

[76] Ibid, 77.

[77] Kong Xiangjun, *The Supreme People's Court Legal Interpretation on Intellectual Property: Understanding and Application* (China Legal Publishing House, 2012) 264.

[78] Art 50 AML.

[79] SPC Interpretation on the Rules of the Application of Law on Civil Dispute Cases Caused by Monopolistic Behaviour, issued on 30 January 2012 and effected on 1 June 2012.

[80] Ibid, Arts 1–2.

[81] Art 53 AML.

[82] An, Jian (n 21) 113.

While the two-tier enforcement framework provides an answer to the power struggle amongst State Council organs, it poses new challenges to the enforcement of the AML in practice. The joint enforcement of the AML by the NDRC, the SAIC and MOFCOM means that the AML enforcement becomes segmented. Further, restraint on competition in the modern market economy has become increasingly complicated, which means that it may not necessarily be able to be differentiated merely in terms of its relevance to pricing. The risks and difficulties faced by the AML in enforcement expose the challenges faced by China as a new competition regulation regime when it attempts to adjust global competition norms to the national context.

VI. CONCLUSION

This chapter has reviewed the preparation and the making of the AML in China. It has shown that the embeddedness of the market regulatory framework in China, the law-making process and the approaches to communicating with international competition law norms have contributed to the outcome of the AML. Consequently, the substance of the AML shows China's efforts in adjusting international legal norms in order to promote its strategic goal. The enforcement structure of the AML shows China's efforts in building up a framework in order to be compatible with China's market regulatory system. However, as a result of adjusting to the national context, the enforcement of the AML faces continuous challenges in practice. Therefore, the manner in which China manages to institutionalize the enforcement of the AML after its enactment remains crucial.

Part III

Global Competition Law Norms and Local AML

6

Institutionalization of the AML Enforcement

I. INTRODUCTION

Part III of this volume examines the institutionalization of the enforcement of the AML and its connection to international competition law norms in enforcement. It aims to illustrate the entangled relationship between the proliferation of global competition rules and China's experience as a new competition law regime. This chapter examines the enforcement of the AML by the government administrative system and by the court system and judicial and administrative review of the AML. It shows that the anti-monopoly authorities capacity building, rationalising of enforcement structure and coordinated segmentation contribute to the institutionalization of the enforcement of the AML in the Chinese society.

II. PUBLIC ENFORCEMENT

Unlike other legal instruments used for market regulation, competition law has long been seen to be *sui generis*. Hence, the institutional setting of competition regulation requires the balance of principles such as independence and accountability, efficiency and the protection of rights, and transparency and confidentiality.[1] To protect the regulation of competition from the realities of politics, the competition authority should be independent. However, measures should be undertaken to safeguard the accountability of the institution in terms of its legitimacy. Efficiency is particularly important in competition regulation because a delay in regulation may result in high costs to business parties, consumers and the economy as a whole. However, the pursuit of administrative efficiency should not be achieved at the expense of the loss of rights of all parties involved, as well as the marginalization of due process. The regulation of competition should be

[1] Michael Trebilock and Edward Iacobucci, 'Designing Competition Law Institutions' (2002) 25(3) *World Competition* 361–94.

transparent at the highest possible level and should have the aim of improving the social awareness of competition regulation in society and increasing the deterrence effect of competition. The confidentiality of information should be given particular attention. As such, it is crucial for competition law enforcement to strike a balance between the instrumentality of competition law for market regulation and the rule of law.[2]

Consequently, the public enforcement of the AML in China faces two challenges. As a new competition regime, it requires the build up of its enforcement capacity systematically. Furthermore, given that the public enforcement of the AML is embedded within the Chinse government administrative system and that this system has been conferred with wide discretion in market regulation, China is under pressure to strike a balance between the instrumentality of the AML and the rule of law in order to safeguard the effectiveness of the enforcement of the AML.

In response to this pressure, from 2008 to 2012, the NDRC, the SAIC and MOFCOM engaged in continuous capacity building in terms of the enforcement of the AML. Furthermore, these three anti-monopoly authorities issued secondary rules with the aim of rationalizing the public enforcement of the AML and clarifying ambiguities. The NDRC issued the Rule on Monopolistic Pricing (Rule No 7) and the Rule on Investigation Procedure on Monopolistic Pricing (Rule No 8) on 29 December 2010 (both of which became effective on 1 February 2011).[3] The SAIC issued the Rule on Investigation Procedure Against the Administrative Power to Exclude or Restrict Competition and the Rule on Investigation Against the Anti-competitive Agreements and Abuse of Dominance (both of which became effective on 1 July 2009). It further issued the Rule on Prohibiting Anti-competitive Agreement, the Rule on Prohibiting the Abuse of Dominance and the Rule on Prohibiting Abuse of Administrative Power to Exclude or Restrict Competition (which became effective on 1 February 2012).[4] MOFCOM issued the MOFCOM Rule on Concentration Notification Threshold (which became effective on 3 August 2008), the Rule on Concentration Investigation (which became effective on 1 January 2009), the Rule on Concentration Notification Procedure (which became effective on 1 January 2009), the Interim Provisions on the Divestiture of Assets or Business in the Concentration of Business Operators (which became effective on 5 July 2009), the Interim Provision on the Evaluation of Concentration's Impact on Competition (which became effective on 5 September 2011) and the Interim Provision on Investigation of Business Operators Which Fail to Notify Concentration According to Law (which became effective on 1 February 2012).[5]

[2] Imelda Maher, 'The Rule of Law and Agency: The Case of Competition Policy', Chatham House International Economic Law Programme Working Paper, 2006, available at:www.chathamhouse.org/publications/papers/view/108207.

[3] NDRC secondary rules on enforcement of the AML: http://jjs.ndrc.gov.cn/fjgld/default.htm.

[4] SAIC secondary rules on enforcement of the AML: www.saic.gov.cn/fldyfbzdjz.

[5] MOFCOM secondary rules on concentration regulation: http://fldj.mofcom.gov.cn/article/c.

The development of the public enforcement of the AML from 2008 to 2012 reveals the efforts made by the anti-monopoly authorities in terms of capacity building with implied competition against each other. In the meantime, the authorities have engaged in coordination to clarify the regulatory competence, case admission, investigation and remedies in the enforcement of the AML through secondary laws.

A. Capacity Building

The NDRC, the SAIC and MOFCOM stand at the frontline of the enforcement of the AML. From 2008 to 2012, the three anti-monopoly authorities have engaged in continuous capacity building in terms of the enforcement of the AML.

In the NDRC, the Bureau of Price Supervision was expanded in 2008 and 2010, with one division regulating monopolist pricing and another regulating market supervision.[6] In 2011, the Price Supervision and Anti-Monopoly Bureau replaced the previous Bureau of Price Supervision and 20 more staff were recruited for the enforcement of the AML. The new Bureau is supported by nine divisions, including three new ones on monopolistic pricing behaviour in the service sector, on monopolistic pricing behaviour in the commodity sector and on researching and drafting the NDRC policy and secondary legislation, international cooperation and administrative monopoly.

In the SAIC, the department for fair trading—responsible for enforcing the Unfair Competition Law—has been transformed into the Department for Anti-Monopoly and Anti-Unfair Competition. The Department contains five divisions, namely: the Division of Enforcement; the Division of Legislation; the Division of Unfair Competition; the Division of Investigation Coordination; and the Division of Administration.

In MOFCOM, a new Anti-Monopoly Bureau was set up to handle concentration regulation soon after the AML was enacted. The Bureau consists of five divisions, namely: the Division of Administration; the Division of Competition Policy; the Division of Law; the Division of Economics, Negotiation and Coordination; and the Division of Supervision of Enforcement. Furthermore, the State Council Anti-Monopoly Commission is physically located in MOFCOM.

By 2012, a vertical enforcement system had been set up by the three authorities in order to enforce the AML nationwide. Article 10 of the AML guarantees that the anti-monopoly authorities, when necessary, can authorize the corresponding authorities within the government administrative system at the provincial level to take charge of the enforcement of the AML.[7] Hence, within the NDRC system, the NDRC oversees the regulation against price-related competition restraints

[6] Xu Kunlin, NDRC Director General, 'Past and Prospect of Anti Monopolistic Pricing' in *Report on Competition Policy and Law in China 2011* (Law Press China, 2011) 7.

[7] Art 10 AML.

nationwide, while the Provincial Governmental Development and Reform Departments (DRDs) and the Pricing Bureau, which is subordinate to the local DRD, are responsible for the investigation of price-related competition restraints within local jurisdictions. The NDRC maintains its regulatory power to investigate cases of national significance. Regarding cross-provincial cases, the NDRC appoints the relevant provincial DRD to handle the case.[8] However, it should be noted that contrary to Article 10 of the AML, the NDRC ensures that within local jurisdictions, the regulatory power can be further delegated to the DRD at the local city level.[9]

The SAIC is the mechanism of enforcement regarding non-price-related, anti-competitive agreements, non-price-related abuse of dominance and non-price-related administrative monopoly. The enforcement can be delegated to local Administration of Industry and Commerce when the restraint in question satisfies one of the three following scenarios: when the restraint happens within the jurisdiction of the local AIC; when the majority of the restraint happens within the jurisdiction of the local AIC; and when the restraint has a cross-provincial nature; or any other scenario when the SAIC sees fit to delegate.[10] However, the SAIC guarantees that it must investigate the restraint on its own when it deems it necessary to do so or when the restraint has a national impact.[11]

MOFCOM's concentration regulation has remained centralized, based on compulsory notification. However, from 2011, MOFCOM has started to seek assistance from the Department of Commerce of provincial governments, in order to investigate in local jurisdictions.[12]

B. Regulatory Competence

The first task faced by the AML public enforcement framework was to clarify regulatory competence among the three authorities. MOFCOM has been instituted as the sole authority to regulate concentration. The NDRC and the SAIC have clarified respective regulatory competences based, primarily, on price theory. With respect to the regulation of agreements and abuse of dominance, the NDRC rules regulate price-fixing agreements and list, in detail, the forms of price-fixing agreements that it aims to regulate.[13] The NDRC guarantees that dominant players are prohibited from abusing their market power through pricing behaviour,

[8] Art 3 NDRC Rule on Investigation Procedure on Monopolistic Pricing (Rule No 8), issued on 29 December 2010.

[9] Ibid, Art 4.

[10] Art 3 SAIC Rule on the Investigation of Anti-Competitive Agreements and Abuse of Dominance 2009.

[11] Ibid.

[12] Art 3 MOFCOM Interim Rule on Investigation on Merger Which Fails to Notify, issued on 30 December 2011.

[13] Art 7 NDRC Rule on Monopolistic Pricing.

such as selling products with unfairly higher or lower than cost prices,[14] exclusive sales through the means of price discounts, adding unreasonable fees in trading[15] and price discrimination.[16] The SAIC ensures that agreements falling under its regulation are those that restrict or fix output and sets out, in detail, the forms of output restriction that it aims to regulate.[17] It further regulates agreements that divide the geographical sales market and agreements that restrict research and development.[18] With respect to the abuse of dominance, the SAIC rule states that dominant players are prohibited from refusing to sell, restricting trading partners to trade, conducting tie-in sales without justifiable reasons and discriminating against trading partners in terms of the quantity of products, etc.[19]

With respect to the administrative monopoly, the NDRC guarantees that the government authorities and organizations are prohibited from abusing their administrative power to obstruct the free movement of products, including setting out discriminatory prices to products from other provinces, discriminatory cost items, discriminatory standards for fee setting, or engaging in other behaviour that sets out prices or fees to obstruct the free movement of products within China.[20] The government authorities and organizations are prohibited from forcing business operators to engage in monopolistic pricing behaviour.[21] They are also prohibited from setting out regulations to exclude or restrict competition.[22]

Echoing the NDRC rule, the SAIC states that government authorities and organizations are prohibited from abusing their power. However its regulation is more detailed, given the fact that the SAIC has been the main authority enforcing the regulations against a government administrative monopoly, based on the Unfair Competition Law since 1993. Apart from prohibiting authorities and public organizations from forcing businesses to engage in anti-competitive behaviour and from issuing rules to restrict or exclude competition, the SAIC sets out detailed rules to prohibit authorities and public organizations from using the administrative power to restrict purchase or trade, to delay or deny market entry, and to discriminate against business operators from outside the local jurisdiction.[23]

Further, the SAIC has extended its regulation against administrative monopoly to the business operators involved. Business operators are prohibited from entering into anti-competitive agreements or abuse of dominances on the grounds that such behaviour is based on administrative restrictions set out by public authorities or organizations with public administration functions; on the grounds that

[14] Ibid, Arts 11 and 12.
[15] Ibid, Art 15.
[16] Ibid, Art 16.
[17] Art 4 SAIC Rule on Prohibiting the Anticompetitive Agreement.
[18] Ibid, Arts 5 and 6.
[19] Arts 4–7 SAIC Rule on Prohibiting Abuse of Dominance.
[20] Art 20 NDRC Rule on Monopolistic Pricing.
[21] Ibid Art 21.
[22] Ibid, Art 22.
[23] Arts 3, 4 and 5 SAIC Rule on Prohibiting Abuse of Administrative Power to Exclude or Restrict Competition.

such behaviour is based on administrative decrees issued by public authorities or organizations with public administration functions.[24]

C. Case Admission

While MOFCOM sets out detailed rules on the notification of concentration, the NDRC and the SAIC have taken into consideration the possibility of duplicated regulation by setting out to examine whether the complaint has been filed with other authorities as a part of its scrutiny when admitting a case. This implies that a competition complaint admitted by one authority may pre-empt its admission by another authority.

The NDRC states that any individual and institution can file a complaint to the NDRC and the DRD at the provincial government level, and that the authorities are under obligation to comply with confidentiality requirements. The NDRC and the DRD scrutinize the complaint in terms of whether the same report has been made to the SAIC and AIC or the MOFCOM or whether a case relating to the same matter has been filed at the court, the complainant's background, the evidence provided by the complainant and other matters.[25] However, the NDRC has been unclear with respect to who has the final say on the admission of the complaint.

The SAIC guarantees that a case in relation to non-price-related monopolistic agreements or non-price-related abuse of dominance can be admitted through a complaint by any institution or individual to the SAIC and the AIC at the provincial government level. A case can also be admitted if it is referred by the superior government authority or transferred from other government authorities.[26] In relation to the complaints on non-price-related anti-competitive agreements and abuse of dominance, the SAIC should scrutinize the following: background information on the complaining party; information on the party complained against; facts on the alleged restriction of competition; relevant evidence; and whether the complaint has been filed with other authorities or whether a case relating to the same matter has been filed at the court.[27]

The provincial AIC is responsible for scrutinizing the complaint from within its own jurisdiction. The provincial AICs should report to the SAIC on a complaint that involves two or more jurisdictions. Unlike the NDRC, the SAIC decides whether or not to admit the complaint and whether to delegate the power of admission to the local AIC.[28] However, the SAIC rule has not set up a complaint mechanism with respect to its enforcement against a non-price-related administrative monopoly.

[24] Ibid, Art 5.

[25] Art 5 NDRC Rule on Investigation Procedure on Price-Related Monopolistic Behaviour.

[26] Art 4 SAIC Rule on Investigation Procedure on Non-Price-Related Monopolistic Agreement and Non-Price-Related Abuse of Dominance.

[27] Ibid, Art 5.

[28] Ibid, Art 8.

MOFCOM has set out compulsory notification requirements for mergers satisfying the revenue threshold.[29] However, it states that when applicants do not satisfy the revenue threshold for notification, the applicant can on a voluntary basis notify MOFCOM of the proposed concentration. MOFCOM should admit the notification when it deems it necessary to do so.[30] It states that a pre-notification consultation can be undertaken with the applicants to the proposed concentration, and that it and the applicants should submit a written application to request a pre-notification consultation. Upon notification, applicants are required to submit an application form, a statement on the impact of the concentration on competition in the relevant market, an agreement to the concentration and other related documents, an annual auditing report provided by an accountancy firm and other documents requested by MOFCOM.[31] Furthermore, MOFCOM has guaranteed that applicants can, on a voluntary basis, provide additional documents that can assist its investigation and decision making, such as the opinions of local government or other government authorities on the proposed concentration.[32] It scrutinizes the submitted documents and informs the applicant in writing about the admission of the notification on the day that it receives all the necessary documents.[33] It is bound by the principle of confidentiality in the pre-notification consultation and the notification process with respect to commercial secrets and other confidential information.[34]

D. Investigation

The NDRC and the SAIC rules have largely converged regarding the investigation in anti-monopoly cases. Both authorities guarantee that the NDRC, the local DRD, the SAIC and the local AICs have the competence to undertake the investigation. The investigation measures include on-site investigation, inquiry with the business operations in question or other related parties, the scrutinization and copying of the certificates, agreements, accountancy books, correspondence and electronic data held by the business operator and related parties, the sealing-up or withholding of relevant evidence and the investigation of the banking account of the business operator in question.[35] The authorities in both systems are required

[29] Art 3 Provisions of the State Council on Thresholds for Prior Notification of Concentrations of Undertakings, issued on 3 August 2008.

[30] Art 16 MOFCOM Rule on Concentration Notification Procedure.

[31] Ibid, Art 10.

[32] Ibid, Art 11.

[33] Ibid, Art 14.

[34] Ibid, Art 17.

[35] Art 6 NDRC Rule on Investigation Procedure on Monopolistic Pricing and Art 10 SAIC Rule on Investigation Procedure on Non-Price-Related Monopolistic Agreement and Non-Price-Related Abuse of Dominance.

to obtain the approval of the official in charge in written form in order to carry out the above-mentioned on-site investigation.[36]

The NDRC and the DRD can undertake an inquiry with the business operators in question and related parties in written form, through a meeting or over the phone. Regarding the latter two options, minutes should be made, read and signed by the party under investigation. Regarding the inquiry in written form, the authority should deliver to the party under investigation the outline of inquiry or the questionnaire.[37] However, the SAIC and the local AIC state that they can undertake the inquiry with the business operator or relevant parties in writing.[38] Although the SAIC provides that the parties under investigation have the right to express their opinions, the SAIC and the local AIC have the competence to scrutinize the facts, justifications and evidence put forward by the parties under investigation.[39]

With respect to investigation against concentration, MOFCOM investigations include the preliminary investigation of 30 days and further investigation stage of 90 days subject to a maximum extension of 60 days.[40] During the preliminary investigation stage, the applicants can make their statements in the form of a letter or a fax to MOFCOM.[41] MOFCOM can consult the opinions of other government authorities, industrial associations, business operators, consumers and individuals when necessary.[42] It has set out detailed rules on hearing, as one channel, to investigate the concentration in question. Upon its own initiative or requests by other parties, it can organize hearings to be attended by the applicants to the concentration and competitors, representatives of the enterprises in the upstream or market or other related enterprises, experts, representatives of industrial associations, representatives of relevant government authorities and representatives of consumers. It has not set out the obligation to rule over the hearing; instead, it states that following statements made by the parties to the hearing, it will conduct an inquiry into the participating parties. By the end of the preliminary investigation, it must decide whether or not to continue the investigation and inform the applicants about its decision in written form. The applicants can proceed with the concentration if MOFCOM decides not to continue with further investigations at this stage.[43]

During the further investigation stage, MOFCOM should inform the applicants of its opinions on the restraints on competition caused by the proposed

[36] Ibid.

[37] Art 7 MOFCOM Rule on Concentration Notification Procedure.

[38] Art 12 SAIC Rule on Investigation Procedure on Non-Price-Related Monopolistic Agreement and Non-Price-Related Abuse of Dominance.

[39] Ibid.

[40] Arts 25 and 26 AML.

[41] Art 5 MOFCOM Rule on Investigation of Concentration.

[42] Ibid, Art 6.

[43] Art 9 MOFCOM Rule on Investigation of Concentration.

concentration and should set out the timeframe for the applicants to provide a defence. If the applicants fail to provide a defence by the deadline, they are regarded as not opposing MOFCOM's opinions.[44]

MOFCOM will inform the applicants in writing of its decision on whether to clear their concentration application. For concentrations that are not cleared, the MOFCOM can decide to confer upon the applicants conditions in order to reduce the restraint of competition arising from concentration. During this process, the parties to the concentration can propose measures in order to reduce or eradicate the effects of eliminating or restricting competition. Both the MOFCOM and the applicants can propose suggestions and make comments on the commitment proposed by the applicants.[45]

Leniency programmes have been set up by the NDRC and the SAIC. The NDRC states that where business operators have reported to the NDRC or to the DRD relevant anti-competitive price-fixing agreements with strong evidence, the NDRC and the DRD can decide to reduce or waive the penalty on the whistleblower. As far as the first whistleblower is concerned, the penalty can be waived, while the second one can have its penalty reduced to be no less than 50 per cent of the original penalty and the rest can receive a reduction of no higher than a 50 per cent reduction.[46] The SAIC provides a similar leniency programme. However, with respect to business operators involved in non-price-related anti-competitive agreements, the SAIC states that it will waive the penalty given to the first whistleblower and will reduce the penalties given to other whistleblowers proportionally.[47] With respect to non-price-related abuse of dominance, it states that where the dominant player proactively ceases the abuse, it has the discretion to waive or reduce the penalty against the player.

E. Exemptions

The AML provides exemption clauses to enforcement of agreement, abuse of dominance and concentration. The exemption clauses have been further developed in terms of the substance and the procedures with the secondary rules issued by the anti-monopoly authorities.

With respect to regulation of agreements, Article 15 of the AML states that agreements can be exempted from the regulation as long as the parties to the agreement can prove that, first, the agreement in question would not significantly

[44] Ibid, Art 10.

[45] Ibid, Art 13.

[46] Art 14 NDRC Rule on Investigation Procedure on Monopolistic Pricing.

[47] Art 11 SAIC Rule on Investigation Procedure on Non-Price-Related Monopolistic Agreement and Non-Price-Related Abuse of Dominance.

restrict competition and would be to the benefit of consumers, and, second, that the agreement satisfies any one of the following seven, broadly defined conditions:

- the improvement of technology and the promotion of research and innovation;
- the improvement of product quality, cost reductions and increases in terms of efficiency;
- the setting up of standards and specifications for products;
- improvement in terms of the competitiveness and efficiency of small and medium-sized operators;
- the reduction of energy, the protection of the environment and the protection of matters in the public interest, such as disaster relief;
- mitigation of serious decrease in sales volume of obviously excessive production during by economic recession;
- any other conditions provided by other laws and regulations.[48]

Furthermore, parties can, without proving the insignificance of the impact of an agreement on competition and its benefits to consumers, have the agreement exempted from the regulation if they can prove that the agreement protects the justified interests in international trade or economic cooperation, or other conditions as set out by law and the State Council.[49]

It can be seen that the exemption clauses aim to provide ample space for China to achieve social equity goals, such as the promotion and development of small and medium-sized enterprises, and public policy goals, such the promotion of environmental protection.

Article 19 of the AML states that a business operator can be presumed to be dominant based on market share. However, where a business operator who has been presumed to have a dominant market position can otherwise prove that it does not have a dominant market position, then it shall not be determined as having a dominant market position.[50]

Based on Article 19 of the AML, the enforcement against the abuse of dominance develops its exemption clauses in two steps: the exemption to the establishment of dominance and the exemption to the abuse of dominance, based on justifiable reasons. The SAIC states that when dominance is established for a business operator, the business operator can prove to the contrary on the grounds that it does not control price, quantity or other transaction conditions, or that it does not have the ability to prevent other operators from entering

[48] Art 15.1–5 AML.
[49] Ibid, Art 15.6.
[50] Ibid, Art 19.

the relevant market.[51] Furthermore, the SAIC states that for operators who are alleged to have abuse their position of dominance, the business operator can have its abuse exempted based on justifiable reasons.[52] Such reasons include the following: if the other party in the trading has a significantly bad credit history or deteriorating performance on a continuous basis which may pose a high risk to the business; if the trading party is able to purchase the same product or an alternative product at a reasonable price from another business operator or is able to sell the product at a reasonable price to other business operators; if the business operators can prove the justifiability of their behaviour;[53] if the alleged abuse is to protect product quality and safety, to maintain brand image or improve services, or to significantly reduce costs, improve efficiency and allow consumers to benefit from it; and other behaviours that can be proven by the business operators to be justified.[54]

Article 28 of the AML states that when MOFCOM wishes to prohibit the proposed concentration, it may decide not to do so if the business operators concerned can prove that the concentration will cause a positive impact rather than a negative impact on competition, or that the concentration is in the public interest. This was reinforced by MOFCOM's Interim Rule on Evaluation of Concentration's Impact on Competition, which states that if the applicants can prove that the concentration has a more positive than a negative impact on competition or that it is compatible with public interest, MOFCOM can decide not to reject the concentration application.[55]

As far as the enforcement against administrative monopoly is concerned, the SAIC states that when the abuse of administrative power on the part of public authorities and organizations that restrict or exclude competition has been provided by other laws and regulations, the other laws and regulations apply.[56] In other words, the public restraint on competition can be exempted on the ground that the abuse is based on laws adopted prior to the AML.

The provision of Article 15 of the AML implies self-regulation by business operators in order to satisfy the threshold set out by the exemption clause. However, the anti-monopoly authorities have centralized the regulation on exemption clauses with secondary rules. Hence, both the NDRC and the SAIC have set out procedures to scrutinize the evidence provided by the business operator to support an application for exemption before granting the exemption.[57]

[51] Art 12 SAIC Rule on the Enforcement against Abuse of Dominance.
[52] Ibid, Art 13.
[53] Ibid.
[54] Ibid, Art 14.
[55] Art 13 MOFCOM Interim Rule on Evaluation of Impact on Competition by Concentration.
[56] Art 9 SAIC Rule on Prohibiting Abuse of Administrative Power to Exclude or Restrict Competition.
[57] Art 13 NDRC Rule on Monopolistic Pricing and Art 14 SAIC Rule on Non-Price-Related Anti-Competitive Agreements.

F. Remedies

Article 45 of the AML provides the basis for the anti-monopoly authorities to impose remedies. It provides that if the business operator(s) under investigation commit to take measures to remove restrictions of competition caused by its business behaviour within the timeframe permitted by the relevant anti-monopoly authority, the relevant anti-monopoly authority can decide to suspend investigation. The anti-monopoly authority's decision to suspend investigation should include the commitments made by business operator(s) and should be issued in the written form.

The anti-monopoly authorities bear the responsibility to supervise the enforcement of the remedies and can decide to terminate investigation if the business operators enforce the remedies. However, the anti-monopoly authority can decide to reopen the investigation if business operator(s) has not enforced the remedy committed, if the factual basis for the decision to suspend the investigation changes or if the decision to suspend the investigation was made on the basis of incomplete or fraudulent information.[58]

The AML provides that if an operator has not complied with an anti-monopoly authority's decision, it can be subject to a fine of 500,000 RMB.[59] It further states that applicants who foster unlawful concentrations can be subject to a fine of 500,000 RMB.[60]

However, secondary legislation has provided all three anti-monopoly authorities the competence to impose remedies on business operators. With respect to price-related anti-competitive agreements, the business operator in question can provide a commitment to the NDRC and the DRD within the timeframe set out by the authorities during the investigation. These commitments should include detailed measures to be undertaken to remove the effects of the behaviour that restricts competition.[61]

The NDRC closely supervises the business operators, who are under an obligation to report their enforcement of the remedies in written form. The NDRC can choose to suspend the investigation if the business operators enforce the committed remedies within the timeframe permitted by the NDRC. It can decide to reopen the investigation if the business operators fail to enforce the commitments within the set timeframe, if substantial changes have occurred to the factual basis for the suspension decision, or if the suspension decision was made based on incomplete or fraudulent information.[62]

With respect to the price-related administrative monopoly, the NDRC makes recommendations to the government authorities which are superior to the

[58] Art 45 AML.
[59] Arts 46 and 47 AML.
[60] Ibid, Art 48 AML.
[61] Art 16 NDRC Rule on Investigation Procedure on Monopolistic Pricing.
[62] Ibid, Arts 16–18.

authorities in question. It sets out detailed forms of recommendations, which include recommending the authority to stop forcing operators to engage in anti-competitive pricing behaviour, to repeal rules that restrict or prevent price competition, to impose disciplinary sanctions on government officials who are directly responsible for this or to make other recommendations.[63]

With respect to non-price-related anti-competitive agreements and the abuse of dominance by business operators, the SAIC will order that the operators cease their anti-competitive behaviour based on the agreement in question, confiscate the income generated by the agreement and impose a fine on business operators of no less than one per cent and no more than 10 per cent of the sales revenue of the preceding year.[64] It will impose a fine of no more than 500,000 RMB on industrial associations which organize members into anti-competitive agreements and can request the relevant government authority to revoke the registration of the association if the industrial association engages in serious anti-competitive restraints.[65] With respect to the administrative monopoly, the SAIC makes recommendations to government authorities that are superior to the authorities in question. However, it has failed to list the recommendations in detail.[66]

MOFCOM states that applicants to the concentration can propose a commitment to adjust the concentration plan, with the aim of removing or reducing the effect of restricting or excluding competition. These commitments include structural remedies, for example, divestiture of business or the capital of parties to the concentration; behavioural conditions such as opening up essential facilities and key technologies held by parties to the concentraion or ceasing exclusive agreements; and comprehensive conditions as in a combination of structural and behavioural conditions.[67] MOFCOM will supervise the applicants' enforcement of commitments and the applicants should report to the MOFCOM on the enforcement within a set timeframe. It can order the applicants to correct their behaviour when the applicants fail to enforce their remedies by setting out a set timeframe. For applicants that fail to correct their behaviour within a set timeframe, it can impose fine of up to 500,000 RMB on the applicants.[68]

Through capacity building and secondary rules, the anti-monopoly authorities have risen to become the main agents in China's competition regulation regime. The regulatory competence has been divided among the three authorities. The case admission procedure implies the pre-emption of the other two authorities once a complaint has been admitted by the other one. The investigation procedure has largely been converged and most importantly the authorities, in particular the

[63] Ibid, Art 19.

[64] Art 10 SAIC Rules on Anti-Competitive Non-Price-Related Agreements and Art 14 SAIC Rules on Abuse of Dominance.

[65] Art 10 SAIC Rules on Anti-Competitive Non-Price-Related Agreements and Art 14 SAIC Rules on Abuse of Dominance.

[66] Art 6 SAIC Rule on Non-Price-Related Administrative Monopoly.

[67] Art 11 MOFCOM Rule on Investigation of Concentration.

[68] Art 15 MOFCOM Rule on Investigation of Concentration and Art 48 AML.

NDRC and MOFCOM, have equipped themselves with various forms of remedy instruments. The attempts to rationalize the public enforcement framework contributes to the institutionalization of the enforcement of the AML practice in China. However, the rising enforcement framework continues to face the challenges brought about by the application of the technicality of the law in the complexity of China's market. Furthermore, the enforcement of the AML in practice touches every sector of the Chinese market system. Despite its rapid development, the public enforcement framework of the AML is embedded within the formal and informal constraints of market governance in China and contains inconsistencies and risks that may undermine the effectiveness of competition law.

G. Public Enforcement of the AML: Embeddedness and Challenges

The enforcement of the AML by the NDRC, the SAIC and MOFCOM reveals China's segmented market regulation practice. However, in practice, the public enforcement of the AML is coordinated amongst the three anti-monopoly authorities and within the framework of the State Council Anti-Monopoly Commission. The coordinated segmentation constitutes the main force which influences the AML public enforcement decisions and institutionalizes the administrative enforcement framework.

First, the State Council Commission is composed of 14 commissioners, representing key government authorities in charge of various aspects of market regulation. The commissioners include the director of the Commission, vice ministers from the NDRC, the Ministry of Industry and Information, the Ministry of Supervision, the Ministry of Finance, the Ministry of Transportation, MOFCOM, the SASAC, the SAIC, the State Bureau of Intellectual Property Protection, the State Council Legislative Affairs Office, the China Banking Supervision Commission, the China Securities Supervision Commission, the China Insurance Supervision Commission, the China Electricity Regulatory Commission, four deputy directors including the Minister of the NDRC, MOFCOM and the SAIC, the Deputy Secretary General of the State Council. While the State Council Anti-Monopoly Commission emphasizes that it does not replace individual government authorities in enforcing the AML,[69] it provides a de facto forum for the government authorities involved in the process to negotiate and coordinate on competition-related issues.

Hence, when the enforcement of the AML by the anti-monopoly authorities touches upon sectors of the Chinese economy, the anti-monopoly authorities are in communication and coordination with sectoral regulators listed in the Commission. The relationships between the anti-monopoly authorities and the sectoral regulators in the coordination have been ad hoc and have varied from

[69] State Council Anti-Monopoly Commission Detailed Rules on AML Enforcement.

case to case. In some cases, the sectoral regulator is better established than the anti-monopoly authorities; as a result, the sectoral regulator leads the investigation and decision-making process, and the anti-monopoly authorities participate in the process.

This can be observed in the enforcement of the AML by the SAIC against QQ.com and 360.cn. QQ.com is a popular webchat provider in China owned by the Tencent plc. By September 2012, QQ.com had 783.9 million registered users in China.[70] www.360.cn is an antivirus software provider owned by the company Qihoo with an annual revenue of $167.9 million in 2011.[71] In 2010, www.360.cn released a free antivirus software program to improve the security of QQ, the instant webchat tool provided by Tencent. In the face of the popular download of the software, Tencent responded by stopping the function of QQ on any computer that had downloaded the antivirus software. The SAIC received complaints accusing Tencent's of abusing its dominant position on the ground of refusing to trade.[72] Despite the controversy over the economic analysis of the market and the restraints on competition, the enforcement of the AML in the case helps to illustrate the relationship between the sectoral regulator and the anti-monopoly authorities.

In this case, it was the Ministry of Industry and Information Technology (MIIT), a member of the State Council Competition Commission, which led the investigation against the two companies. The SAIC participated in the process. The MITT is the sole regulator of the Internet sector and oversees the development of the Internet market in China. The investigation resulted in a decision issued by the MITT on 20 November 2010.[73] Pursuant to the MITT's decision, the MITT joined with other authorities, in this case the SAIC, to investigate the case. It attempted to find a resolution for the dispute with the aim of protecting the interests of consumers and market order. In its decision, QQ.com and www.360.cn were required to apologize to consumers and to ensure the coexistence and compatibility of the software provided by the two. The MITT would supervise the enforcement of the decision as far as the two companies are concerned.

The MITT directly regulates the Internet sector and plays an influential role in adjudicating over the disputes arising between business operators in the Internet sector. The SAIC's investigation into and decisions on business operators in the Internet sector, under the framework of the AML, requires the consultation and to a certain extent approval of the relevant sectoral regulator, namely the MITT. The SAIC joining forces with the MITT in this case benefits from the MITT's

[70] Tencent Financial Report in the Third Quarter 201, available at: www.tencent.com/zh-cn/content/at/2012/attachments/20121114.pdf.

[71] Qihoo Financial Report 2011 available at: http://ir.360.cn/phoenix.zhtml?c=243376&p=irol-newsArticle&id=1664125.

[72] Art 17 AML.

[73] MITT Decision on Tecent and Qihoo, available at: www.miit.gov.cn/n11293472/n11293862/n11376336/n11638290/13501758.html.

institutional resources from the MITT's role as the sectoral regulator in decision making and enforcement.

While the regulatory competence of the anti-monopoly authorities has been clarified by the secondary rules, the NDRC, the SAIC and MOFCOM are in regular communication with each other during the case admission, the investigation, the decision-making process and in the event of the imposition of remedies. Each authority has set up offices or staff to be in charge of the coordination. Decisions made by a single anti-monopoly authority have been submitted to review by the other two authorities and, if necessary, by the sectoral regulator of the State Council Anti-Monopoly Commission for comment and feedback.

Hence, the AML public enforcement is de facto led by the coordination among segmented market regulators under the umbrella of the State Council Anti-Monopoly Commission. This approach helps China as a new competition regime to avoid friction amongst the AML authorities and between the AML authorities and the sectoral regulators. However, the coordinated segmentation enforcement is embedded within the government administrative system. This framework, when used in the enforcement of the AML, can be vulnerable to the intervention by politics at high levels, may add an invisible enforcement cost to the AML authorities and undermine administrative efficiency, and can subject the enforcement of the AML to China's sectoral developmental goals, influenced by the power relations between the AML authorities and sectoral regulators.

As well as being constrained by the embeddedness of China's market regulation, the public enforcement of the AML faces challenges in terms of developing into an effective regime. The anti-monopoly authorities are conferred with a wide discretion and are subject to non-stringent accountability checks. The AML has not conferred upon anti-monopoly authorities the obligation to publicize all decisions; instead, it is the choice of the authorities as to which decisions they publicize.[74] MOFCOM's decisions to clear the concentration with commitments or to reject the concentration are published on its website in Chinese. The NDRC and the SAIC have so far revealed their decisions on the enforcement of the AML mainly in the form of news and on a selective basis. The discretion that authorities have regarding the publicizing of decisions means that business operators' access to information is not equally protected throughout the AML enforcement process.

Furthermore, inconsistency exists in the public enforcement framework. With respect to case admissions, though the NDRC and the SAIC have required the complaining party to indicate whether the complaint has been submitted to another anti-monopoly authority before the admission, neither of the authorities has explained clearly how the case admission will be handled should the complaint be duplicated. Before further rules are issued, this ambiguity implies that the final decision on case admission may be subject to informal coordination among the three authorities.

[74] Art 44 AML.

With respect to the remedy imposed by the anti-monopoly authorities, the development suggests that all three authorities can impose remedies. However, nneither the AML nor the secondary legislation have provided to subject the imposition of remedies to proportionality test so far. Further, MOFCOM has a consultation mechanism with the applicants to discuss the remedies before the final decision. Business operators accused of price-related competition restraints have fewer opportunities to have their voices heard than applicants to the concentration during the investigation. Regarding administrative monopoly, the NDRC provides recommendations in explicit form on how the government authorities in question should change their behaviour, while the SAIC makes recommendations in general. Further, the NDRC and MOFCOM bear the responsibility of supervising business operators in their compliance with remedies, while the SAIC provides no such administrative duties so far.

The rapid development of the public enforcement framework reveals the AML's reliance on administrative enforcement in China. In this process, the three anti-monopoly authorities have made efforts to rationalize the public enforcement framework on the frontline by developing secondary rules. However, public enforcement is subject to coordinated segmentation amongst government regulators, under the umbrella of the State Council Anti-Monopoly Commission. This shows that although China has embraced competition law as a modern legal instrument for market governance, the enforcement of this legal instrument remains a matter of China's own market regulation embeddedness.

III. PRIVATE ENFORCEMENT

In line with the development of the public enforcement of the AML, the AML's private enforcement has been developed by the SPC. Based on the AML (2007), the Contract Law (1999), the Civil Procedure Law (1991) and the Tort Law of China (2009), the SPC issued the legal interpretation on the Rules on the Application of Law on Civil Dispute Cases Caused by Monopolistic Behaviour, which became effective on 1 June 2012.[75] The SPC's legal interpretation sets out the main legal basis for the private enforcement of the AML.

Pursuant to the SPC's interpretation, civil disputes arising from the AML are broadly defined to include the following: disputes on damages caused by monopolistic behaviour; disputes arising from the legality of the content of contract; and disputes over articles of association of the industrial association based on the AML. Natural or legal persons and other institutions can file a civil suit to the SPC.[76]

[75] The SPC Legal Interpretation on the Application of Law on Civil Dispute Cases Caused by Monopolistic Behaviour, issued on 3 May 2012 and effected on 1 June 2012.

[76] Art 1 SPC Legal Interpretation.

Consequently, a party has three routes to access the court in order to resolve civil disputes arising from the AML. The first two routes are when the claimant files a suit directly with the court or files a suit after a decision has been made and effected by the anti-monopoly authorities in China.[77] The third route is when in a lawsuit not involving anti-monopoly issues, the defendant files a counterclaim against the claimant with evidence or files as a protest against the claimant on the ground that the latter has conducted monopolistic behaviour during the litigation process.[78]

The SPC's legal interpretation sets out different requirements for the burden of proof in civil disputes with respect to enforcement against anti-competitive agreements and against abuse of dominance. With respect to anti-competitive agreements, the defendant bears the burden to prove that the restraint on competition does not have the effect of excluding or restraining competition as provided by Article 13.1–5 of the AML.[79] Article 13.1–5 of the AML regulates horizontal anti-competitive agreements that fix prices, limit output, divide markets, restrict new technological developments and boycott transactions.[80] The SPC states that the horizontal agreements are hardcore restraints of competition. To levy the burden of proof on the claimant will confer an excessive burden on the claimant and will undermine the efficiency of the private enforcement by the court. Consequently, the court requires the claimant to prove that the defendant has enforced the agreement in question, and the defendant bears the burden of proving that the agreement has not excluded or restricted competition.[81]

With respect to the abuse of dominance, the claimant has the burden of proving that the defendant has a dominant position by delineating the relevant market and of proving that the defendant has abused its market power to restrict or exclude competition pursuant to Article 17 of the AML.[82] However, the SPC states that for SOEs or other business operators that have obtained dominance lawfully, the court can rule that the SOEs have dominance based on the analysis of the market structure and competition, unless the SOEs and the business operator can provide evidence to the contrary.[83] Furthermore, the defendant can prove that the abuse is justified during the litigation.[84]

With regard to the evidence, the claimant can rely on the information publicized by the defendant for evidence.[85] The parties to the dispute can apply to the court to invite expert witnesses and can apply to the court to appoint certain

[77] Ibid, Art 2.
[78] Ibid, Art 5.
[79] Ibid, Art 7.
[80] Art 13 AML.
[81] Kong Xiangjun, *The Supreme People's Court Legal Interpretation on Intellectual Property: Understanding and Application* (Beijing, China Legal Publishing House, 2012) 269.
[82] See above n 76, Art 8.
[83] See above n 76, Art 8.
[84] See above n 76, Art 9.
[85] See above n 76, Art 10.

institutions to undertake market investigation or produce economic analysis reports. The parties to the dispute can agree on the institution to be appointed, subject to the approval of the court. Where such agreement cannot be reached, an institution will be appointed by the court. The court maintains its competence to scrutinize the market investigation and the economics analysis report, pursuant to China's Civil Procedure Law and previous interpretations by the SPC.[86]

The SPC's interpretation states that the court should rule that the contract or the articles of industrial association are void once the contract or the articles of industrial association are established to have breached the AML;[87] is proven to impose civil liabilities on business operators who have caused damage to other parties due to their monopolistic behavior. The SPC's interpretation provides for tortious damages and applies the tort law principle of non-fault liability. In other words, in order to be awarded a remedy, the claimant is required to prove that the defendant has undertaken monopolistic behavior, that the claimant has suffered loss and that there is a causal relationship between the monopolistic behaviour and the loss. Given this background, the court can impose the liability of ceasing the monopolistic behaviour, as tortious behavior, or of compensation.[88]

From 2008 to the end of 2011, the Chinese courts admitted 61 anti-monopoly civil suits and ruled on 53 of them.[89] However, the main hurdle faced by private enforcement remains the burden of proof placed on the claimant. This is particularly the case in the enforcement against abuse of dominance, where the claimant faces the formidable task of market delineation and the establishment of dominance and abuse.

Although the private enforcement of the AML aims to handle civil disputes arising from the AML, the court recognizes that the claimant can file the lawsuit directly with the court without resorting to the competition authorities first.[90] Hence, consistent with international practice, the private enforcement of the AML exists in parallel to the public enforcement, but is not secondary to the public enforcement by the government administrative system.[91] Public and private enforcement has revealed a certain convergence. For example, public enforcement provides that the SOE, which is alleged to hold dominance on the marketplace has the opportunity to prove the contrary. The same technique is used in the private enforcement against SOEs in terms of abuse of dominance.[92] Whereas public enforcement provides the opportunity for the SOEs to justify their abuse of dominance, the same is provided by private enforcement, though the SOEs bear the burden of proving the justification.[93]

[86] Art 13, see above n 76.
[87] Art 15, see above n 76.
[88] Art 14, see above n 76.
[89] Kong Xiangjun, 261.
[90] Art 2, see above n 76.
[91] Kong Xiangjun, 266.
[92] See above n 76, Art 9.
[93] See above n 76, Art 8.

Parallel public and private enforcement means that both the government administrative system and the court system are put under pressure in terms of resources, knowledge and expertise. Furthermore, some competition restraints, such as anti-competitive concentration, which are below the notification threshold or which are cleared by the competition authorities upon conditions may still be challenged by the claimant through private enforcement. Given the unitary feature of China's market governance, Chinese authorities enforcing the AML have attempted to find innovative solutions to these challenges. One such initiative was taken by Yun Nan Provincial AIC and the provincial People's Higher Court, which set up a Joint Working Committee in August 2012. This Committee aims to set up joint meetings between the local AIC and the local courts, to exchange information, to set up a regular mechanism for the AIC and the courts to communicate, and to set up an institution for the AIC representative to attend court proceedings.[94]

IV. ADMINISTRATIVE AND JUDICIAL REVIEW

The AML provides administrative review and judicial review on the decisions by the anti-monopoly authorities to private parties.[95] Pursuant to the doctrines of the Chinese administrative law, administrative acts are divided into intangible administrative acts and tangible administrative acts.[96] Intangible administrative acts refer to legally binding administrative acts, which are generally applicable, such as laws, regulations and soft law government documents. Tangible administrative acts refer to acts directed at a specific purpose or a party in which the interest of one party is directly involved.[97]

With respect to tangible administrative acts, applicants can apply to the administrative institution—which is superior to the administrative institution responsible for issuing the tangible act—to review the act in question within 60 days of receiving an administrative decision.[98] The remedy is called administrative review. Administrative review may lead to the repeal or modification of the act in question. The applicant can challenge the act either directly before the court without turning to administrative review or after challenging the act unsuccessfully with an administrative review.[99]

With respect to the intangible administrative acts, the Chinese administrative law system has basically excluded these acts from both administrative and judicial

[94] News Release, *China Administration of Industry and Commerce Newspaper*, available at: http://www.saic.gov.cn/jgzf/fldyfbzljz/201210/t20121011_130114.html.

[95] Art 53 AML.

[96] Art 5 Administrative Review Law of China.

[97] Ibid.

[98] Art 6 Law for Administrative Review of China.

[99] Ibid, Art 8. However, applicants who turn to the courts for judicial review cannot apply for administrative review afterwards.

review. Intangible administrative acts can be indirectly reviewed by the superior administrative institution, by the NPC and its standing committee, and by the corresponding local People's Congresses.[100] Thus, it is difficult for legal or natural persons, including the anti-monopoly authority, to challenge intangible acts before the courts.[101]

Pursuant to the Law for Administrative Review of China, any natural or legal person who believes that their lawful rights and interests are impinged by the tangible administrative acts can apply for an administrative review of the acts in question within 60 days of the party being informed about the act.[102] The administrative review is free of charge, provides no requirement on applicant's standing, and makes legally binding decisions.[103] The review has to start within five days following the application and be completed within 60 days, which guarantees the efficiency of the remedy.[104] Furthermore, the superior administrative authority has the competence to impose an injunction upon the decision in question.[105] However, administrative review by superior authorities subjects the review to the substantial discretion of an authority which is closely linked with the one in question, and may therefore be flawed by corruption and protectionism.

Parties can bring the act directly to court or within 15 days of receiving the decision of the administrative review. With judicial review, parties can claim damage before the local courts and are guaranteed a strong enforcement mechanism.[106] However, compared with administrative review, judicial review is expensive and has the requirement of the admission of the case; namely, the burden is on the applicant to prove that he or she is the party whose interests are impaired by the act under challenge, that there exists a specific administrative institution to serve as the respondent to the challenge and that the review is within the court's jurisdiction.[107] Furthermore, the dependence of the local judiciary on the local government executive serves as another factor which affects the outcome of the judgment when a local interest is involved.[108]

Consequently, the decisions of anti-monopoly authorities can be challenged by private parties through administrative and/or judicial review provided that the private parties satisfy the relevant standings. However, whereas the public administrative authorities are proscribed from adopting regulations and rules containing anti-competitive content under the framework of the AML, private

[100] Ibid. However, this indirect review is in itself limited as constitutions for state ministries and local governments are excluded from the indirect review.

[101] Questions on the inconsistency between intangible administrative acts and general laws of China can only be submitted by the highest People's Courts to the State Council for interpretation. In other words, it is the State Council as the top-level administrative institution that makes the final ruling.

[102] Art 9 Administrative Review Law of China.

[103] Ibid, Arts 9, 31 and 39.

[104] Ibid, Art 31.

[105] Ibid, Art 21.

[106] Arts 65 and 67 Administrative Procedure Law of China.

[107] Ibid, Art 41.

[108] See ch 3.

parties would not be able to challenge these regulations and rules per se before the court, as they are intangible administrative acts.

Further, with respect to enforcement against administrative monopoly, anti-monopoly authorities only have the competence to make recommendations to authorities superior to the administrative authority in question. The recommendation has no legally binding effect. This makes it impossible for private parties to challenge the advice by anti-monopoly authorities through administrative or judicial review, as the advice does not constitute an administrative act.

In August 2008, one month after the AML became effective, four Chinese high-technology companies headed by Beijing Zhao Xing Information Technology Company filed an application to the Beijing Intermediate Court to challenge the decision by the General Administration of Quality Supervision Inspection and Quarantine of the PRC (AQSIQ) on the ground of the abuse of administrative power which prevented or restricted competition on the market.[109]

All four high-technology companies are engaged in the online anti-counterfeit product service business. They alleged that the AQSIQ had abused its administrative power and required enterprises to purchase the online product authenticity verification service provided by the CITIC information technology company (CITICITC), a company belonging to the CITIC as a state-owned investment business group.[110] The four companies, which are in competition against the CITICITC in the same business, alleged that the AQSIQ issued a notice in December 2007, which required that enterprises producing any of the 69 products listed in the notice must label their products with verification provided by the CITICIC. Without this, these products could not be allowed to be produced or sold on the market.[111]

It can be seen that the AQSIQ's decision and notice used administrative rules to require enterprises to undertake specific purchases. This breaches Article 32 of the AML. Hence, the challenge of the AQSIQ decision by the four companies created excitement in the Chinese public arena with regard to the AML's regulation against public restraints. Nevertheless, the Beijing Intermediate Court issued a ruling that the application would not be admitted, on the ground that the application had not been filed within the three-month time limit for judicial review of tangible administrative acts, as provided by the Chinese Administrative Litigation Law.[112]

The result of the case shows that whereas secondary legislation with respect to the regulation against the public restraint of competition is yet to be adopted, the Chinese court is reluctant to be involved in the scrutiny of public restraints on competition. However, the court's refusal to admit the case, based on the procedural ground of the application, somehow implies that applicants may have the

[109] http://news.p5w.net/gncj/200808/t1818892.htm.
[110] www.95001111.com/websiteserv/web/index.jsp.
[111] AQSIQ notice on the enforcement of strengthening product safety, issued in December 2007.
[112] Art 39 Chinese Administrative Litigation Law.

standing to challenge public restraint on competition should the applicants bring their challenge within the timeframe.

V. CONCLUSION

The AML consequently builds up its public and private enforcement in parallel to each other, which is consistent with the international practices of competition regulation. The anti-monopoly authorities have striven to build up their enforcement capacity and to rationalize the public enforcement framework. However, the functioning of the public enforcement has, to a large extent, been shaped by coordinated segmentation under the umbrella of the State Council Anti-Monopoly Commission. The rationalization and the coordinated segmentation of public enforcement are the two main factors that facilitate the institutionalization of the localized public enforcement of the AML. However, the enforcement of the AML is a demanding task for China, not only due to the technicality of the law and the demand for resources, but also because the law touches upon the fundamental rationale of China's market economy, which China has been in search of since 1978. It remains to be seen to what extent international competition law norms impact on the substance of the enforcement of the AML.

7

Global Competition Law Norms in the AML Enforcement

I. INTRODUCTION

In the context of globalization, China is faced with multiple challenges in terms of its market governance. The challenges include, but are not limited to how to increase the social welfare generated by the functioning of the economy and tackle the challenges brought by its continuous reforms, and how to ameliorate the fairness and equity in the market environment and maintain the leading role played by SOEs in China's strategic development. What complicates the situation is that China is forced to handle the challenges of conflicting interests at the same time.

Faced with pluralistic sources of competition law norms, the enforcement of the AML refers to leading competition law norms, including the pursuit of allocative efficiency, based on the economic analysis of the market and the market-access-oriented non-discrimination principle. China has referred to both norms in the substance of the enforcement of the AML. However, both the norms face challenges in serving as the guiding principles for China's AML enforcement, given the embeddedness of China's market governance and legal doctrines.

II. THE AML AND THE PURSUIT OF ALLOCATIVE EFFICIENCY

From 2008 to 2012, the NDRC, the SAIC and MOFCOM became visible anti-monopoly authorities in the global economy. Within the AML framework, the NDRC and the local DRDs have established themselves as aggressive anti-monopoly authorities by tackling a couple of high-profile investigations in relation to price-related competition restraints. The SAIC and the local AIC have dealt with 18 investigations in relation to non-price-related competition restraints. MOFCOM has received 474 concentration notifications, among which 457 were approved with no conditions, 16 were approved with commitments and one application was rejected.[1] The NDRC and the SAIC publish decisions on a selective basis and in the form of news releases with the aim of setting an example for future enforcement. MOFCOM has published 17 decisions on the conditional approval or rejection of concentration applications.

In terms of price-related agreements, the NDRC has published news releases on price-fixing agreements issued by the Paper Manufacturing Industrial Associations of Zhe Jiang Province, Fu Yang City in 2010,[2] price-fixing agreements between rice noodle manufacturers in the cities of Nan Ning and Liu Zhou of Guang Xi Province in 2010[3] and price-fixing agreements among six international LED monitor manufacturers in 2011.[4]

With respect to the abuse of dominance, the NDRC has publicized news releases on the abuse of dominance by Shang Dong Wei Fang Shun Tong Pharmaceutical Company and Shang Dong Hua Xing Pharmaceutical Trading Company in 2011,[5] the abuse of dominance by Wu Chang Salt Subsidiary Company of Hu Bei Provincial Salt Corporation,[6] and the abuse of dominance by China Telecom and China Unicom.[7] With respect to administrative monopoly, the SAIC published news releases on the Guang Dong local city government and the Global Positioning System (GPS) provider in 2012.[8]

With respect to concentration regulation, MOFCOM has published decisions on Coca Cola and Hui Yuan (18 March 2009), Inbev and Anheuser-Bush (18 November 2008), Mitsubishi Rayon and Lucite International (24 April 2009), General Motors and Delphi (28 September 2009), Pfizer and Wyeth (29 September 2009), Panasonic and Sanyo (30 October 2009), Novartis and Alcon (13 August 2010), Uralkali and Silvinit (2 June 2011), Alpha V and Savio (31 October 2011), GE and Shenhua JV (10 November 2011), Seagate and Samsung (Tiande-Henkel JV (9 February 2012), Western Digital and Hitachi (2 March 2012), Google/Motorola Mobility (19 May 2012), UTC and Goodrich (15 June 2012), Wal Mart and Newheight Holdings (13 August 2012) and ARM, Giesecke & Devrient andt Euronext NL (6 December 2012).[9]

Based on the publicized decisions of the anti-monopoly authorities, it can be seen that MOFCOM's decisions have increasingly shown a desire to conduct market delineation and the economic evaluation of market power and competition restraints. In comparison, the NDRC and the SAIC's enforcement against

[1] MOFCOM statistics on concentrations approved with no conditions: http://fldj.mofcom.gov.cn/article/zcfb/201211/20121108437868.shtml.

[2] http://jjs.ndrc.gov.cn/fjgld/t20120306_465488.htm.

[3] http://jjs.ndrc.gov.cn/fjgld/t20100331_338262.htm.

[4] http://jjs.ndrc.gov.cn/gzdt/t20130117_523203.htm.

[5] http://jjs.ndrc.gov.cn/fjgld/t20120306_465386.htm.

[6] http://jjs.ndrc.gov.cn/gzdt/t20101115_380421.htm.

[7] *Annual Report on China's Competition Law and Policy of China* (Law Press of China, 2012) 73.

[8] www.competitionlaw.cn/show.aspx?id=6047&cid=35.

[9] For MOFCOM decisions to reject or approve concentrations with conditions from 2009 to 2012 in Chinese, see http://fldj.mofcom.gov.cn/article/ztxx.

agreements, dominance and administrative monopolies show limited economic analysis of the market and competition, and its application remains more formal and legalistic.

A. Economic Analysis in the Enforcement of the AML

Part I of this volume argued that convergence between US antitrust law and EU competition law has generated soft law norms, which have influenced the development of competition law around the world. Among these norms, the most influential one is the pursuit of allocative efficiency leading to the maximization of consumer welfare by competition law. The economic analysis of competition serves as the main framework to achieve this goal and has developed under the influence of different schools of economic thought, with the Chicago School being the most influential.

Based on the development of US antitrust law and EU competition law, the framework of economic analysis of competition is based on two main steps: the definition of the relevant market and the assessment of market power. The definition of the relevant market refers to the definition of product and geographical markets for each player involved in the competition case, and serves as the prerequisite to the economic assessment of market power. The US and the EU experience reveal that the delineation of markets has been transformed from being based on simple product substitution towards systematic econometric analysis of price changes. In 1982, the US Merger Guideline proposed the *Small but Significant and Nontransitory Increase in Price* (SSNIP) test to be used to delineate the smallest possible antitrust market for assessing the market power held by the players in question.[10]

The 1997 US Merger Guideline states that the delineation of the market should include the product and geographical markets, both of which are to be carried out simultaneously and can be undertaken by demand or supply substitution. It provides that the competition authority should start with a narrowly defined product in the first instance and ask what would happen if a hypothetical monopoly of that product were to impose a small but significant and non-transitory increase in price. If the reduction in sales of the product would be large enough that the monopoly would not find it profitable to impose the price increase, then the next best substitute for the product is established. A successive repetition of the test should be continued until a group of products is identified which come within the monopoly, over which a small SSNIP test can be profitably imposed.[11]

[10] US Merger Guideline 1982.
[11] S 1.11 US Merger Guideline 1997.

In consideration of the reaction of buyers to the price increase, the US Competition Agency should consider all relevant evidence, including but not limited to the following:

- evidence that buyers have shifted or have considered shifting purchases between products in response to relative changes in price or other competitive variables;
- evidence that sellers base business decisions on the prospect of buyer substitution between products in response to relative changes in price or other competitive variables;
- the influence of downstream competition faced by buyers in their output markets; and
- the timing and costs involved in switching products.[12]

The US Merger Guideline adopted on 19 August 2010 downplayed the importance of market share and market definition in the evaluation of the constraints on competition caused by mergers. This signalled a more effects-oriented but less formalistic approach in undertaking the necessary economic analysis in merger control.

The EU officially proposed to use the SSNIP test by the issuing of the *Commission Notice on the definition of relevant market for the purposes of Community competition law*.[13] Pursuant to the Commission Notice, a relevant market can be delineated by demand substitution, supply substitution and potential competition. An SSNIP test is introduced as the main framework for the delineation.[14]

However, the Commission's proposition that the SSNIP test should be incorporated into EU competition law has been criticized for injecting new economic insights into a legal straitjacket, as the old-style market definition based on product characteristics, price and interchangeability is still upheld as the main tone of the notice. It remains unclear whether the supply-side substitution should serve as the criteria for the market definition. The potential competition is neglected at the stage of market definition, and products and geographical markets are delineated consecutively rather than simultaneously.[15]

The assessment of market power based on the delineation of markets can be undertaken by two approaches: the traditional approach examining market conditions and the econometric methods for directly assessing market power.[16] The discussion here focuses on the traditional approach, which includes the

[12] Ibid.

[13] OJ C372, 9 December 1997, 5–13.

[14] Art 15 Commission Notice.

[15] Roger Van den Bergh and Peter Camesasca, *European Competition Law and Economics: A Comparative Analysis* (Sweet & Maxwell, 2006) 125–31.

[16] The econometric technique used for market power assessment includes residual demand elasticities and logic demand models. See Massimo Motta, *Competition Policy: Theory and Practice* (Cambridge University Press, 2004) 124.

examination of, among other things, the market share of the player(s) in the case; the likelihood and ease of entry into the market (market entry barrier), and the buyer power on the market. It is subject to the discretion of the competition authorities as to the weight assigned to each factor in the assessment. However, both EU and US practice shows that whereas the market share derived from the sales of players on the market acts as the main screening device for competition regulation, sufficient analysis must be undertaken to examine the specific conditions of the market, including the market structure, entry barrier and buyer power.[17]

The economic analysis framework thus provides a common platform for competition regimes to communicate with and influence each other. With its extensive communication with international competition regimes, the AML has been well informed and updated on the economic analysis of competition employed in the competition laws of the US and the EU.

Whereas the press releases of the NDRC and the SAIC reveal limited information on delineating relevant product or geographical markets, the MOFCOM decisions have started to show the delineation of product and geographical markets since the case of Mitsubishi Rayon and Lucite in April 2009.[18] However, MOFCOM reveals limited information on the methods used in market definition. Based on this, the NDRC, the SAIC and MOFCOM have shown various degrees of economic analysis in their respective enforcement of the AML.

i. Agreements

With respect to regulation of agreement, the AML attempts to make unlawful, outright, horizontal agreements that fix price, restrict output or sales, allocate the sales market or the supply market, restrict the purchase of technology and equipment, restrict research and development, and boycott certain transactions.[19] It does the same for vertical agreements that fix the reselling price to the third party, amongst others.[20] Hence, the enforcement does not require the examination of the effect of the market power held by the agreements based on economic analysis of the market share, market entry barriers and buyer power in the case in question.

This can be observed in the NDRC's enforcement. The NDRC stated that the Paper Manufacturing Industrial Association in Fu Yang City, the Rice Noodle Manufactures in Nanning City and Liu Zhou City and the group of six LED monitor producers, including Samsung, LG and four producers from Taiwan,

[17] See ch 1.

[18] MOFCOM Decision on Concentration Proposal by Mistubishi Rayon and Lucite, issued on 24 April 2009, available at: http://fldj.mofcom.gov.cn/article/ztxx/200904/20090406198805.shtml.

[19] Art 13 AML.

[20] Ibid, Art 14.

have been caught by the AML, simply on the ground that these parties initiated and participated in price-fixing agreements.[21]

ii. Abuse of Dominance

With respect to the abuse of dominance, the AML states that market dominance refers to the power held by the player to control product price, quantity or transaction conditions, or the power to prevent other competitors from entering the market.[22] By using market share as a main criterion, it sets out that the threshold for market dominance is as follows: one operator is established to be dominant when it holds over half the market share in the relevant market; two operators hold collective dominance if they hold, jointly, over two-thirds of the market share of the relevant market; and three operators hold collective dominance if they hold, jointly, three-quarters of the market share of the relevant market.[23] Furthermore, the regulation requires anti-monopoly authorities to consider factors including the operators' control over distribution and the supply market, the operators' financial and technological capacity, other operators' reliance on the operator and how easy it is for other operators to enter the market.[24]

The NDRC has enforced the AML against the abuse of dominance on the part of private business operators and SOEs. In both instances, the NDRC has not engaged in economic analysis of competition, nor has it provided the operators with the opportunity to prove that they do not hold dominance. Instead, the NDRC established the dominance of the operators based on the fact that they were the sole operators in the market or that they were the monopolistic SOEs.

Two pharmaceutical companies based in Shang Dong Province signed exclusive sales contracts with the only two producers of promethazine hydrochloride, a key material for a medicine widely used for treating high blood pressure, with an annual consumption volume of 8–9 billion tablets in China. The NDRC established the dominance of the two pharmaceutical companies based on the fact that the companies were the only two agents selling the product in China. It found that without the permission of the two pharmaceutical companies, the two producers could not sell promethazine hydrochloride to third parties. The two pharmaceutical companies had subsequently increased the retail price of promethazine hydrochloride from less than 200 RMB per kg up to 1,350 RMB per kg. As a result, manufacturers of the high blood pressure medicine based on this raw material were forced to stop manufacturing by July 2011, which has caused disruption to the market in China. The NDRC ruled that that the two pharmaceutical companies

[21] Ibid (nn 2, 3 and 4).
[22] Art 17 AML.
[23] Ibid, Art 19.
[24] Ibid, Art 18.

had breached the AML because they have committed anti-competitive pricing behaviour based on their dominant position in the market.[25]

In the *Hubei Salt* case, the NDRC authorized the Hu Bei Provincial Government Development and Reform Commission Pricing Bureau to investigate the alleged tie-in sales by Hu Bei State Owned Salt Company Wu Chang Subsidiary in 2010. The local DRC established the dominance held by Wu Chang Salt Subsidiary on the ground that the salt industry was monopolized by state trading and that the Wu Chang Salt Subsidiary monopolized the trading of salt within Wu Chang area. The Wu Chang Salt Subsidiary forced wholesalers to purchase washing powder and other non-salt products along with salt, and the tie-in behaviour was found by the Hu Bei Provincial Pricing Bureau to be in breach of the AML.

In the China Telecom and China Unicom investigation, the NDRC launched a high-profile investigation against the pricing behaviour by China Telecom and Unicom in 2011. China Telecom and Unicom were the two SOEs that monopolized the provision of CDMA and WCDMA broadband in China. The NDRC established the two as dominant players based on the market shares criteria set out by the AML. China Telecom and China Unicom have charged different Internet service provider (ISP) fees to rival and non-rival broadband operators. The marginal squeeze behaviour of the two companies towards the operators in the downstream market was caught by the NDRC on the ground of charging an excessively high price as an abuse of dominance.[26] The NDRC's investigations reveal that it is motivated to handle high-profile players but it also catches lower layers whose dominance is self-evident, and uses pricing behaviour as the main criteria to evaluate competition restraints.

iii. Concentration Regulation

With respect to concentration regulation, Article 27 of the AML provides that the anti-monopoly authority, in examining the lawfulness of the notified concentration, should consider the following factors: the market share and power held by parties to the concentration; the market concentration ratio in the relevant market; the impact by the concentration on market entry and on technological progress; and the impact of concentration on consumers and other factors influencing competition which must be considered by the authority.[27] However, starting from the Novartis decision in 2010, MOFCOM's decisions show that in order to evaluate the restraints on competition in the proposed concentration, it considers the market share held by parties to the concentration, the market concentration ratio on the relevant market, the impact of concentration on market entry and technological improvement, the impact of concentration

[25] See n 5 above.
[26] Art 17 AML.
[27] Ibid, Art 27.

on consumers and other business operators, and the impact of concentration on national economic development. The MOFCOM practice reveals that in its decision making, it will take into consideration the public policy element in relation to China's economic development.

The State Council has issued a decree on the threshold for concentration notification, which states that it is obligatory for parties to notify MOFCOM of the concentration, based on their total annual turnover in China.[28] The decree provides that parties to the concentration must notify MOFCOM regarding the concentration when:

- the combined worldwide turnover of all the undertakings concerned in the preceding financial year is more than RMB 10 billion, and the nationwide turnover within China of each of at least two of the undertakings concerned in the preceding financial year is more than RMB 400 million; or
- the combined nationwide turnover within China of all the undertakings concerned in the preceding financial year is more than RMB 2 billion, and the nationwide turnover within China of each of at least two of the undertakings concerned in the preceding financial year is more than RMB 400 million.

In November 2009, the MOFCOM issued *rules on concentration notification*,[29] which provide further explanation as to the requirements for concentration notification procedure. It clarifies the calculation of the annual turnover of parties by stating that the annual turnover of each party to the concentration refers to the after net tax revenue for product and service sales by the party in the last financial year.[30] The revenue should include that of all operators controlled by the party to the concentration;[31] however, the calculation of turnover excludes the revenue generated from transactions between the party to the concentration and the operators controlled by the party.[32] Furthermore, it sets out clear requirements for the content of the notification, which requires the parties to provide detailed information on the transaction of the proposed concentration, the relevant market definition, the market share and power held by parties to the concentration, the main competitors and their market share, the market concentration level, market entry barriers, industrial information on the impact of the concentration on market structure, industrial development, technological development, the national economy, and consumers and other operators.[33]

[28] Decree of the State Council of the People's Republic of China, No 529. Available at: http://fldj.MOFCOM.gov.cn/aarticle/c/200903/20090306071501.html?2037849016=719177432.

[29] http://fldj.MOFCOM.gov.cn/aarticle/c/200911/20091106639149.html?91823032=719177432.

[30] Art 4 MOFCOM Rules on Concentration Notification.

[31] Ibid, Art 5.

[32] Ibid, Art 6.

[33] Ibid, Art 10.

The MOFCOM decisions show that it has often relied on statements submitted by parties to the concentration in determining market shares. The market share held by parties in the global market can be used as a reference to scrutinize the parties' market share on the Chinese market, such as in the case of Seagate and Samsung and of Western Digital and Hitachi.[34] MOFCOM recognizes and uses the HHI submitted by parties to the concentration, as in the case of Tiande and Henkel and of UTC and Goodwich.[35]

In examining the effect of concentration on competition, MOFCOM seems to consistently emphasize the effect of the concentration on future market entry, namely whether the proposed concentration will cause difficulty for new entrants to enter the post-concentration market; in other words, hindering or restricting competition. This can be observed in the Uralkali and Silvinit,[36] Alpha V and Savio,[37] GE and Shenhua JV[38] and Seagate and Samsung decisions.[39]

What should be noted is that MOFCOM has not differentiated its evaluation of the effect of concentration on competition in relation to horizontal, vertical and conglomerate mergers. Prevention of market entry by potential competitors continues to be the main criterion to be considered in MOFCOM's evaluation of the effect of concentration on competition. In the GE and Shenhua decision, MOFCOM indicated that Shenhua was the biggest coal provider in the upstream market and that the GE was the largest operator developing the coal water slurry (CWS) gasification technique in the downstream market. The concentration of GE and Shenhua would raise the highly technical entry barrier and would prevent new companies from entering the developing CWS gasification technique market.[40]

Similar approach can be observed in the MOFCOM decision on ARM, Giesecke & Devrient (G&D) and Euronext NL.[41] This decision involves the proposed

[34] MOFCOM decision to approve Seagate and Samsung concentration proposal with conditions, issued on 12 December 2011. Available at: http://fldj.mofcom.gov.cn/article/ztxx/201112/20111207874274.shtml.

[35] MOFCOM decision to approve concentration proposal with conditions on Tiande and Henkel, issued on 19 February 2012. Available at: http://fldj.mofcom.gov.cn/article/ztxx/201202/20120207960466.shtml; MOFCOM decision to approve UTC and Goodwich concentration proposal with conditions, issued on 15 June 2012. Available at: http://fldj.mofcom.gov.cn/article/ztxx/201206/20120608181083.shtml.

[36] MOFCOM decision to approve Uralkali and Silvinit concentration proposal with conditions, issued on 2 June 2011. Available at: http://fldj.mofcom.gov.cn/article/ztxx/201106/20110607583288.shtml.

[37] MOFCOM decision to approve Alpha V and Savio concentration proposal with conditions, issued on 31 October 2011. Available at: http://fldj.mofcom.gov.cn/article/ztxx/201111/20111107855585.shtml.

[38] MOFCOM decision to approve GE and Shenhua JV concentration proposal with conditions, issued on 10 November 2011. Available at: http://fldj.mofcom.gov.cn/article/ztxx/201111/20111107855595.shtml.

[39] See n 34 above.

[40] See n 38 above.

[41] MOFCOM decision to approve ARM, Giesecke & Devrient (G&D) and Euronext NL concentration Proposal with conditions, issued on 6 December 2012. Available at: http://fldj.mofcom.gov.cn/article/ztxx/201212/20121208469841.shtml.

concentration between ARM in the upstream market and G&D and Euronext in the downstream market for the promotion of Trusted Execution Environment (TEE), a data security solution that can provide an independent environment surrounding the operation system inside the processors. MOFCOM decided that the proposed concentration relied on TrustZone technology held by the ARM that has been a dominant player on the upper stream market. The ARM may discriminate against other TEE operators and prevent other competitors from entering the post concentrated downstream market. Consequently, MOFCOM failed to carry out any examination of efficiency gains against the loss of consumer surplus and total social welfare in vertical mergers.

Given the increasing interconnectedness of the world markets and the rise of China in the world economy, MOFCOM has become increasingly visible and assertive in concentration regulation. This can be observed in the decisions of Seagate and Samsung as well as in the decision of Western Digital and Hitachi. Seagate, Samsung, Western Digital and Hitachi are world-leading producers of hard disks. They filed multiple notifications to global competition authorities, including the US, the EU and China. While the US and the EU cleared the Seagate and Samsung concentration,[42] MOFCOM decided that the concentration was anti-competitive and imposed remedies. While the EU imposed remedies on Western Digital and Hitatchi, MOFCOM imposed further remedies.[43]

Seagate, as a global manufacturer and seller of hard disk drives (HDDs), proposed taking over the HDD business of Samsung. In examining the competition issues, MOFCOM decided that HDD constituted its own relevant market and could be subdivided into hard disk markets for enterprises, for personal use, for portable computers and for electronic products, and that the geographical market was the global market. The price of HDDs is largely impacted or shaped by the purchase mode of large computer manufacturers. With bilateral negotiations, the large computer manufacturers allocate their purchase orders proportionately between two and four HDD producers. In the bidding, which is only open to HDD producers, the most competitive tender from the HDD producers will obtain the largest order from the computer manufacturers. The purchase mode of the computer manufacturers, according to MOFCOM, is very important in terms of maintaining competition in the HDD market. Further, it ruled that the HDD market has high product homogeneity, high transparency and high technical entry barriers. More importantly, unlike computer manufacturers, who can transfer the price rise cost of HDDs to consumers, individual buyers of HDDs have relatively weaker buying power and are hit the hardest. This led to the position that the incumbent HDD producers had obvious influence on the price making of HDDs. The concentration between Seagate and Samsung, two HDD producers with a market share of 33 per cent and 10 per cent, respectively, would

[42] Decision C (2011) 7592 final in COMP/M.6214 Seagate/HDD Business of Samsung ('EU Seagate/Samsung Decisions').

[43] See n 34 above.

reduce the number of competitors in the market and strengthen the power held by the HDD producers. MOFCOM felt strongly on this, as China is one of the largest consuming countries for computers and HDDs. Following its investigation, MOFCOM found that HDD prices had risen up to 100 per cent due to the drought in Thailand, which would be eventually transferred to individual consumers. Based on this, it decided that the concentration would lead to coordination between Seagate and Samsung, which would restrict competition. It adopted a similar approach in examining competition issues relating to Western Digital and Hitachi and reached the same decision. It can be seen that MOFCOM scrutinizes the competition issues based on China's market in the global economy and no longer simply refers to the decisions of leading competition authorities for reference. To this end, its decisions show China's assertiveness in regulating concentration on the global market.

iv. Remedies

In China's AML regulation, the anti-monopoly authorities are frequent users of remedies, irrespective of the area of regulation. In the NDRC's investigation against price-related agreements, the six LED monitor producers made a commitment to the NDRC to strictly comply with Chinese law in order to maintain the market order and protect consumer benefits, to make their best efforts to supply on a fair basis to Chinese television manufacturers, to provide all customers with high-tech products on an equal basis and to extend the warranties on monitors to Chinese television manufacturers from 18 months to 36 months.[44]

The same attitude can be observed in MOFCOM's decisions. Since 2008, it has been willing to impose remedies on parties to concentration. In INBEV, the first decision published by the Ministry of Commerce, INBEV made commitments not to increase its incumbent shareholding in the Chinese State Owned Tsingtao Beer Ltd Co and the Chinese Zhujiang Beer Ltd Co, and not to acquire equity shares of Chinese Huaru Snow-white Beer Ltd Co and of Beijing Yanjing Beer Co Ltd.[45] In the following 15 decisions of conditional approval, the majority of the remedies imposed by MOFCOM were behavioural or a combination of behavioural and structural in nature.

Remedies in the Western Digital and Hitachi decision attracted international attention, as the MOFCOM decision on this differed from that of the EU.[46] While

[44] See n 4 above.

[45] MOFCOM decision to approve Inbev and ANHEUSER-BUSCH concentration proposal with conditions, issued on 18 November 2008. Available at: http://fldj. MOFCOM.gov.cn/aarticle/ztxx/200811/20081105899216.html.

[46] MOFCOM decision to approve Western Digital and Hitachi concentration proposal with conditions, issued on 2 March 2012. Available at: http://fldj.mofcom.gov.cn/article/ztxx/201203/20120307993758.shtml.

the EU imposed a divestiture remedy,[47] MOFCOM set out detailed behavioural and structural remedies for Western Digital, Hitachi and Vivitie (a wholly owned subsidiary of Hitachi), which were the parties to the concentration. Based on this, Vivitie has committed to remain an independent competitor with an independent legal personality and its own research and development capacity. Western Digital and Vivitie will build up a firewall to prevent them from exchanging information on competition, with the incumbent production line, they will decide output based on market demand and report to MOFCOM, they will not be able to change their business mode in substance and force clients to purchase their HDDs exclusively and they will continue to undertake research and development for innovation, while Western Digital has committed to divest the assets for 3.5 inch HDDs to the third party within six months after the issue of the decision. The commitment will last for two years and Western Digital can apply to MOFCOM to remove the first two commitments at the end of the two-year period. The intense behavioural remedies imposed on Vivtie and Western Digital by MOFCOM has raised questions on effectiveness and cost of monitoring, given that MOFCOM is a new concentration regulator. Nevertheless, the anti-monopoly authorities' keenness to impose remedies and, in particular, behavioural remedies shows that they do not hesitate in projecting themselves as a global regulator and dare to differ from leading competition authorities.

B. Enforcement of the AML and Pursuit of Allocative Efficiency: Challenges

Based on the foregoing, it can be seen that the AML is in the process of developing the economic analysis of competition by building up the steps of market delineation and the economic analysis of market power in the investigations. However, the authorities use market share as the main criteria to establish the market power of the player in question and evaluate the restraint on competition mainly in terms of its impact on market entry. In terms of the economic analysis of market power, the anti-monopoly authorities have adopted a simplified approach based primarily on classic price theory.

More importantly, given the lack of transparency of data and statistics on market development in China, and the high technicality and fast development of economic analysis of competition in leading competition regimes, the anti-monopoly authorities and the Chinese court system have found it an overwhelming task to undertake effective market delineation in China.

[47] 'Commission Clears Western Digital's Acquisition of Hitachi's Hard Disk Drive Business Subject to Conditions', press release, 23 November 2011. Available at: http://europa.eu/rapid/press-release_IP-11-1395_en.htm.

In May 2009, the State Council Anti-Monopoly Commission issued the Guideline on the Definition of Relevant Market, which is applicable to all anti-monopoly authorities.[48] The Guideline contains five parts, including general purposes (Chapter I), the foundation of the definition of the relevant market (Chapter II), the methods for the definition of the relevant market (Chapter III), the rationale of the methods (Chapter IV) and the practical questions (Chapter V).

The Guideline states that the definition of markets includes that of the product and geographical markets based on demand and supply substitution.[49] It further states that the definition of the relevant market refers to the delineation of the sphere for operators to compete against each other, and that it is important in terms of the AML's application to anti-competitive agreements, the abuse of dominance and concentration.[50]

The Guideline reveals its embrace of the core principles of economic analysis of competition law. First, it introduces the SSNIP test as the main instrument for market definition. Then it sets out that the delineation of product or geographical markets works with a hypothetical monopoly and aims to analyse whether the monopoly can manage to keep increasing the product's price in a small range (5–10 per cent) on a continuous basis (in one year). Consequently, if consumers switch to other products, which causes the reduction of the sales of the product in the test, but enables the monopolist to keep making a profit, then these other products are treated as being part of the same product market as the product in the test. When the monopolist's loss of sales cannot be covered by its profits, then the product is added to the product group as the next best substitutes. Successive iterations of the price increase test would be performed until a group of products is identified, so that a hypothetical monopolist controlling the group can impose a profitable SSNIP test over the group. Hence, a product market is delineated.[51] A similar method is provided for the delineation of the geographical market.[52]

Furthermore, the Guideline emphasizes that there is no single way to define the relevant market and requires the competition authorities to rely on economic analysis on the one hand and to consider factors influencing the behaviour of operators on the market on a flexible, case-by-case basis on the other hand.[53] By doing so, the anti-monopoly authorities are required to take into consideration factors specific to Chinese markets when undertaking the delineation task.

[48] The Guideline on the Definition of Relevant Market: www.gov.cn/zwhd/2009-07/07/content_1355288.htm.

[49] Ibid, Art 3.

[50] Ibid, Art 2.

[51] Ibid, Art 10.

[52] Ibid.

[53] Ibid, Art 7.

In terms of the definition of product markets based on demand substitutability, competition authorities should consider the following factors, amongst others:

- the evidence of consumers switching or considering switching to other products due to a price increase or other factors of competition;
- the appearance, function, quality and technical features of the product;
- price difference among products;
- sale and distribution of the product;
- other factors, including consumer preference, consumer reliance on the product, cost, obstacle and risk factors which prevent consumers from switching to substitutes to the product and price discrimination.[54]

In terms of the definition of the product market based on supply substitutability, competition authorities should take into consideration the following factors, including evidence of the supplier's reaction due to a price increase:

- the production process of other suppliers;
- the level of difficulty in switching to the production of other products, including cost, distribution and the competitiveness of a new product.[55]

In terms of the definition of the geographical market based on demand substitutability, competition authorities should take into consideration the following factors, amongst others:

- evidence of consumers switching to other products due to price-related or non-price-related factors;
- the cost and characteristics of the transportation of the product;
- the actual geographical area for consumption and the geographical distribution of suppliers;
- regional trade barriers, including tariffs, local rules, environmental protection requirements, technical elements, etc;
- other factors, for example, the special consumer preference in a particular geographical area and the quantity of products imported or exported from that geographical area.

In terms of defining the relevant geographical market based on supply substitutability, the Guideline states that the competition authority must take into consideration factors such as:

- evidence of reaction by suppliers in other areas to the price change of the product; and
- the possibility for operators in other areas to supply or sell the relevant product, including costs incurred when the order is transferred to non-local operators.

[54] Ibid, Art 8.

[55] Ibid.

Second, the Guideline is informed by the practice of US antitrust law and EU competition law, and has made an effort to avoid the imperfections exposed by the two practices. It sets out when demand substitution and supply substitution should be used as the criteria for the delineations. It also states that while demand substitution serves as the main criterion for market definition, supply substitution is relied on when it exerts a similar restraint on competition, among operators, as the demand substitution does. In particular, it states that supply substitution should be used as the main criteria when other suppliers face low investment costs to act as the alternative supplier and do so speedily.[56] Moreover, unlike the EU practice of delineating geographical markets based on the conventional notion of the homogeneity of competition conditions, the Guideline states that the methods used for delineating products and geographical markets are the same, in which factors such as consumer preference and transportation costs are taken into account.[57] Furthermore, taking into consideration the faultlines of the SSNIP test, exposed in the US and the EU competition case law, the Guideline provides that whereas the price used as the basis for the SSNIP test is the current price, under market competition, in abuse of dominance and concentration cases, when the current price obviously deviates from the competitive price, the competition authority should make relevant adjustments to select a more competitive price as the yardstick for the SSNIP test.[58] This has shown China's awareness of the *cellophane fallacy*[59] of the SSNIP test and its aim to avoid the fallacy in its own enforcement.

However, the Chinese Guideline on the definition of the relevant market has its limits in facilitating the AML to achieve the allocative efficiency. First, the SSNIP test proposed by the US Merger Guideline explicitly states that the test is based on the precondition of perfect competition, namely that price discrimination would not be profitable to the hypothetical monopolist.[60] Where the hypothetical monopolist can profit from price discrimination, the US Merger Guideline provides that a different form of analysis should apply to consider additional relevant product markets, consisting of a particular use or uses, by groups of buyers of the product.[61]

However, in the Chinese Guideline, price discrimination is only one element to be considered when the product market is delineated, based on demand substitution.[62] The Guideline has also not provided how price discrimination would affect the SSNIP test. This implies that the SSNIP test under the Chinese AML does not provide a separate set of rules for market definition, under the price

[56] Ibid, Art 6.
[57] Ibid, Art 9.
[58] Ibid, Art 11.
[59] *US v EL du Pont de Nemours & Co*, 351 US 377 (1956). In the case, the SSNIP test faces limits where it cannot identify if the current price is already a monopoly price resulting from market power.
[60] Section A, US Merger Guideline 1982.
[61] Ibid.
[62] Art 8 Guideline.

discrimination or imperfect competition condition, which may risk distorting the theoretical basis of the test and undermining the accuracy of the delineation.

Second, the Guideline has attempted to respond to the social embeddedness of Chinese market development in the delineation of relevant markets. For example, the Chinese domestic market remains largely disintegrated due to local protectionism on the part of local governments. Government distortions of the market, through regulations, rules and administrative acts, have become one of the main reasons for the foreclosure of the regional markets in China. Therefore, it is understandable that the Guideline has stressed the consideration of the regional trade barriers, including local government rules and regulatory measures, in the delineation of geographical markets based on demand substitution.

However, although the market element has been introduced to all sectors of the Chinese economy and the Chinese government has opened up markets in all sectors, particularly after it joined the WTO, the government has remained the dominant player in China's construction of a market economy. Government distortion of the market has occurred frequently, which has influenced the operation of players.

With respect to the delineation of product markets based on demand substitution, the Guideline requires the anti-monopoly authorities to consider evidence of consumers switching, price difference, sales and distribution, and other factors in relation to the business behaviour of players. However, it should be noted that in China's market governance with various degrees of marketization, government intervention in the market often influences the buyers' decisions. This can be seen when government forces the latter to make particular purchases, to intervene in the sale and distribution on the local market or to influence the price-setting of products by controlling the factors market or controlling the utilities market. This undoubtedly raises challenges to the application of SSNIP in the enforcement of the AML.

With respect to the delineation of the geographical market based on supply substitution, the Guideline has attempted to respond to the social embeddedness of market governance and requires anti-monopoly authorities to consider the trade barriers among different regions, which include tariffs, local rules, environmental protection factors and technological factors.[63] However, in the consideration of other factors, including the evidence of buyers switching, transportation costs and the distribution of suppliers, the Guideline has failed to address the government distortion of and influence on buyers switching to products in other areas. These distortions may include, for example, subsidies for the transportation and distribution of local products provided by local governments or industrial associations.

With respect to the delineation of product and geographical markets based on supply substitution, economic theories in particular, have required the

[63] Art 9 Guideline.

examination of the market entry barrier factor. This is because the failure to do so may cause a narrower definition of the market and pose more of a challenge for the competition authorities in terms of justifying why a firm with a considerable market share does not have a corresponding market power.[64] The Chinese Guideline has stated that in the delineation of the market, based on supply substitution factors including difficulty, cost and risk, the time spent in switching to other products should be considered.[65] This has to a certain extent required the de facto examination of the entry barrier factor. However, this requirement has focused on business behaviour-related entry barrier alone and has not addressed the entry barriers caused by local protectionism or local government distortion of the market, which constitutes an important part of the entry barriers in China.

The adoption of the Guideline on the definition of the relevant market in May 2009 marked the beginning of China's efforts to establish a framework for the assessment of competition based on economic analysis. However, there are potential problems for delineation as the guideline on market definition has failed to provide sufficient consideration of the embeddedness of market governance, in particular, the distortion, intervention and influence on the part of government authorities in the marketplace.

However, the AML has set out to pursue a diversity of goals at the same time. What the authorities have found most challenging in enforcing the AML is the pursuit of goals other than efficiency. In this scenario, price theory-based economic analysis faces limits when China attempts to utilize the AML to pursue macro-economic developmental goals. The NDRC and the SAIC's formal and legalistic enforcement reveals not only the difficulties involved in building up the economic analysis of markets in China, but also their cautious attitude in referring to international competition law norms to pursue the non-efficiency goals and their intention to search for alternative enforcement methods. To this end, it remains to be seen to what extent the principle of non-discrimination is referred to by the anti-monopoly authorities in their pursuit of macro-developmental goals.

III. THE AML AND NON-DISCRIMINATION

In the making process of the AML, the Chinese government was motivated to utilize the law to achieve fairness in its marketplace in order to push through deadlocked political reforms and to respond to the social outcry for fairness. Hence, the AML has provided to apply to SOEs with lawfully granted market power on the market and to restraints on competition caused by the abuse of

[64] Motta (n 16) 104.

[65] Arts 8 and 9 Guideline.

power held by the government authorities. However, the market access-oriented non-discrimination principle has not been built upon a well-developed conceptual framework in terms of its enforcement in competition regulation. Furthermore, in the anti-monopoly authorities' enforcement of the AML, as far as macro-developmental goals are concerned, the non-discrimination principle faces constraints resulting from Chinese legal doctrine and the embeddedness of China's market governance.

A. The AML and SOEs

SOEs as public enterprises is defined as a government-owned (more than 50 per cent) and controlled entity, which earns most of its revenue from the sale of goods and services, and is self-accounting and has a separate legal personality.[66] Public enterprises therefore often engage in natural monopolistic industries, although they are not restricted to this. Nevertheless, it has been argued that SOEs can have strong incentives to engage in anti-competitive activities, as their aim is to increase the scale and scope of their operations. In this situation, they can normally afford to set the selling price below cost, with the aim of squeezing competitors out of the sector, when profit making is not their priority concern.[67] Therefore, it has been advocated that public enterprises should be subject to competition regulation.[68]

Discussion on market governance reveals that Chinese SOEs have the main aim of pursuing economic return. Based on China's economic development strategy, the SOEs in key sectors are encouraged to expand their scales of size and business by developing into incorporated public listed companies or business groups. SOEs in China are granted monopolistic powers through laws and regulations in areas such as market access and price setting. The market environment consequently treats SOEs, FIEs and PDEs on a legitimate discriminatory basis.

In the China Telecom and China Unicom case, the NDRC has referred to the non-discrimination principle and ruled that the pricing behaviour by China Telecom and China Unicom was unlawful, as they had conducted price discrimination towards downstream business operators. In the Hu Bei Salt case, the Hu Bei Provincial Government Pricing Bureau found that the Wu Chang Salt Subsidiary had abused its state granted dominant position in the form of tie-in sales. In consolidating its decision, the NDRC and the local DRD referred to Article 7 of the AML, which states that operators in exclusive trading 'shall lawfully operate,

[66] John Wellis and Sunita Kikeri, 'Public Enterprise Reform: Privatization and the World Bank' (1989) 17(5) *World Development* 659–72.

[67] John R Lott, Jr, 'Predation by Public Enterprises' (1990) 43(2) *Journal of Public Economics* 237–51.

[68] David EM Sappington and J Gregory Sidak, 'Competition Law for State Owned Enterprises' (2003) 2 *Antitrust Law Journal* 479–524.

be honest and faithful, be strictly self-disciplined, accept social supervision, and shall not damage the interests of consumers by virtue of their dominant or exclusive positions'.[69] This implies that SOEs bear the responsibility of not engaging in monopolistic pricing behaviour based on Article 7 of the AML.

The NDRC ruled that the Wu Chang Salt Subsidiary committed tie-in sales, which are prohibited by Article 17 of the AML.[70] It ruled that China Telecom and China Unicom had committed price discrimination, which falls within the abuse of dominance prohibited by Article 16 of the NDRC Regulation against Monopolistic Pricing.[71] However, the NDRC did not scrutinize the legality of the dominant position held by the Wu Chang Salt Subsidiary and China Telecom and China Unicom in the decisions, and the dominant positions held by the latter remains unchallenged.

The application of the AML to the SOEs focuses on pricing-related behaviour that restricts competition, instead of examining the advantageous positions held by the SOEs in the Chinese market. This can be explained mainly by the economic law doctrine of the Chinese legal system and the embeddedness of China's market regulation.

China's construction of a market economy has seen the transformation of the relationship between the state, the law and the market. With the state retreating from direct control of the economy through planning, economic law has become an important instrument used by the state to facilitate the construction of the market economy that the state aims to build up. Economic law in a socialist legal system provides the regulation of private transactions from a public viewpoint and often bases its regulation upon ownership.[72] In other words, economic law provides different regulations for public and non-public-owned enterprises, and plays a significant role in controlling the functioning of the economy in socialist states. The role of economic law in China's market development is further defined by China's Constitution. Article 15 of the Constitution provides that the state should strengthen the making of economic law in order to improve the macro-adjustment of the economy, and that the state should prohibit any organization or individual from distorting the social and economic order.[73] While it remains unclear on the delineation of a social and economic order, it provides that the state-owned economy is the leading force of the national economy and that the state guarantees the consolidation and development of the state-owned economy.[74]

The AML is conceived as one economic law instrument within the Chinese legal system. Consequently, it has the rationale of facilitating the Chinese government to oversee the functioning of a socialist market economy, in

[69] See n 6 above.
[70] Art 17 AML.
[71] Art 16 NDRC Regulation against Monopolistic Pricing.
[72] Masanobu Kato, 'Civil and Economic Law in the People's Republic of China' (1982) 30(3) *American Journal of Comparative Law* 429.
[73] Art 15 Constitution.
[74] Ibid, Art 7.

which the state-owned sector plays a leading role. The AML therefore provides differentiated treatment to players of public ownership and players of non-public ownership on the market.

Against this background, Article 7 of the AML has been added into the AML as a result of deliberation by the NPCSC, as discussed in chapter 5. It provides that:

> With respect to the industries controlled by the state-owned economy and concerning the lifeline of the national economy and national security or the industries implementing exclusive operation and sales according to law, the state protects the lawful business operations conducted by the business operators therein. The state also lawfully regulates and controls their business operations and the prices of their commodities and services so as to safeguard the interests of consumers and promote technical progresses.
>
> The business operators as mentioned above shall lawfully operate, be honest and faithful, be strictly self-disciplined, accept social supervision, and shall not damage the interests of consumers by virtue of their dominant or exclusive positions.

The NPCSC's interpretation of the AML states that the lawful business behaviour of the SOEs in key sectors should be protected; however, the pricing behaviour of these SOEs restricting competition can be subject to regulation by the AML.[75]

The economic law rationale of the AML further explains the development of exemption clauses to the regulation on the abuse of dominance and concentration regulation under the AML framework. The exemption clauses to the establishment of dominance, to the abuse of dominance based on justified reasons and to the evaluation of restraint on competition in concentration regulation confirm that the authorities give priority to the safeguarding of public interests through the exemption clauses in the regulation of competition in China. The exemption clauses hence provide the best possible mechanism for the SOEs to be exempted from the enforcement against abuse of dominance and/or concentration.

The Chinese anti-monopoly authorities' reference to the non-discrimination principle against SOEs faces further constraints emanating from the embeddedness of China's market governance. As shown in the making process of the AML, ministries of the State Council have increasingly become strategic actors aiming to expand their respective regulatory power through law making. However, within the government administrative system, the government regulators have different statuses with subtle nuances.

Among the three anti-monopoly authorities, MOFCOM is an active regulator in communicating with international actors and thus is more visible in the international community. The SAIC, as a new ministerial level institution, has relatively less resources in enforcing its regulatory tasks. When the SOEs engage in anti-competitive behaviour in the marketplace, it is often backed by market power granted by State Council ministries in the form of laws and regulations, based

[75] An, Jian, *Interpretation of the Antimonopoly Law of the P.R.China* (Beijing, China Law Press, 2007) 152.

on the state economic development strategy. In comparison to the State Council sectoral regulators, the SAIC and MOFCOM occupy lower positions within the State Council administrative system and have no competence to scrutinize the competence of these sectoral regulators. Hence, MOFCOM and the SAIC have no competence to examine the legality of the power granted by the sectoral regulators. Consequently, regulation in this sphere often leads to joint investigation by the relevant State Council ministry as the sectoral regulator and the SAIC and MOFCOM as the anti-monopoly authority.

The NDRC acts as the main agent controlling marketization in China, and is superior to government authorities within the State Council administrative system. Apart from setting out the sectoral development catalogue and industrial policies, it has the competence to decide upon investment projects outside these spheres when these projects have a significant impact on society, when they are restricted by industrial policies, when they are beneficial to economic and social development where relevant regulars cannot reach a consensus on approval, or when required by the State Council.[76] Given its status within the State Council administrative system, the NDRC is able to handle a couple of high-profile investigations against SOEs, as discussed above. However, its investigations are restricted to price-related restraints of competition on the part of SOEs.

Therefore, the economic law rationale of the Chinese legal system serves as the legal doctrine that restricts the application of the non-discrimination principle in the enforcement of the AML against the SOEs. The market regulation embeddedness and, in particular, the status held by the NDRC within the State Council administrative system explains why the application of the AML against SOEs focuses primarily on the pricing behaviour of SOEs.

B. The AML and Administrative Monopolies

The AML, in line with the WTO trade policy review recommendation for China, explicitly attempts to tackle the abuse of administrative power on the part of public authorities which would restrict or prohibit competition in the market.[77]

The AML's provision on administrative monopoly regulates the public administrative authority or the authority conferred with competence for public administration from restricting or preventing competition by abusing their power. To this end, public authorities are prevented from engaging in three categories of anti-competitive behaviour: first, public authorities are proscribed from intervening in the daily operation of business operators and, in particular, requiring operators to purchase from particular product providers or requiring operators

[76] NDRC Rules on Changing and Improving the Approval Procedure for Investment Project, 2005.
[77] Chapter V AML.

to engage in anti-competitive activities regulated by the AML;[78] second, public authorities are proscribed from adopting rules which contain anti-competitive content;[79] and, third, public authorities should not abuse their power to cause discriminatory treatment to local business operators which would prevent the free movement of products, services and establishments on the Chinese national market.[80] Hence, the AML refers explicitly to the non-discrimination principle to regulate administrative monopoly.

In the case of the AML's regulation against the abuse of public administrative power, the AML states that the anti-monopoly authorities have the competence to investigate anti-competitive behaviour in the market.[81] However, when the public authorities are found to have abused their power and to have restricted and prohibited competition on the market, the anti-monopoly authorities do not have the power to issue legally binding decisions on the abuse. It is the superior public administrative authorities that are responsible for overseeing that the abuse is corrected, while the anti-monopoly authorities have the competence to provide suggestions to the superior administrative authority on the action to be taken.[82] Consequently, even if one public authority is found to be in breach of the AML, it is not subject to direct regulation by the anti-monopoly authorities, but to political negotiation and coordination between the anti-monopoly authorities and the superior authority.

The inclusion of the regulation of abuse by public authorities has been applauded by the international community.[83] As shown earlier in the volume, government distortion of the market has been one unfailing, if not more serious, source of the restriction on competition on the market. However, the anti-monopoly authorities have released limited information on the enforcement of the AML against the administrative monopoly. So far, the SAIC has released one investigation against the abuse of administrative power by a local government in restricting competition in the local market, namely the case of the Guang Dong Province local government and a GPS provider in 2011.[84]

In January 2011, the city government of Guang Dong Province set out a policy document with the aim of promoting the use of GPS systems in the transportation administration in the city. The policy required that the GPS system provided by the Xin Shi Kong GPS Science and Technology Company would be used as the city's GPS system provider. The GPS providers in the city were required to upload their user information to Xin Shi Kong and these users were obliged to pay up to 30 RMB a month in order to connect to Xin Shi Kong's GPS system. The requirement was

[78] Ibid, Arts 32 and 36.
[79] Ibid, Art 37.
[80] Ibid, Art 33–35.
[81] Ibid, Art 38.
[82] Ibid, Art 51.
[83] Eleanor Fox, 'An Anti-Monopoly Law for China: Scaling the Walls of Protectionist Government Restraints' (2008) 74 *Antitrust Law Journal* 173–194.
[84] See n 8 above.

written into the minutes of the government meeting and was distributed to other relevant government authorities for enforcement. In 2011, three automobile GPS providers in the city complained to the Guang Dong Provincial Administration of Industry and Commerce about the abuse of administrative power on the part of the local government.

The local AIC undertook an investigation into the complaint. It first identified whether the business operator in question bore the public administration function and whether its business behaviour was based on the need for public administration. After ruling that Xin Shi Kong had no public administration function, the local AIC then moved on to analyse whether the behaviour of the local government had caused the effect of restricting competition. To this end, the local AIC focused on analysing the impact of government behaviour on the freedom of business providers in the market. It concluded that the local government had restricted the freedom of business providers and distorted the market order in China. It submitted its investigation report to the SAIC for approval, which was granted. With the support of the SAIC, the Guang Dong Provincial AIC made recommendations to the Guang Dong Provincial Government on how to bring the behaviour of the local government into line with the AML. Based on the recommendations, the Guang Dong Provincial Government Legislative Affairs Office decided that the local government policy is a tangible administrative act, that the act is inconsistent with Articles 8 and 32 of the AML, and that it should be revoked. The local government has since revoked its policy. The case shows that the anti-monopoly authorities are not hesitant in using the law to tackle an administrative monopoly when necessary. However, what should be noted is that the company involved in the case was not an SOE and possessed no public administration functions. Hence, the company held no advantages granted by other laws and regulations, which made the investigations undertaken by the local AIC and the SAIC more straightforward.

Nevertheless, the AML's regulation of other forms of administrative monopoly, for example government's rules with anti-competitive content and government's discriminatory treatment to business operators on the market, continues to face challenges in their enforcement.

First, the AML states that its regulation on public restraint does not prevail over the regulation on the abuse of administrative power, which was adopted prior to its own adoption.[85] This means that where the public restraints on competition have already been regulated by other government administrative agencies, the AML does not have the competence to regulate. This also restricts the application of the AML with respect to administrative abuse.

Second, the anti-monopoly authorities face challenges in enforcing the AML based merely on the non-discrimination principle when this principle is not supported by a developed conceptual framework for enforcement. This is

[85] Art 51 AML.

particularly the case when the authorities enforce the AML against the government's discriminatory treatment of business operators motivated by the protection of local business operators. Whereas the anti-monopoly authorities have not revealed information on their enforcement in this respect, they have shown a cautious attitude in handling administrative monopolies based on local protection.

Furthermore, Chinese legal doctrines have set out restrictions for the AML to directly scrutinize the content of government rules in terms of their compatibility with the AML. The government rules of general application fall within the category of intangible administrative acts. As discussed in the previous chapter, the tangible administrative act is not subject to judicial review. The interpretation of tangible administrative acts set out by the government administrative system falls within the competence of the LAO of the State Council.[86] The State Council organs and local governments can submit the request to the State Council for the interpretation of regulations and rules set out by the government administrative system as intangible administrative acts.[87] It further sets out that for questions arising from the application of regulations and rules as such, the State Council LAO can reply directly or should obtain the approval of the State Council based on its recommendations when significant issues are involved.[88] The State Council's legal interpretations of its own regulations and rules bear equal legally binding effect as the State Council regulations and rules do.[89] The State Council internal review of the central government authorities' and local governments' intangible acts means that the compatibility of government regulations and rules' content with the AML is subject to scrutiny by the State Council rather than by the anti-monopoly authorities.

Based on the foregoing, it can be seen that the AML has referred to the principle of non-discrimination in its pursuit of fair competition in enforcement. However, the AML's regulation of SOEs is restricted by the economic law doctrines of the Chinese legal system and by the embeddedness of Chinese market regulation. Consequently, its enforcement against the SOEs is restricted to the monopolistic pricing behaviour of the SOEs enforced by the NDRC. In addition, its regulation against administrative monopoly is restricted by the administrative law doctrines of the Chinese legal system and the lack of a conceptual framework of the non-discrimination principle in enforcement. Consequently, ita enforcement faces challenges in tackling government rules with anti-competitive content and discriminatory government rules backed by local protection. As a result, the non-discrimination principle, which aims to increase market access in the Chinese market, faces limits to achieve its purpose in lifting market access in the state controlled markets.

[86] Art 31 Regulation on the Procedures for Administrative Regulation Making, issued by the State Council on 16 November 2001 and effected on 1 January 2002.

[87] Ibid, Art 32.

[88] Ibid, Art 33.

[89] Ibid, Art 31.

The experience that China has had in enforcing the AML from 2008 to 2012 shows that as a new competition regime, it has set its AML to pursue both efficiency and non-efficiency goals in terms of its own development. The pursuit of allocative efficiency and the maximization of consumer benefits are based on neo-classical micro-economic price theory. In the construction of its own market economy, China is looking for ways to adjust the economic analysis framework in order to be conducive to the context of its market economy construction. In the meantime, the price theory-based economic analysis increasingly faces its limits and cannot be overstretched to serve as the methodology used by China to pursue non-efficiency goals in the enforcement of the AML. However, as revealed by China's experience, the non-discrimination principle, as another influential international competition law norm, has not provided China with an effective normative framework to pursue its non-efficiency goals in the enforcement of the AML.

The enforcement of competition regulation based on classic price theory aims to pursue the maximization of the social welfare of the economy based on economic analysis of the market. The enforcement of competition regulation based on the non-discrimination principle aims to improve the macro-economic environment, which is, in turn, conducive to generating the welfare of the economy. Hence, it can be argued that the two competition law norms aim to lead to the development of the economy from different directions. However, China's experience confirms that there is a theoretical and empirical gap between the two norms when China, as a new competition regime, aims to pursue efficiency and non-efficiency-related goals at the same time. The gap consequently confers upon the new competition regulation regimes the challenge of searching for a conceptual framework to support its pursuit of multiple goals.

What should be noted is that while faced with the constraints resulting from the gap between the international competition law norms, China has not stopped searching and developing its own conceptual framework for the enforcement of the AML. The above analysis shows that in relation to this enforcement, MOFCOM undertakes a more economic analysis-based approach, while the NDRC and the SAIC undertake a relatively formal and legalistic approach. The result can again be explained by the difficulties that China has had in developing its own conceptual framework for the AML. However, it should be indicated that the NDRC, the SAIC and MOFCOM have engaged in active communication with international organizations and corresponding competition authorities, and that the authorities are well informed with regard to leading international competition law norms. The different approaches taken by the anti-monopoly authorities show the cautious attitude of the NDRC and the SAIC when enforcing the AML to achieve non-efficiency goals and the authorities' intention to search for alternative enforcement methods. Consequently, while building up its own normative framework, China applies a dual-track enforcement of its AML to pursue different goals at the same time. In other words, it is searching for its own conceptual framework to enable the AML to pursue efficiency and non-efficiency goals within one single framework. In the meantime, the enforcement of the AML has chosen to align more with the international practice of the economic analysis of the market when pursuing efficiency goals and chosen to effect China's strategic development planning, based on public interest grounds when pursuing non-efficiency goals.

IV. CONCLUSION

Part III of this volume has examined how the localized competition regulation of China becomes institutionalized through capacity building and secondary legislation issued by the three anti-monopoly authorities: the NDRC, the SAIC and MOFCOM. However, it is the coordinated segmentation among the authorities and within the State Council Anti-Monopoly Commission that largely shapes the outcome of the enforcement of the AML. Based on this, it reveals that China as a new competition regime aims to pursue efficiency and non-efficiency-related goals at the same time within the framework of the AML. In this process, China refers to the principle of the pursuit of allocative efficiency based on the economic analysis of competition and to the principle of non-discrimination as the normative framework. However, the reference to the two principles faces challenges resulting from the embeddedness of China's market governance and its own legal doctrines. More importantly, the theoretical and empirical gap existing between the two principles is unable to provide China with an effective and realistic tool to pursue its diversified developmental goals at the same time. Consequently, China is searching for its own conceptual framework for its regulation of competition on the one hand and applies a dual-track enforcement of the AML on the other.

Conclusion

身是菩提树，心如明镜台，时时常拂拭，勿使染尘埃。

My body is a Bohdi tree, my heart is a dressing table mirror, wash and care them often and leave them to no dirt.

菩提本无树，明镜亦非台，本来无一物，何处染尘埃？

Bohdi never is a tree, nor is mirror a table, there has been no such existence, from where the dirt comes?

—Wisdom from Chinese Buddhism, *Chan Zong*, seventh century AD[1]

This book has examined China's experience in developing its AML in the context of globalization. However, it does not aim to answer the question as to whether competition laws like the AML should be harmonized or converged with international competition law norms and, if so, how. Nor does it aim to provide an answer as to what form of competition law China should adopt in a globalized world.

Rather, it attempts to use competition law and the Chinese experience of globalization as an angle to approach, understand and, if possible, explain the complexity resulting from the structural development and the interaction of hybrid legal spaces in the globalization process. These complexities can be observed in the forms of harmonization, convergence, cross-reference or territorialization of hard and soft legal norms at the same/different locations and in the same and different time periods. However, what really invites exploration is probably not the forms of legal development, but rather the hidden wisdom behind it, ie, the reasons or elements that impact, influence or even shape this complexity.

For years, China has been regarded as the opposite of normality and its economic reform has attracted much debate. With its rise, its attempt to adopt a law to protect competition has raised questions, suspicion and uncertainty amongst international actors as well as international business players.

China's experience shows that in the world of legal pluralism, a new competition regime is no longer a passive recipient of norms. Instead, the generators of competition law norms are in subtle coordination with and competition against each other to influence China's AML development. Where the development of global competition law increasingly stresses the response to the embeddedness

[1] Translation by the author.

of the new competition regime, new competition regimes such as China have instrumentally adjusted global competition law norms to advance their own strategic interests and have quickly institutionalized the localized competition law in their own context.

China's experience further shows that in the world of pluralistic sources of competition law norms, new competition regulation regimes may choose to converge more with certain norms than others. However, when international competition law norms fail to provide China with a systematic normative framework for it to pursue both efficiency and non-efficiency goals under the AML, it seeks to develop a conceptual framework for the AML on its own by referring back to its strategic development plan, market regulatory practice and legal doctrines. This can be observed in the speech delivered by Zhou Bohua, Minister of the SAIC, one of the anti-monopoly authorities, in the second BRICS International Competition Law Conference held in 2011 in Beijing. Mr Zhou advocated to the fellow BRICS members that in enforcing the AML, the following principles should be pursued: macro-economic interests and public moral values take precedence over local or individual interests; long-term benefits are more valuable than short-term ones; and mutual benefit and non-detrimentality to others take priority over benefits at the expense of others.[2]

China's experience also shows that in the pluralistic world of global competition law, where no single player is dominant in terms of the generation of norms, new competition law regimes are not hesitant to seek the opportunity to export their own competition law normative framework. This can be seen by the Chinese anti-monopoly authorities' active participation in cooperation with international competition regimes in the past four years, and especially by MOFCOM's visit to competition authorities in Kenya, Zambia and Zimbabwe in June 2012.[3]

In the world of legal pluralism, China's experience of developing its AML shows that domestic market governance can no longer be isolated from international legal norms. Hence, the development of China's competition regime is subject to peer review by other competition law norms generators. However, the pluralistic legal world has given China, as a new competition regime, the resources to strategically advance its own interests by referring to international legal norms on the one hand and the opportunity to rise as a global competition regime on its own on the other. In this process, China has became a resilient, strategic and increasingly assertive actor in global market governance. The development of China as a competition regime on its own thus, in turn, influences the development of global competition law in an increasingly interconnected global market. This raises one significant and challenging task for the global competition law community. That is, how to work with increasingly assertive new competition law regimes through communication and collaboration, while recognising the existence of plural forms of competition laws. It is in this context that this book invites one to consider taking a small step further rather than focusing on the magnificent Budho trees in order to better understand the dynamic and complex development of global competition law.

[2] www.brics2011.org.cn/english/dhqk_en/201109/t20110927_119804.html.

[3] http://fldj.mofcom.gov.cn/article/xxfb/201207/20120708222645.shtml.

BIBLIOGRAPHY

BOOKS

Adenas, M and Andersen, Camilla Baasch (eds). *Theory and Practice of Harmonisation* (Cheltenham, Edward Elgar, 2012).

Amato, G, 1997. *Antitrust and the Bound of Power*, Oxford University Press.

An, Jian, 2007. *Interpretation of the Antimonopoly Law of the P.R.China*, Law Press China.

Bain, JS, 1956. *Barriers to New Competition*, Cambridge University Press.

Barnard, Catherine (ed), 2008. *The Cambridge Yearbook of European Legal Studies 2007–2008*, Hart Publishing.

Bauer, Martin and Gaskell, George, 2000. *Qualitative Researching with Text, Image and Sound: A Practical Handbook*, Sage Publications.

Bellis, JF, 2001. *The Community Competition Policy in the Face of Globalisation and the Enlargement of the European Union*, Nomos.

Bhattasali, Deepak, Li, Shangton and Martin, (eds), *2008. China and the WTO: Accession, Policy Reform and Poverty Reduction*, World Bank.

Bork, Robert, 1993. *Antitrust Paradox*, Free Press.

Bramall, Chris, 2000. Sources *of Chinese Economic Growth, 1978–1996*, Oxford University Press.

Branstetter, Lee and Lardy, Nicholas, 2008. 'China's Embrace of Globalization' in Brandt, L and Rawski, T (eds), *China's Great Economic Transformation*, Cambridge University Press.

Bridge, Gary and Watson, Sophie, *2002. The Blackwell City Reader*, Blackwell.

Broadman, Harry, 1995. *Meeting the Challenge of Chinese Enterprise Reform*, World Bank.

Broder, Douglas, 2005. *A Guide to US Antitrust Law*, Sweet & Maxwell.

Brodsgaard, Kjed Erik and Yongnian, Zheng (eds), 2006. *The Chinese Communist Party in Reform*, Routledge.

Brown, William, 1950. *The United States and the Restoration of World Trade*, Brookings Institution.

Brusick, Phillippe, Alvarez, Ana Maria, Cernat, Lucian and Holmes, Peter (eds), 2005. *Competition, Competitiveness and Development: Lessons from Developing Countries*, (New York and Geneva, UNCTAD).

Cao, Tianyu (ed), 2005. *The Chinese Model of Modern Development*, Routledge.

Chen, Jian and Yao, Shujie, 2006. *Globalization, Competition and Growth in China*, Routledge.

Chen, Jianfu, 2008. *Chinese Law: Context and Transformation*, Martinus Nijhoff.

Cheng, Feng, 1993. *Economic Transition and Political Legitimacy in Post-Mao China*, State University of New York.

Clifton, Judith et al, 2003. *Privatization in the European Union: Public Enterprises and Integration*, Springer.

Collins, Hugh, 1982. *Marxism and Law*, Oxford University Press.

Cucinotta, Antonio, Pardolesi, Roberto and Van den Bergh, Roger, 2003. *Post-Chicago Development in Antirust Law*, Edward Elgar.

Culter, A Claire et al, 1999. *Private Authority and International Affairs*, State University of New York Press.

Eisner, Marc Allen and Stryker, Robin, 1991. *Antitrust and the Triumph of Economics: Institutions, Expertise and Policy Change*, University of North Carolina Press.

Erich, Adrian, Rudomino, Vassily and Regazzini, Jose, 2012. *Competition Law in the BRICS Countries*, Kluwer Law International.

Fleisher, Belton, Hope, Nicholas, Pena, Anti Alves and Yang, Dennis Tao, 2008 (ed), Policy Reform and Chinese Markets: Progress and Challenges, Edward Elgar.

Furse, Mark, 2006. *Competition Law of the EC and UK*, Oxford University Press.

Gavil, Andrew, Kovacic, William E and Baker, Jonathan B, 2002. *Antitrust Law in Perspective: Cases, Concepts and Problems in Contemporary Policy*, West Group.

Gerber, David, 1998. *Law and Competition in Twentieth Century Europe: Protecting Prometheus*, Oxford University Press.

Giddens, Anthony, 1999. *The Third Way*, Polity Press.

Gilbert, Nigel, 2008. *Researching Social Life*, Sage Publications.

Gillingham, John, 2003. *European Integration, 1950–2003: Superstate or New Market Economy?* Cambridge University Press.

Global Merger Studies Center, 2008. *China 2008 Merger and Acquisition Yearbook*, Pst&T Telecom Press.

Grisay, D, 2005. *International Competition Policy from Extra Territoriality to Multilaterality*, Mimeo.

Guzzini, Stefano, 1998. *Realism in International Relations and International Political Economy*, Routledge.

Harris, Michael and Stephen, Harris, 2001. *Competition Laws Outside the United States*, American Bar Association.

Harvey, David, 2005. *A Brief History of Neoliberalism*, Oxford University Press.

Hay, Donald, H, Morris, Derek, Liu, Guy and Yao, Shujie, 1994. *Economic Reform and State Owned Enterprises in China: 1979–1987*, Clarendon Press.

He, Qinglian, 1998. *Xian dai huai de xian jing* (*Pitfalls of Modernization*), Today China Press.

Held, David and McGrew, Anthony, 2000. *The Global Transformation Reader*, Polity Press.

High, Jack and Gable, Wayne, 1992. *A Century of the Sherman Act, American Economic Opinion*, George Mason University Press.

Hope, Nicholas C, Yang, Dennis Tao and Li MuYang (eds), 2003. *How Far Across the River?: Chinese Policy Reform the Millennium*, Stanford University Press.

Howell, Jude, 2004. *Governance in China*, Rowman & Littlefield.

Huang, Yaseng, 2008. *Capitalism with Chinese Characteristics: Entrepreneurship and the State*, Cambridge University Press.

Hutcheson, Allan C and Monahan, Patrick (eds), 2004. *The Rule of Law: Ideal or Ideology*, Carsell.

Kegley, Charles, 2007. *World Politics: Trend and Transformation*, Wadsworth Publishing.

Kenen, Peter, 1994. *Managing the World Economy: Fifty Years after Bretton Woods*, Institute for International Economics.

Knight, John and Song, Lina, 2005. *Towards a Labour Market in China*, Oxford University Press.

Komesar, N, 1994. *Imperfect Alternatives: Choosing Institutions in Law, Economics and Public Policy*, University of Chicago Press.

Kong Xiangjun, 2012. *The Supreme People's Court Legal Interpretation on Intellectual Property: Understanding and Application*, China Legal Publishing House.

Korah, Valentine, 2006. *Cases, Materials on EC Competition Law*, Hart Publishing.

Kovaleff, Theodore, 1994. *The Antitrust Impulse: An Economic, Historical and Legal Analysis*, ME Sharpe.

Kuhn, Thomas, 1996. *The Structure of Scientific Revolution*, University of Chicago Press.

Lam, Willy Wo Lap, 2006. Chinese Politics in Hu Jiantao Era: New Leaders, Chinese Challenges, ME Sharpe.

Lardy, Nicolas, 2002. *Integrating China into the Global Economy*, Brookings Institution.

Latridis, Demetrius and Hopps, Gary, 1998. *Privatization in Central and Eastern Europe: Perspective and Approaches*, Greenwood Publishing.

Li, Changping, 2002. *Wo Xiang Zong Li Shuo Shi Hua (Telling the Premier the Truth)* Guang Ming Daily Press, China.

Li, Xiaoli (ed), 2006. *Assessing the Extent of China's Marketization*, Ashgate.

Lin, Chun, 2006. *The Transformation of Chinese Socialism*, Duke University Press.

Lin, George C, 1997. *Red Capitalism in South China: Growth and Development of Pearl River Delta*, UBC Press.

Lin, Justin Yifu, Cai, Fang, and Li Zhou, 1996. *The China Miracle: Development Strategy and Economic Reform*, Chinese University of Hong Kong Press.

Lu, Xiaobu and Perry, Elizabeth, 1997. *The Changing Chinese Workplace in Historical and Comparative Perspective*, Eastgate.

Lubman, Stanley, 1999. *A Bird in a Cage: Legal Reform in China after Mao*, Stanford University Press.

Majone, G (ed), 1996. *Regulating Europe*, Routledge.

Marsden, Philip, 2003. *A Competition Policy for the WTO*, Cameron May.

Mason, Edward, 1957. *Economic Concentration and the Monopoly Problem*, Harvard University Press.

Michalopoulos, Constantine, 2001. *The WTO and Developing Countries*, Palgrave.

Monti, Giorgio, 2007. *EC Competition Law*, Cambridge University Press.

Moore, Sally Falk, 1978. *Law as Process: An Anthropological Approach*, Routledge & Kegan Paul.

Motta, Massimo, 2004, *Competition Policy, Theory and Practice*, Cambridge University Press.

Naughton, Barry, 2007. *The Chinese Economy: Transition and Growth*, MIT Press.

Neale, AD, 1970. *The Antitrust Law of the United States of America: A Study of Competition Enforced by Law*, Cambridge University Press.

Nobles, Richard and Schiff, David, 2006. *A Sociology of Jurisprudence*. Hart Publishing.

Papadopoulos Anestis S, 2010. *The International Dimension of EU Competition Law and Policy*, Cambridge University Press.

Peacock, Alan and Willgerodt, Hani (eds), 1989. *German Neo-liberal and the Social Market Economy*, Macmillan.

Peerenboom, Randall, 2002. *China's Long March Toward Rule of Law*, Cambridge University Press.

—— (ed), 2009. *Judicial Independence in China, Lessons for Global Rule of Law Promotion*, Cambridge University Press.

Pelkmans, Jacques, 2006. *European Integration: Methods and Economic Analysis*, Pearson Education.

Peritz, Rudolph JR, 1996. *Competition Policy in America, 1888–1992: History, Rhetoric, Law*, Oxford University Press.

Pitofsky, Robert (ed), 2008. *How the Chicago School Overshot the Mark, The Effect of Conservative Economic Analysis on U.S. Antitrust*, Oxford University Press.

Posner, Richard, 1976. *Antitrust Law, an Economic Perspective*, University of Chicago Press.

Pryce, Roy, 1987. *The Dynamics of European Union*, Croom Helm.

Rawski, Thomas and Brandt, Loren, 2008. *China's Great Economic Transformation*, Cambridge University Press.

Risse, Thomas, 1999. *The Power of Human Rights: International Norms and Domestic Change*, Cambridge University Press.

Roberts, Simon and Palmer, Michael, 2005. *ADR and Primary Forms of Decision Making*, Cambridge University Press.

Robinson, Joan, 1993. *Economics of Imperfect Competition*, Macmillan.

Sarat, Austin, 2004. 'Economic Globalization and the Law in the Twenty-First Century' in *Blackwell Companion to Law and Society*, Blackwell.

Sauter, Wolf, 1997. *Competition Law and Industrial Policy in the EU*, Oxford University Press.

Schmidt, Ingo and Rittaler, Jan B, 1989. *A Critical Evaluation of Chicago School of Antitrust Analysis*, Kluwer.

Shambough, David, 2008. *China's Communist Party: Atrophy and Adaptation*, University of California Press.

Shirk Suzan, 1993. *The Political Logic of Economic Reform in China*, University of California Press.

Smith, Adam, 1954. *The Wealth of Nations*, Modern Library.

Snyder, Francis, 2009. *The European Union and China, 1949–2008: Basic Documents and Commentary*, Hart Publishing.

——, 2010. *The EU, the WTO and China: Legal Pluralism and International Trade Regulation*, Hart Publishing.

Stigler, George, 1983. *The Organization of Industry*, University of Chicago Press.

Stiglitz, Joseph, 2002. *Globalization and its Discontents*, Penguin.

Streeck, Wolfgang and Thelen, Kathleen (ed), 2005. *Beyond Continuity: Institutional Change in Advanced Political Economies*, Oxford University Press.

Tamanaha, Brian, 2004. *On the Rule of Law: History, Politics, Theory*, Cambridge University Press.

Taylor, Martyn, 2006. *International Competition Law: A New Dimension for the WTO?* Cambridge University Press.

Teubner, Gunther (ed), 1997. *Global Law without a State*, Dartmouth.

——, 1988. *Autopoietic Law: A New Approach to Law and Society*, Walter De Gruyter.

Thomas, Chantal and Trachtman, Joel P, 2009. *Trade and Competition Policy in the Developing World: Is there a Role for WTO, in Developing Countries in the WTO Legal System*, Oxford University Press.

Tian, Xiaowen, 2007. *Managing International Business in China*, Cambridge University Press.

Tseng, Wanda and Rodlauer, Markus, 2003. *China Competing in the Global Economy*, IMF.

Tuthrie, Doug, 2006. *China and Globalization, the Social, Economic and Political Transformation of Chinese Society*, Routledge.

Twinning, William, 2000. *Globalization and Legal Theory*, Butterworths.

Van den Bergh, Roger and Camesasca, Peter, 2006. *European Competition Law and Economics: A Comparative Analysis*, Sweet & Maxwell.
Van den Bossche, Peter, 2005. *The Law and Policy of World Trade Organization*, Cambridge University Press.
Walder, Andrew, 1988. *Communist Neo-Traditionalism: Work and Authority in Chinese Industry*, Berkeley.
Warner, Malcolm, 2005. *Human Resource Management in China Revisited*, Routledge.
Watson, Alan, 1993. *Legal Transplants: An Approach to Comparative Law*, University of Georgia Press.
Weber, Max, 1981. *General Economic History*, Brunswick.
Wesseling, Rein, 2008. *Modernization of EC Antitrust Law*, Hart Publishing.
Lam, Willy Wo Lap, 2006. *Chinese Politics in Hu Jintao Era: New Leaders, New Challenges*, Eastgate.
Wish, Richard, 2009. *Competition Law*, Oxford University Press.
Wolf, Charles Jr, Yeh, KC, Zycher, Benjamin, Eberstadt, Nicholas and Lee, Sung-Ho, 2003. *Fault Lines in China's Economic Terrain*, Rand.
Xiao Zhou, Kate, 1996, *How the Farmers Changed China: Power of the People*, Westview Press.
Yu, Keping, 2008. *Globalization and Changes in China's Governance*, Brill.
——, 2009. *Democracy is a Good Thing, Essays on Politics, Society and Culture in Contemporary China*, Brookings Institution.
Zheng, Yongnian, 1999. *Discovering Chinese Nationalism in China, Modernization, Identity and International Relations*, Cambridge University Press.
Zhu, Suli, 1996. *Fa Zhi Ji Qi Ben Tu Zi Yuan (The Rule of Law and its Local Resources)*, China Politics and Law University.
Zimmerman, James, 2004. *China Law Deskbook*, ABA Association.

JOURNALS AND WORKING PAPERS

Adams, Walter and Brock, James, 1994. 'Antitrust, Ideology, and the Arabesque of Economic Theory', 66 *University of Colorado Law Review* 257.
Akman, Pinar, 2009. 'Consumer Welfare and Art. 82 EC: Practice and Rhetoric', 3(1) *World Competition* 71.
Appleton, Simon, Knight, John, Song, Lina and Xia, Qingjie, 2002. 'Labour Retrenchment, Determinants and Consequences', 13(2–3) *China Economic Review* 252.
Backer, Larry Catá, 2006. 'The Rule of Law, the Chinese Communist Party, and Ideological Campaigns: Sange Daibiao (the "Three Represents"), Socialist Rule of Law, and Modern Chinese Constitutionalism', 16(1) *Journal of Transnational Law and Contemporary Problems* 29.
Basedow, Jürgen, 1999–2000. 'Jurgen International Antitrust: From Extraterritorial Application to Harmonization', 60 *Layola Law Review* 1037.
Bercero, Ignacio Garcia and Amarasinha, Stefan D, 2001. 'Moving the Trade and Competition Debate Forward', 4(3) Journal *of International Economic Law* 481.
Berman, Paul Schiff, 2007. 'Global Legal Pluralism', 80 *Southern California Review* 1155.

Bhattacharjea, Aditya, 2006. 'The Case for a Multilateral Agreement on Competition Policy: A Developing Country Perspective', 9 *Journal of International Economic Law* 293.

Bork, Robert H, 1966. 'Legislative Intent and the Policy of the Sherman Act', 9 *Journal of Law and Economics* 7.

Bratton, William and McCahery, Joseph, 1999. 'Comparative Corporate Governance and the Theory of the Firm: The Case against Global Cross Reference', 38(2) *Columbia Journal of Transnational Law* 213.

Briones, Juan, 2009. 'A Balance of the Impact of Economic Analysis on the EU Competition Policy', 32(1) *World Competition* 27.

Chan, Anita, 2006. 'Globalization, China's Free Labour Market and the Chinese Trade Unions' 6(3–4) *Asia Pacific Business Review* 261.

Chen, Baizhu and Yi, Feng, 2000. 'Determinants of Economic Growth in China: Private Enterprises, Education and Openness', 11 *China Economic Review* 1.

Chen, Shaofeng, 2006. 'State Regulated Marketization: China's Oil Pricing Regime', 7(3) *Perspectives* 151.

Chen, YF and Funke, MF, 2009. 'China's New Labour Contract Law: No Harm to Employment?' 20 *China Economic Review* 558.

Chung, JH, Lai, H and Joo, JH, 2009, 'Assessing the "Revive the Northeast" (zhenxing dongbei) Program: Origins, Policies and Implementation', 197 *China Quarterly* 108.

Clark, Donald, 2007. 'Legislating for a Market Economy in China', 191 *China Quarterly* 567.

Clark, John Maurice, 1940. 'Towards a Concept of Workable Competition', 30 *American Economic Review* 243.

Cooper, James C, Froeb, Luke M, O'Brien, Dan and Vita, Michael G, 2005. 'Vertical Antitrust Policy as a Problem of Inference', 23(7–8) *International Journal of Industrial Organization* 639.

Cooper, James C, Froeb, Luke M, O'Brien Dan and Vita, Michael G, 2005. 'A Comparative Study of United States and European Union Approaches to Vertical Policy', Vanderbilt University Law School, *Law and Economics working paper* number 05–11.

Daniels, Robert and Trebilcock, Michael, 2004. 'The Political Economy of Rule of Law Reform in Developing Countries', 26 *Michigan Journal of International Law* 99.

Demaret, Paul, 1996. 'The Metamorphoses of the GATT: From the Havana Charter to the World Trade Organization', 34 *Columbia Journal of Transnational Law* 123.

Du, Julan and Wei, Shang-Jin, 2004. 'Does Insider Trading Raise Market Volatility?', 114(498) *Economic Journal* 916.

Dutz, Mark et al, 1999. 'Does More Intense Competition Lead to Higher Growth?', World Bank Policy Research Working Paper, No 2320, available at: http://ssrn.com/abstract=630693.

Eeckhout, Piet, 2002. 'Judicial Enforcement of WTO Law in the European Union: Some Further Reflections', *Journal of International Economic Law* 91.

Evans, Peter, 1997. 'The Eclipse of the State? Reflections on Stateness in an Era of Globalization', 50(1) *World Politics* 62.

Evenett, Simon, 2005. 'Links between Development and Competition Law in Developing Countries', in *Case Studies for the World Development Report on Investment Climate, Growth and Property*. https://www.alexandria.unisg.ch/export/DL/22249.pdf

Ewald, William, 1995. 'Comparative Jurisprudence (II): The Logic of Legal Transplants', 43(4) *American Journal of Comparative Law* 489.

Falke, Andreas, 2005. 'EU-USA Trade Relations in the Doha Development Round Market Access', 10 *European Foreign Affairs Review* 1.

Farrell, Joseph and Shapiro, Carl, 2000. 'Scale Economies and Synergies in Horizontal Merger Analysis', 68 *Antitrust Law Journal* 685.

Fenton, Christopher R, 2003. 'U.S. Policy towards Foreign Direct Investment Post-September 11: Exon-Florio in the Age of Transnational Security', 41 *Columbia Journal of Transnational Law* 195.

Fernandez, Borja Martinez, Hashi, Iraj and Jergers, Marc, 2004. 'The Implementation of the European Commission's Merger Regulation 2004: An Empirical Analysis', 4(3) *Journal of Competition Law and Economics* 791.

Fisher, Franklin, 1979. 'Diagnosing Monopoly', 23 *Quarterly Review of Economics and Businesses* 19.

Fligstein, Neil and Drita, Iona Mara, 1996. 'How to Make a Market: Reflections on the European Union's Single Market Program', 102 *American Journal of Sociology* 1.

Flynn, John J, 1977. 'Antitrust Jurisprudence: A Symposium on the Economic, Political and Social Goals of Antitrust Policy', 125(6) *University of Pennsylvania Law Review* 1182.

Fox, Eleanor, 2000. 'Equality, Discrimination, and Competition Law: Lessons from and for South Africa and Indonesia', 41 *Harvard International Law Journal* 579.

Fox, Eleanor, 2003. 'We Protect Competition, You Protect Competitors', 26 *World Competition* 149.

——, 2007. 'Economic Development, Poverty and Antitrust: The Other Path', 13 *Southwestern Journal of Law & Trade in Americas* 211.

——, 2007. 'An Anti-Monopoly Law for China: Scaling the Walls of Protectionist Government Restraints' 74 *Antitrust Law Journal*, 173.

Furse, Mark, 2007. 'Competition Law Choice in China', 30(2) *World Competition* 323.

Gal, June, 2004. 'The Ecology of Antitrust Preconditions for Competition Law Enforcement in Developing Countries', *Competition, Competitiveness and Development*, UNCTAD.

Gray Jack, 2006. 'Mao in Perspective', 187 *China Quarterly* 659.

Gerber, David, 1994. 'The Transformation of European Community Competition Law', 35(1) *Harvard International Law Journal* 97.

Gifford, Daniel J and Sullivan, E Thomas, 2000. 'Can International Antitrust Be Saved for the Post-Boeing Merger World: A Proposal to Minimize International Conflict and to Rescue Antitrust from Misuse', 45 *Antitrust Bulletin* 55.

Griffin, Joseph, 1999. 'Extraterritoriality in U.S. and EU Antitrust Enforcement', 67 *Antitrust Law Journal* 159.

Griffiths, John, 1986. 'What is Legal Pluralism?', 24 *Journal of Legal Pluralism* 1.

Hassard, John, Morris, Jonathan, Sheehan, Jackie and Yuxin, Xiao, 2006. 'Downsizing the Danwei: Chinese State-Enterprise Reform and the Surplus Labour Question', 17(8) *International Journal of Human Resource Management* 1441.

Hawk, B, 1995. 'System Failure: Vertical Restraints and EC Competition Law', 32 *Common Market Law Review* 973.

Ho, Virginia, 2009, 'From Contracts to Compliance? An Early Look at Implementation Under China's New Labor Legislation', 23 *Columbia Journal of Asian Law* 35.

Hongzhi, Tang, 1984. 'Arbitration a Method Used by China to Settle Foreign Trade and Economic Disputes', 4(3) *Pace Law Review* 519.

Hovenkamp, Herbert, 2008. 'Neoclassical Crisis in Competition Policy 1890–1955', University of Iowa Legal Studies Research Paper No 08-32.

Hu, Xiaobo, 2000. 'The State, Enterprises, and Society in Post-Deng China: Impact of the New Round of SOE Reform', 40(4) *Asian Survey* 641.

Huang, Yong, 2008. 'Pursuing the Second Best: The History, Momentum, and Remaining Issues of China's Anti-Monopoly Law', 75 *Antitrust Law Journal* 117.

Huang, Phillip CC, 1993. 'Between Informal Mediation and Formal Adjudication: The Third Realm of Qing Civil Justice', 19(3) *Modern China* 251.

Hung, Veron Mei-Ying, 2004. 'China's WTO Commitment on Independent Judicial Review: Impact on Legal and Political Reform' 52(1) *American Journal of Comparative Law* 77.

Johnson, Arthur M, 1959. 'Theodore Roosevelt and the Bureau of Corporations', 45(4) *Mississippi Valley Historical Review* 571.

Kelleher, Grant, 1967. 'The Common Market Antitrust Laws: The First Ten Years', *Antitrust Bulletin* 1219.

Killion, M Ulric, 2004. 'Post-WTO China and Independent Judicial Review', 26(3) *Houston Journal of International Law* 507.

Kim, Samuel S, 1987. 'The Development of International Law in Post-Mao China: Change and Continuity', 7 *Journal of Chinese Law* 117.

Korah, Valentine, 1990. 'EEC Competition Law: Legal Form or Economic Efficiency?', 35 *Antitrust Bulletin* 1009.

Kovacic, William, 1997–98. 'Getting Started: Creating New Competition Policy Institutions in Transition Economies', 23 *Brooklyn Journal of International Law* 403.

——, 2001–02. 'Institutional Foundations for Economic Legal Reform in Transition Economies: The Case of Competition Policy and Antitrust Enforcement', 77 *Chicago Kent Law Review* 265.

Kovacic William and Chapiro, Carl, 1999. 'Antitrust Policy: A Century of Economic and Legal Thinking', University of California, Working Paper No CPC99-09.

Kronthale, Franz, 2007. 'Effectiveness of Competition Law: A Panel Data Analysis', IWH discussion paper, available at: www.iwh-halle.de/d/publik/disc/7-07.pdf.

Lang, Andrew, 2007. 'Rethinking Trade and Human Right', 15(2) *Tulane Journal of International and Comparative Law* 335.

Larner, Wendy, 2000. 'Neoliberalism: Policy, Ideology and Governmentality', 63 *Studies in Political Economy* 5.

Legrand, Pierre, 1997. 'Impossibility of Legal Transplant', 4 *Maastricht Journal of European and Comparative Law* 111.

Li, David D, 1988. 'Changing Incentives of the Chinese Bureaucracy', 88(2) *American Economic Review* 393.

Linton, Katherine Connor, 2008. 'Access to Capital in China: Competitive Condition for Foreign and Domestic Firms', 1 *Journal of International Commerce and Economics* 27.

Lott, John R, Jr, 1990. 'Predation by Public Enterprises', 43(2) *Journal of Public Economics* 237.

Lubman, Stanley, 2006. 'Looking for Law in China', 20 *Columbia Journal of Asian Law* 1.

Ludema, Robert, 2002. 'WTO Agreement on Competition Policy: Prospects and Pitfalls', *USITC International Economic Review,* 3506.

Luo, and Chen, Min, 1997. 'Does Guanxi Influence Firm Performance?', 14 *Asia Pacific Journal of Management* 1.

Ma, Jie and Zhang, Weiying, 1999. 'Ownership Distortion as a Cause for Excessive Competition', *Economic Research Journal* 11.

Maher, Imelda, 2000. 'Re-imaging the Story of European Competition Law', 20(1) *Oxford Journal of Legal Studies* 155.

——, 2002. 'Competition Law in the International Domain: Networks as a New Form of Governance', 29(1) *Journal of Law and Society* 112.

——, 2006. 'The Rule of Law and Agency: The Case of Competition Policy', Chatham House International Economic Law Programme Working Paper.

Maier, Charles, S, 1981. 'The Two Postwar Eras and the Conditions for Stability in Twentieth-Century Western Europe', 86(2) *American Historical Review* 327.

Marsden, Philip, 2004. 'WTO Decides its First Competition Cases with Disappointing Results', *Competition Law Insight*, May 2004, www.biicl.org/files/1106_comp_law_insight_-_wto_article.pdf

Masanobu, Kato, 1982. 'Civil and Economic Law in the People's Republic of China' 30(3) *American Journal of Comparative Law* 429.

May, James, 1989. 'Antitrust in the Formative Era: Political and Economic Theory in Constitutional and Antitrust Analysis, 1890–1918', 50 *Ohio State Law Journal* 258.

McGee, John S, 1958. 'Predatory Price Cutting: The Standard Oil Case', 1 *Journal of Law and Economics* 137.

McNulty, Paul, 1968. 'Economic Theory and the Meaning of Competition', 82(4) *Quarterly Journal of Economics* 639.

Mei-Ying Hung, Veron, 2004. 'China's WTO Commitment on Independent Judicial Review: Impact on Legal and Political Reform', 52(1) *American Journal of Comparative Law* 77.

Merry, Sally Engle, 1988. 'Legal Pluralism', 22(5) *Law & Society Review* 869.

Melamed, Douglas, 2000. 'Promoting Sound Antitrust Enforcement in the Global Economy', available at: www.justice.gov/atr/public/speeches/6785.htm.

Michaels, Ralf, 2007. 'The True *Lex Mercatoria*, Law Beyond the State', 14(2) *Indiana Journal of Global Legal Studies* 447.

Monti, Giogio, 2002. 'Article 81 EC and Public Policy', 39(5) *Common Market Law Review* 1057.

Naughton, Barry, 1994. 'What is Distinctive about China's Economic Transformation? State Enterprise Reform and Overall System Transformation', 18 *Journal of Comparative Economics* 470.

Nee, Victor, 2000. 'The Role of the State in Making a Market Economy', 156 *Journal of Institutional and Theoretical Economics* 64.

Nolan, Peter, 2005. 'China and Global Business Revolution', 1 *Journal of Cambridge Economics* 119.

O'Rourke, Kevin and Wiliamson, Jeffery, 2002. 'When Did Economic Globalization Begin?', 6(1) *European Review of Economic History* 23.

Oi, Jean C, 1992. 'Fiscal Reform and the Economic Foundations of Local State Corporatism in China', 45(10) *World Politics* 99.

——, 1999, 'Two Decades of Rural Reform in China: An Overview and Assessment', 159 *China Quarterly* 616.

Owen, Bruce M, Sun, Su and Zheng, Wentong, 2008. 'China's Competition Policy Reforms: The Anti-Monopoly Law and Beyond', 75 *Antitrust Law Journal* 231.

Paler, Laura, 2005. 'China's Legislation Law and the Making of a More Orderly and Representative Legislative System', 182 *China Quarterly* 301.

Palim, Mark, 1998. 'Worldwide Growth of Competition Law: An Empirical Analysis', 43 *Antitrust Bulletin* 105.

Palmer, Michael, 2006. 'Controlling the State? Mediation in Administrative Litigation in the People's Republic of China', 16(1) *Transnational Law & Contemporary Problems* 165.

Perkins, Dwight, 1994. 'Completing China's Move to the Market', 8(2) *Journal of Economic Perspectives* 23.

Petersmann, EU, 2007. 'Multi-level Judicial Governance of International Trade Requires a Common Conception of the Rule of Law and Justice', 10(3) *Journal of International Economic Law* 529.

Petrusic, Michael, 2006. 'Oil and National Security: CNOOC's Failed Bid to Purchase Unocal', 84 *North Carolina Law Review* 1373.

Pitofsky, Robert, 1978–79. 'The Political Content of Antitrust', 127 *University of Pennsylvania Law Review* 1051.

Pitofsky, Robert, 2002–03. 'Antitrust at the Turn of the Twenty-First Century: The Matter of Remedies', *91 Georgetown Law Journal* 169.

Pocet, Sandra, 2005. 'A Fragmented China: Measure and Determinants of Chinese Domestic Market Disintegration', 3(3) *Review of International Economics* 409.

Potter, Pitman B, 2007. 'China and the International Legal System: Challenges of Participation', 191 *China Quarterly* 699.

Qin, Julia Ya, 2003. '"WTO-Plus" Obligations and their Implications for the World Trade Organization Legal System: An Appraisal of the China Accession Protocol', 37(3) *Journal of World Trade* 483.

Ruskola, Teemu, 2002. 'Legal Orientalism', 101 *Michigan Law Review* 79.

Sach, Jeffrey and Woo, Wing Thye, 1994. 'Experience in the Transition to a Market Economy', 18(3) *Journal of Comparative Economics* 271.

Sappington, David EM and Sidak, J Gregory, 2003. 'Competition Law for State-Owned Enterprises', 71(2) *Antitrust Law Journal* 479.

Sasso, R, 1991. 'Legal Formats: A Dynamic Approach to Comparative Law (II)', 39 *American Journal of Comparative Law* 398.

Schurmann, Franz, 1963. 'Economic Policy and Political Power in Communist China', 349 *Annals of the American Academy of Political and Social Science* 49.

Schweitzer, Heike, 2007. 'Competition Law and Public Policy: Reconsidering an Uneasy Relationship: The Example of Art. 81', available at: http://ssrn.com/abstract=1092883.

Schweitzer, Heike, 2007. 'Parallels and Differences in the Attitudes towards Single Firm Conduct: What are the Reasons? The History, Interpretation and Underlying Principles of Sec. 2 Sherman Act and Art. 82 EC', EU Working Paper. http://cadmus.eui.eu/handle/1814/7626

Seldon, Mark and Gray, Jack, 2006. 'Mao Zedong and the Political Economy of Chinese Development', 187 *China Quarterly* 680.

Shambough, David, 2004. 'China Engages Asia: Reshaping the Regional Order', 29(30) *International Security* 64.

Shang Ming, 2009. 'Antitrust in China: A Constantly Evolving Subject', 5(1) *Competition Law International* 4–11.

Snyder, Francis, 1999. 'Governing Economic Globalization: Global Legal Pluralism and European Union Law', *European Law Journal* 334.

Snyder, Francis, 2009. 'China, Regional Trade Agreements and WTO Law', 43(1) *Journal of World Trade* 1.

Streel, Alexdandre de, 2003. 'The Integration of Competition Law Principles in the New European Regulatory Framework for Electronic Communications', 26(3) *World Competition* 489.

Sun, Qian and Tong, Wilson HS, 2003. 'China Share Issues Privatization: The Extent of its Success', 70 *Journal of Financial Economics* 183.

Tang, Hongzhi, 1984. 'Arbitration a Method Used by China to Settle Foreign Trade and Economic Disputes', 4(3) *Pace Law Review* 519.

Tang, Wenfang, 2002. 'Political and Social Trends in the Post-Deng Urban China: Crisis or Stability?', *China Quarterly* 890.

Tang Yijie, 2007. 'The Contemporary Understanding of Confucius Harmonious Society', 2 Theory and Reference 21.
Tam, On Kit, 1991. 'Capital Market Development in China', 19(5) *World Development* 511.
Tamanaha, Brian, 2007. 'Understanding Legal Pluralism: Past to Present, Local to Global', 29 *Sydney Law Review* 375.
Teubner, Gunther, 1998. 'Legal Irritants: Good Faith in British Law or How Unifying Law Ends Up in New Differences', 61 *Modern Law Review* 11.
——, 2002. 'Breaking Frames: Economic Globalization and the Emergence of *Lex Mercatoria*', 5(2) *European Journal of Social Theory* 199.
Todoino, Mario, 2003. 'International Competition Network: The State of Play after Naples', 26(20) *World Competition* 283.
Trebilock, Michael and Iacobucci, Edward, 2002. 'Designing Competition Law Institutions', 25(3) *World Competition* 361–94.
Tsang, Steve, 2009. 'Consultative Leninism: China's New Political Framework', 18(62) *Journal of Contemporary China* 865.
Van Kraay, Frans GA, 1984. 'Public Enterprises and the EEC Competition Rules: The British Telecommunication Decision', 33(3) *International & Comparative Law Quarterly* 1022.
Vincent, Andrew, 1993. 'Marx and Law', 20(4) *Journal of Law and Society* 371.
Wallerstein, Immanuel, 2005. 'After Developmentalism and Globalization, What?', 83(3) *Social Forces* 1263.
Wei, Shang-Jin and Wang, Tao, 1997. 'The Siamese Twins: Do State-Owned Banks Favor State-Owned Enterprises in China?', 8(1) *China Economic Review* 19.
Wei, Yingqi, Bo Liu and Liu, Xiaming, 2005. 'Entry Modes of Foreign Direct Investment in China: A Multinomial Logic Approach', 58(11) *Journal of Business Research* 1495.
Wellis, John and Kikeri, Sunita, 1989. 'Public Enterprise Reform: Privatization and the World Bank', 17(5) *World Development* 659.
West, Jeremy K, 2005. 'Barriers to Entry', OECD Roundtables on Competition Policy, Working Paper No 58.
Wong, Siuyun, 1993. 'Chinese Family Business, A Model', 6(3) *Family Business Review* 327.
Wood, Diane, 1995. 'The Internationalization of Antitrust Law: Options for the Future', available at: www.justice.gov/atr/public/speeches/0099.htm.
Wu, Qianlan, 2007. 'The Making of a Market Economy in China: Transformation of Government Regulation of Market Development', 13(5) *European Law Journal* 750.
——, 2012. 'EU-China Competition Dialogue: A New Step in the Internationalisation of EU Competition Law?', 18(3) *European Law Journal* 461.
Xiao, Gongqin, 1996. 'A Reflection on Radicalism in China's Transition', *Ming Pao* (9 December).
Xu, Chenggang and Weitzman, Martin L, 1994. 'Chinese Township Village Enterprises as Vaguely Defined Cooperatives', 18(2) *Journal of Comparative Economics* 121.
Xue, Hanqin and Jin, Qian, 2009. 'International Treaties in the Chinese Domestic Legal System', 18(2) *China Journal of International Law* 299.
Ya Qin, Julia, 2003. '"WTO-Plus" Obligations and their Implications for the World Trade Organization Legal System: An Appraisal of the China Accession Protocol', 37(3) *Journal of World Trade* 483.
——, 2007. 'Investment and Beyond: The Impact of WTO Accession on China's Legal System', 191 *China Quarterly* 720.
Yang, Jijian, 2002. 'Market Power in China: Manifestations, Effects and Legislation', 21 *Review of Industrial Organization* 167.

Yiu, Daphne, Bruton, Garry D and Lu, Yuan, 2005. 'Understanding Business Groups Performance in an Emerging Economy: Acquiring Resources and Capabilities in Order to Prosper', 42(1) *Journal of Management Studies* 183.

Yueh, Linda and Knight, John, 2009. 'Competition or Segmentation in China's Urban Labour Market?', 33(1) *Cambridge Journal of Economics* 79.

Zhang, Mo, 2000. 'Freedom of Contract with Chinese Legal Characteristics: A Closer Look at China's New Contract Law', 14 *Temple International & Comparative Law Journal* 237.

Zheng, Yongnian, 2012. 'Where Does the Chinese Communist Party Go from Here? Challenges and Opportunities' 10(2) *China: An International Journal* 84.

Zhu, Xueqing, 2009. 'Wo Men De Jing Sheng JiaYuan Zai Na Li' (Where is Our Spiritual Dock?'), 1 Fa Zhi Zi Xun (*Legal Information*) 20–21.

INDEX